*Sexual Health
in
Recovery*

A Professional Counselor's Manual

Douglas Braun-Harvey, MFT, CGP, is a licensed marriage and family therapist. In 1993, he founded the Sexual Dependency Institute of San Diego (SDI). SDI provides individual and group therapy to clients concerned about their out-of-control sexual behavior. Since 1985, Mr. Braun-Harvey has traveled nationally and internationally, conducting hundreds of workshops and trainings in areas of human sexuality, sexual orientation, chemical dependency, sexual dependency, and group psychotherapy.

He contributed a chapter, "Sexual Dependence Among Recovering Substance-Abusing Men," in *Gender and Addictions: Men and Women in Treatment* (Jason Aronson, 1997). His published articles include "Integration of Client HIV Status in Sexual Dependency Outpatient Treatment: What Is Your Relationship with HIV?" and "Culturally Relevant Assessment and Treatment for Gay Men's Online Sexual Activity."

Since 2003, Douglas Braun-Harvey has presented sexual health in recovery trainings and workshops in forums as diverse as the Society for the Scientific Study of Sexuality (SSSS), American Association of Sexuality Educators, Counselors and Therapists (ASECT), Society for the Advancement of Sexual Health (SASH), National Conference on Methamphetamine, HIV and Hepatitis, Hazelden Graduate School, California Association of Marriage and Family Therapists (CAMFT), California Association of Drug and Alcohol Counselors (CAADAC), National Association of Addiction Treatment Providers (NAATP), American Psychiatric Association (APA), Maryland State Office of AIDS, and the Whitman Walker Clinic in Washington, DC. He is the author of *Sexual Health in Drug and Alcohol Treatment: Group Facilitator's Manual* (Springer Publishing Company, 2009).

Sexual Health in Recovery

A Professional Counselor's Manual

Douglas Braun-Harvey, MFT, CGP

Copyright © 2011 Springer Publishing Company, LLC

All rights reserved.

No part of this publication may be reproduced, stored in a retrieval system, or transmitted in any form or by any means, electronic, mechanical, photocopying, recording, or otherwise, without the prior permission of Springer Publishing Company, LLC, or authorization through payment of the appropriate fees to the Copyright Clearance Center, Inc., 222 Rosewood Drive, Danvers, MA 01923, 978-750-8400; fax 978-646-8600; info@copyright.com or on the Web at www.copyright.com.

Springer Publishing Company, LLC
11 West 42nd Street
New York, NY 10036
www.springerpub.com

Acquisitions Editor: Jennifer Perillo
Senior Editor: Rose Mary Piscitelli
Cover design: Steven Pisano
Project Manager: Gil Rafanan
Composition: Absolute Service, Inc.

ISBN: 978-0-8261-2017-5
E-book ISBN: 978-0-8261-2018-2

10 11 12 13/ 5 4 3 2 1

The author and the publisher of this work have made every effort to use sources believed to be reliable to provide information that is accurate and compatible with the standards generally accepted at the time of publication. The author and publisher shall not be liable for any special, consequential, or exemplary damages resulting, in whole or in part, from the readers' use of, or reliance on, the information contained in this book. The publisher has no responsibility for the persistence or accuracy of URLs for external or third-party Internet Web sites referred to in this publication and does not guarantee that any content on such Web sites is, or will remain, accurate or appropriate.

Library of Congress Cataloging-in-Publication Data

Sexual health in recovery : a professional counselor's manual / Douglas Braun-Harvey.
    p. ; cm.
Includes bibliographical references and index.
ISBN 978-0-8261-2017-5 — ISBN 978-0-8261-2018-2 (e-book)
1. Drug addiction—Treatment. 2. Sex. 3. Counseling. I. Title.
[DNLM: 1. Sexual Behavior—psychology. 2. Substance-Related Disorders—therapy. 3. Counseling—methods. WM 270]
RC564.B718 2011
616.85'83—dc22
                              2010050308

> Special discounts on bulk quantities of our books are available to corporations, professional associations, pharmaceutical companies, health care organizations, and other qualifying groups.
>
> If you are interested in a custom book, including chapters from more than one of our titles, we can provide that service as well.
>
> **For details, please contact:**
> Special Sales Department, Springer Publishing Company, LLC
> 11 West 42nd Street, 15th Floor, New York, NY 10036-8002
> Phone: 877-687-7476 or 212-431-4370; Fax: 212-941-7842
> Email: sales@springerpub.com

Printed in the United States of America by Gasch Printing

To my grandfather George E. Braun, who at 47 died alone, his car crashing into a bridge post after a union meeting in Minneapolis on June 23, 1949. Although we never met, his story of alcoholism and sexuality is an intergenerational family saga that continues to reverberate in these pages and finds a voice in my passion for improving the lives of men and women seeking the gift of recovery and sexual health.

Contents

Foreword ix
Acknowledgments xiii
Introduction xxi

PART I: COUNSELOR READINESS

1. What Is "Sexual Health in Recovery"?   **3**
2. Eight Key Concepts of Sexual Health in Recovery   **21**
3. Are You Ambivalent About Sexual Health in Recovery?   **47**

PART II: SEXUAL HEALTH IN RECOVERY ASSESSMENT

4. Preparing for Sexual Health in Recovery   **81**
5. Assessing Sex/Drug-Linked Relapse Risk   **105**
6. The Sexual Health in Recovery Assessment   **121**
7. The Sexual Health in Recovery Assessment Feedback Session   **157**

PART III: SEXUAL HEALTH IN RECOVERY COUNSELING SKILLS

8. Sex-Positive Drug and Alcohol Counseling   **189**
9. Improving Counselor Confidence in Talking About Sex   **209**
10. Sexual Health in Recovery Counseling   **235**

References 281
Index 289

Foreword

Sexual Health in Recovery by Doug Braun-Harvey is a very welcome new contribution to the literature on chemical dependency treatment. This is a valuable new resource that fills a significant gap in our understanding of recovery and one that clinicians (and individuals in recovery) will find enormously useful. This book is written in a practical way that illustrates the challenges and processes of both sexual health and recovery through solid scientific information, personal stories of individuals in recovery, and the vast clinical experience of Doug Braun-Harvey.

I have been concerned for a long time that the two fields of drug and alcohol treatment and sexual health have not had a better understanding of each other's wealth of knowledge and experience. Here, Mr. Braun-Harvey bridges that gap and brings the essential knowledge from the two fields that can be so important for many people in recovery.

I have long believed that chemical dependency and intimacy dysfunction have been inextricably linked. Despite this link, the sexual and intimacy concerns of chemically dependent individuals and their family members are rarely addressed in drug and alcohol assessment, treatment, and rehabilitation. At the same time, people in the sexual health field have often ignored the profound effect that alcohol and/or drug abuse or dependency can have on sexual and intimacy functioning. Many individuals never achieve chemical sobriety or sexual health because these issues are not addressed in an integrated manner. In the attempt to achieve recovery, many people relapse because of unresolved sexual and intimacy issues. Or others obtain a chemical sobriety, but remain frozen in their insecurity and inability to form healthy sexual and intimate relationships.

I emphasize sexual and intimate relationships because the term sexual health is still a source of confusion and misunderstanding among health care professionals and clients alike. For many people, sexual health simply means the absence of some sexually transmitted infection. But as Doug Braun-Harvey points out, sexual health is a much broader concept and the ability to be comfortable with one's sexual and gender identity, to be able to communicate desires, to have satisfying and pleasurable sexual activity, to negotiate roles and rules of an intimate relationship, and to have meaningful and fulfilling and nonexploitative intimate relationships. Sexual health is inclusive of reproductive health. It is a very broad concept that comes down to a mind-body-spirit feeling of comfort, integration, and wellness in relation to sex, sexuality, and intimacy.

I view sexuality as a very broad concept that encompasses sex, pleasure, and intimacy. Our sexuality encompasses our physical, gender, sex-role, and sexual orientation identity—and our physical attractions and our needs for warmth, tenderness, touch, and love. We are sexual in all that we do, and therefore sexuality is always a part of our relationships as well as our sexual activity.

While sexual dysfunction refers to problems of sexual desire, arousal, orgasm, or pain during sex, the intimacy problems that many alcohol- and drug-dependent persons face are so much broader than sexual functioning. Intimacy dysfunction is a developmental or pathological barrier to engaging in intimate relationships. It can take the form of (1) physical abuse, emotional neglect, or sexual abuse of children, (2) psychosexual disorders such as problems with gender or sexual identity, sexual functioning, or impulsive or compulsive sexual behavior, (3) relationship discord as a result of conflict, violence, codependency, confusion or conflict in roles, communication problem, unhealthy altitudes regarding sexual activity and intimacy, and sexual dysfunction. All of these intimacy dysfunctions have been found to be highly correlated with chemical abuse and dependency.

Unfortunately most of our sexuality education emphasizes learning about "the plumbing" and the most limited and rudimentary aspects of reproductive health. Most Americans are not equipped with the basic knowledge of sexuality and sexual health to form healthy sexual and intimate relationships. In addition to the general crippling effect of basic sexual illiteracy, individuals who are chemically dependent often come from very dysfunctional families where intimacy dysfunction is often the norm. Chemicals often become a coping mechanism for intimacy dysfunction. Then, in recovery, the person is faced with the challenges and difficulties of past experiences of intimacy dysfunction and the problems they have had in developing healthy sexual and intimate relationships as adolescents or adults.

It is critical that people in recovery are armed with the knowledge and learn the skills of sexual health and intimacy function.

I am so grateful that Doug Braun-Harvey has written this book to not only give everyone the knowledge of these issues but to provide extremely helpful and practical information on how to overcome these difficulties and challenges in recovery. Not only will this information improve the likelihood of recovery but it will increase the quality of recovery.

The ability to feel good in one's body, to feel good about one's sexuality, and to know how to connect with other individuals to experience deep, satisfying, and meaningful intimate relationships is a goal of everyone and everyone's right, including the rights of men and women in recovery. The ability to experience this is not always intuitive. Sexual health is a learned process that is not achieved overnight. Doug Braun-Harvey has poignantly described the process of bridging sexual science with recovery from drug and alcohol dependency and provided real guidance and hope to professional counselors and their clients with a vision of sexual health as vital to living in recovery.

Eli Coleman, PhD
Academic Chair in Sexual Health
Professor and Director
Program in Human Sexuality
University of Minnesota Medical School

Acknowledgments

As a psychotherapist seeking to grow in my ability to treat sexual problems and disorders among my clients, I found the world of psychotherapy training to be quite stifling and limiting. We sure learned about all the sexual disorders and major sexual problems; yet as a therapist, I knew nothing about what sexual health looked like. I had to enter the world of sex research, HIV research, sex education, sex therapy, public health, and most importantly sexual health. Fortunately, there are a number of experts whose groundbreaking research and clinical practice wisdom greatly inform my own work in combining the principles of sexual health and recovery. Some I have met personally; others have influenced me through their research, writings, and presentations. All are doing amazing work that is worth further exploration by anyone interested in recovery and sexual health.

Dr. John Bancroft describes his research as "the interaction between psychological/psychosocial and biological processes in reproductive and sexual behaviour" (from www.kinseyinstitute.org, downloaded August 31, 2009). In his current role as Senior Research Fellow at the Kinsey Institute, Dr. Bancroft and his associates have collaborated to develop an important new model for understanding women and men's sexual response. His "Dual Control" model for sexual response has been integral in expanding sexual health principles within my work as a sex therapist and psychotherapist.

Dr. Donald Calsyn is a Research Affiliate of the Alcohol and Drug Abuse Institute and a Professor of Psychiatry and Behavioral Science at the University of Washington School of Medicine. He is widely published and referenced for his work in HIV prevention among drug-dependent men and women. His critical thinking and substantive research in sex/HIV/substance abuse have led to the National Institute on Drug Abuse Clinical Trials Network evaluating his approaches to reducing HIV/STD risk behaviors for men in drug abuse treatment. His journal articles envision further research and protocols within addiction treatment to develop, assess, and evaluate sex/drug-linked addiction assessment and treatment protocols. He is an essential voice for the future of sexual health in recovery.

Dr. Eli Coleman's mission and life's work are improving sexual health on our planet. He is the inaugural holder of the University of Minnesota's Academic Chair in Sexual Health, the first of its kind in the world. He promotes sexual health as a congruency between sexual health knowledge, attitudes, values, and beliefs within the relationships and behavior of governments, public policy makers, public health leaders, and multiple health care delivery systems. He is a mentor, friend, and the consummate sexual health in recovery ally.

Dr. Stephanie Covington is a mentor, friend, colleague, inspiration, and role model. Dr. Covington and I have engaged in a wide array of sexual health conversations. She is a national expert on gender-responsive and trauma-informed drug and alcohol treatment interventions for women. She has been a pioneer in advocating recovery for incarcerated women and understanding the role of poverty and shame in a high percentage of female addicts. Her groundbreaking 1991 book *Awakening Your Sexuality* invited recovering women to look at their relationship with their body, genitals, pleasure, sexual feelings, and the messages women in recovery have been taught to feel about these aspects of womanhood. For over 25 years she has been challenging the recovery community to stop neglecting sexuality and gender as a core issue in addiction recovery.

Sallie Foley, MSW, is coauthor of *Sex Matters for Women* (the foremost guide on taking care of your sexual self, for men *and* women) and a sexual health social worker. As the director of both the University of Michigan Health System's center for sexual health and the Michigan Sexual Health Certificate program, she provides sex therapy and trains future sex therapists. "There is no lack of information about sex, but there is a lack of *relevant* information" (Sally Foley Web page, http://salliefoley.com/index.html, downloaded September 1, 2009). Her words became an important guiding principle in creating sexual health in recovery. Men and women in recovery do receive information about sexuality. It is just not relevant to the key issues of relapse prevention.

Reverend Debra Haffner is a serious bridge builder. She is a sexologist and a minister. After 12 years as President and CEO for the Sexuality Information and Education Council of the United States (SIECUS), she went to Union Theological Seminary and has been a Unitarian Universalist minister since 2003. I am inspired when listening to her present or quietly reading her expansive thinking on bridging concepts of religion and sexual health. Her discourse with faith communities about sexuality is imbedded in the sections of this book covering spirituality and sexuality in recovery.

Magnus Hirshfeld was the original bridge builder between sex, medicine, and society. He lived in Germany and died in exile in 1935. His motto was "Justice through Science." He was homosexual (to use a term of his times) and believed that hostility toward homosexuality would subside as a result of scientific understanding. This principle remains central to more recent research on the link between shame and stigma associated with sexuality.

Dr. Thomas Lewis is Professor of Psychiatry at the University of California, San Francisco, School of Medicine, and coauthor of the nonfiction book *A General Theory of Love*. Dr. Lewis is passionate about using science (of all things) to demonstrate the wisdom of emotions as the key to our lives. His book transformed the way I think about love. I find his invitation to understand the process of emotional healing through relationships enormously reflective of the basic beliefs of recovery and sexual health. His sister is veterinarian to our dog, Tux. (No kidding!)

Sexual health ally and colleague John di Miranda is the current CEO of Stepping Stone of San Diego, where he has flawlessly accepted the baton of sexual health approaches to drug and alcohol treatment. From day one, he assumed his sexual health leadership role at the treatment program where this intervention was first piloted and studied. He intuitively grasped the value of sex-positive treatment and has generously espoused the many benefits of the Discovering Sexual Health program that has been a central treatment program at Stepping Stone for over 8 years. His quiet strength is an asset when asserting sexual health conversations among key leaders in the national recovery movement. I am grateful for his vision of sexual health in drug and alcohol recovery.

If you have ever used or heard the phrase "gender role," then you have been influenced by Dr. John Money. Dr. Money defined *gender* as a combination of biological and societal influences acting together at critical periods of development to form our social presentation of either male or female. Our gender role matters a great deal throughout active addiction and during the entire recovery process. John Money died in 2006, but he left behind a new science for understanding sexual development.

I did not know what it meant to truly be a sex-positive man until I read *The Erotic Mind* by Dr. Jack Morin (in its first edition back in 1995). His book changed the way I thought about sex and psychotherapy. As a result of a landmark investigation into peak erotic experiences as the window into understanding our individual erotic nature as well as the common human themes that run throughout Eros, Dr. Morin is now a leading expert on erotic fantasies and their relationship with our real-life sexuality and relationships. By focusing on the most positive and memorable of sexual experiences as essential windows into sexual health, this book liberated me from my pathology-based, problem-focused, "only talk about sex when it is a problem" straightjacket given to me by the psychotherapy profession. He is one of many fellow colleagues and friends within the Western Region of the Society for the Scientific Study of Sexuality (www.WRSSSS.org).

Dr. Richard Rawson is Associate Director of the UCLA Integrated Substance Abuse Programs in the Institute for Neuroscience & Human Behavior at UCLA and the David Geffen School of Medicine at UCLA. His studies include clinical trials in psychosocial addiction treatment and how to effectively apply new drug and alcohol treatments. As a result of his studies among crystal meth-addicted men, he has recommended the development of valid and reliable measures to identify and intervene with sex/drug-linked addiction patterns. He represents the best in the country in drug abuse research, critical thinking, and a vision for integration of sexual health to better addiction treatment outcomes.

Dr. Mark Schoen is an expert in human sexuality education. Since 1975, he has produced over 25 sex education films for colleges and universities. He is a world leader in his commitment to film as a means of increasing and clarifying sexual knowledge. His films can be found online at the Sinclair Intimacy Institute (http://www.intimacyinstitute.com). His recent project "SexSmartFilms" (http://www.sexsmartfilms.com) is a Web-based distribution for free and uploadable sex education films.

I met Richard and Larry Siegel, Florida certified sex therapists and educators, several years ago at a national sex therapy and education conference. Their expertise in combining chemical dependency treatment and sexual health meant I was meeting important sexual health in recovery allies. As a result of their tireless commitment to providing sex education groups in Florida drug and alcohol treatment programs, they have witnessed firsthand the current treatment gap in addressing client sex/drug-linked addiction patterns. They are original proponents of sex/drug-linked relapse prevention.

Dr. Susan Tross is an Associate Professor of Clinical Psychology in the Departments of Psychiatry and Pediatrics at Columbia University. She meets the challenges of global HIV/AIDS at the intersection of gender, sexuality, and mental health. Her research has led to the National Institute on Drug Abuse Clinical Trials Network evaluating her gender-informed approaches to reducing HIV/STD risk behaviors for women in recovery. Her vision of sexual health in drug and alcohol treatment bridges the many challenges of addressing proactive harm reduction skill building within current approaches to treating women addicted to drugs and alcohol. She is a fierce voice for sexual health in drug and alcohol treatment.

Dr. Gail Wyatt, professor at the University of California in the Department of Psychiatry and Biobehavioral Sciences, Los Angeles, examines consensual and abusive relationships and how they impact psychological well-being and risk for sexually transmitted infections and HIV. She studies the interactions between culture, ethnicity, gender, race, and sexual orientation and history of sexual violence, sexual abuse, substance abuse, HIV, and AIDS.

I heard Dr. Wyatt present a paper at a conference for sexual researchers and scientists. I was struck by her practical knowledge and detailed understanding of the lives of drug-addicted women. She has been a silent mentor ever since; her work has helped me integrate gender and cultural factors in formulating the relapse prevention tools for sexual health in recovery.

Alan Wertheimer is a very clear thinker. His book *Consent to Sexual Relations* has afforded me the language and critical thinking to discuss sexual ethics in recovery. His determination and steadfastness in consistent thinking about sexual boundaries related to consent, exploitation, and coercion have been indispensable in my maturation as a therapist, writer, and advocate for sexual health for every person in drug and alcohol treatment.

Since the publication of *Sexual Health in Drug and Alcohol Treatment* in 2009, I have trained hundreds of enthusiastic and vibrant treatment professionals who intuitively grasp the presence of sex/drug-linked addiction patterns among the women and men they treat. They arrive with curiosity and often leave relieved that their perceptions, frustrations, and discouragement with drug and alcohol treatment to address this high-frequency, treatment-failure client population are no longer invisibly ignored. Some specific treatment centers and programs have stepped forward and entrusted the principles set forth in the psychoeducational curriculum to give their clients sex/drug-linked relapse prevention skills.

Douglas Place, a multi-acuity-level drug and alcohol treatment facility for men and women in residential and outpatient treatment in East Grand Forks, Minnesota, invited me to train their staff, community, and region in sexual health approaches for drug and alcohol treatment. Just prior to the winter thaw, people traveled from the tri-state area to learn and expand their vision of sexual health as an ally in treatment. I am grateful for their confidence and was inspired by their determination to implement sex/drug-linked relapse prevention throughout their impressive facility.

What appeared to be almost single-handedly, Los Angeles drug and alcohol counselor Sara Frank convinced Woodland Hills, California-based Sober College young adult drug and alcohol treatment and recovery center that their treatment program would improve by implementing the sex/drug-linked relapse prevention curriculum and counseling. She is a determined example of a sexual health ally and dedicated advocate for improving drug and alcohol treatment.

Since the publication of the first of this two-part companion series on sexual health approaches to substance abuse treatment, a diverse range of professional forums such as the Summit for Clinical Excellence: Advanced Clinical Training for Counselors and Therapists, Western Region of the Society for the Scientific Study of Sexuality, San Diego Chapter of the American Association of Marriage and Family Therapists, University of Utah School of Medicine School on Alcoholism and Other Drug Dependencies, Sierra Tucson Hospital, National Conference on Addiction Disorders, and the Center for Family Life Education (sex educator and training conference) have invited me to teach sexual health in recovery.

The support of many friends, colleagues, and family remains the backbone of my strength and determination to complete this companion book on sexual health assessment and counseling in drug and alcohol treatment. Stepping Stone of San Diego was begun in 2001 in response to Cheryl Houk asking me to help her to improve dismal client retention and demoralizing approaches to sex/drug-linked addiction. The intervening 9 years has culminated in these companion texts. Something had to adjust to make this happen.

Family traditions have been omitted from the calendar; weekend upon weekend my husband and my dear friends have been sweetly and graciously encouraging me in my quest to complete this project. Their encouragement, interest, and patience with my absorption in this book are a gift for which I can only begin to say thank you.

A sexual health counseling training manual cannot be written without camouflaged evidence of the thousands of hours in clinical relationship with men and women entrusting me with their narratives and motivations for sexual healing. Although they are fictional, the time spent in providing individual and group psychotherapy informs these client narratives and counselor profiles. The hours of attentive presence, changing each other, changing lives, and changing sexual health are evident in these fictional vignettes as an homage to the hours of our attentive presence together. As I like to tell my clients when ending a course in treatment, I was in the room every appointment as well. Thank you for trusting me to practice my passion for sexual health.

I have been fortunate indeed to have once again the same sharp mind and eye for detail in my editor Jennifer Perillo. Her guidance is reflected in many important suggestions in structure, organization, and format. I could not have coherently discussed the many ideas in this book without her enthusiastic attention.

In closing, my husband Al has seen me through the entire 9 years of this project. It is now my turn to rest from writing and begin to realign our home to the repose of fortunate living. I won the one "real" lottery 23 years ago and continue enjoying my good luck each day.

Introduction
The Origins of *Sexual Health* in Recovery

The concepts and methods described in this book originate in 2001 when Cheryl Houk, a leader in drug and alcohol treatment in San Diego, approached me at a party. At the time Cheryl was the Executive Director of Stepping Stone of San Diego, a residential program for men and women, and she knew me as a licensed Marriage and Family Therapist who specialized in treating men with out-of-control sexual behavior. Over the years, several residents of Stepping Stone had been clients in my group and individual treatment program.

Cheryl knew of my work with her residents and wanted to discuss a serious problem at her center: sex and drug addiction. In Cheryl's view, the men and women at Stepping Stone were being forced to leave treatment as a result of violating residential program rules about sexual behavior. "Too many of our residents are relapsing because of their sexual behavior," Cheryl declared. "We can do better." She wanted to find a way to address sexual behavior during and after treatment to "stop the dying."

I offered to volunteer a few hours a month to assess the situation and offer recommendations. Our goal was to not only address treatment termination in response to client sexual behavior but to also see why, after 6 to 9 months of living clean and sober, residents relapsed because of sexually motivated drug-using situations. Sometimes this relapse occurred within days or weeks of completing treatment. On a few tragic occasions, recently discharged residents were found dead of overdose.

It did not take us long to find there was indeed a significant subset of Stepping Stone residents whose treatment failure was inextricably linked with their sexual behavior. We quickly came to call this *sex/drug-linked behavior*. For many addicts, drug use prolonged their sexual activity and enhanced their libido. Others were able to pursue unconventional sexual habits only after using drugs. In recovery, residents missed these sexual activities, and their treatment program did not prepare them for the absence of this sexual intensity.

We discovered that a high percentage of sex/drug-linked residents failed to complete treatment. However, treatment failure was not always due to a drug relapse. Many times it was due to sexual behavior that violated treatment program policies.

Two coexisting problems began to emerge. First, the program lacked specific interventions for the high sex/drug-linked clients in treatment. Second, we began to realize that Stepping Stone (like most other treatment programs) relied on impulsive, judgmental, reactive, and outdated procedures in addressing sexual concerns among their residents. Key to both of these problems was the strong negative feelings among the staff and their resolve that to do nothing was unacceptable.

THE DISCOVERING SEXUAL HEALTH PROGRAM AT STEPPING STONE

Stepping Stone is a San Diego County Drug and Alcohol Services funded program. It works within a social model for recovery. It relies heavily upon volunteers, other men and women in recovery, and a small professional staff. Founded in 1976, Stepping Stone currently operates both a residential and a nonresidential nonprofit social model recovery program. The residential program is located in an urban residential neighborhood in central San Diego. Stepping Stone relies on the 12 steps of Alcoholics Anonymous and peer interaction and involvement to create a social environment in which clients help each other in the recovery process. Stepping Stone has a reputation for integrating new approaches to recovery. About 25% of the clients at Stepping Stone identify as heterosexual. More than half of the men in treatment are living with HIV infection. It is a diverse group.

My initial conversations with Cheryl eventually led to a wonderful cross-disciplinary collaboration. At the time, little to nothing was published on sexual health-based relapse prevention. There was very little for us to go on. So I went around the country speaking to experts on drug and alcohol addiction, sexual health professionals, sex addiction treatment leaders, and sex and recovery authors and trainers. They all agreed that the concept of relapse prevention based upon sexual health skills was a valid proposal and a hypothesis worth studying.

Armed with their endorsements, in 2002 we received a grant to create what would become the Discovering Sexual Health Program. The 3-year grant, funded by the California Endowment, enabled us to study the problem of sex/drug-linked relapse and to develop a psychoeducational group intervention combined with changing treatment center policy, procedure, and education related to sexuality and recovery. We hypothesized that client retention would increase and sex/drug-linked relapse behavior would decrease when drug and alcohol treatment provided sexual health-based relapse prevention skills in a sex-positive, recovery-oriented system of care. Our primary goal at Stepping Stone was to increase residential client retention by 50% over 3 years and to decrease client termination due to sex/drug-linked behavior or relapse.

To meet this goal, we created a program that included a 12-week psychoeducational group curriculum, one-on-one counseling sessions between clients and staff, staff training, and instituting policies and procedures that supported a sex-positive treatment environment. The group curriculum is detailed in my book *Sexual Health in Drug and Alcohol Treatment: Group Facilitator's Manual* (Springer Publishing Company, 2009). This book is an integral part of the overall Sexual Health in Recovery Pathway I will introduce in Chapter 8. Although it is not necessary to read my first book in order to understand sexual health in recovery, I do recommend it for anyone looking for more information about how to implement psychoeducational group interventions for teaching sex/drug-linked relapse prevention in drug and alcohol treatment settings. Many of the relapse prevention skill sets introduced in the curriculum are adapted for sex/drug-linked relapse prevention counseling approaches discussed in this book.

As we planned our relapse prevention intervention, we wanted to produce an outcome evaluation that would provide useful, statistically significant data to measure change in retention and possibly identify variables associated with sex/drug-linked relapse to propose for further study. Most importantly, we hoped to improve treatment outcomes for the many clients at Stepping Stone with high sex/drug-linked addiction who were failing in treatment at a time when they had little room for error given the devastation of their lives from addiction.

CHALLENGES IN IMPLEMENTING THE DISCOVERING SEXUAL HEALTH PROGRAM

There were many obstacles in moving Stepping Stone from their traditional approaches to sex and recovery. Our first one was that no one had done this before. We had no evidence other than the demoralized consequences from watching too many men and women fail treatment, be asked to leave, or just never return from an afternoon job interview and know that this premature end to treatment was linked to sex and drugs.

I had my own ambivalence to address. I was not sure we could find people to implement and oversee the program. What would be the priority for these unique positions? Would they first and foremost be addiction treatment specialists who would be taught sexual health content? Or rather someone with specialized training in sexuality invited to enter drug treatment as a sex expert? They would have to be certain of the importance of this work.

I became much less ambivalent after I clarified my own priorities about how to best address delivering sexual health programming in a drug treatment center. It would be the *mental attitude* of the experienced drug and alcohol professional or the experienced sexual health professional that was central, not the field they came from. I drew from my training as a sex therapist. Sex therapists can be well trained, excellently informed and scientifically sound in their work, but without certain attitudes, values, self-awareness, and an ability to self-reflect, positive sexual health interactions will be obstructed.

My experience at Stepping Stone supports these findings. When the staff understood the potentially important treatment improvement outcomes for the clients and the program, and when they were given a sense of self-efficacy and support for coping with the many psychological, emotional, and attitudinal states of mind provoked by the sexual health in recovery program, they expressed a high degree of readiness, enthusiasm, and skill in instituting these changes.

Stepping Stone relies on a large volunteer program to provide daily support for residents. The staff is composed primarily of paraprofessionals and certified drug and alcoholism counselors; most have high school diplomas or bachelor's degrees. Three master's-level counselors who had just completed their schooling taught the curriculum to the sexual health in recovery group. I supervised the implementation of the sexual health in recovery program. None of the staff had specialized training in human sexuality; in fact, only one of sexual relapse prevention counselors had taken any advanced sexuality coursework at a master's degree level. And of course no one had taught a psychoeducational group on sexual health approaches to relapse. This meant that all were given training in sexuality, the goals of the program, and instituting policies and procedures that supported a sex-positive treatment environment. This process will be the focus of many of the chapters of this book.

One of the most encouraging and inspiring outcomes of this project was seeing the Stepping Stone counselors, staff, volunteers, and administration enthusiastically integrate sex-positive and sexual health relapse prevention program changes. The sexual health in recovery project was presented as a pioneering opportunity to see if changing from a sex-negative to a sex-positive treatment environment could improve client recovery and retention; it also challenged the increasing feeling of hopelessness that had pervaded the program surrounding crystal meth and other sex/drug-linked addictions.

RESULTS OF THE DISCOVERING SEXUAL HEALTH PROGRAM AT STEPPING STONE

Jim Zians, PhD, an evaluation specialist, led the team in designing an assessment measure to identify clients with high sex/drug-linked addiction as well as to measure client retention. Dr. Zians assembled a wide range of psychological measures to glean potential correlated psychological factors specific to high sex/drug-linked clients. If we could identify what stands out among the high sex/drug-linked clients, we could perhaps identify which component of the intervention was most correlated with change. The most exciting possibility would be to use our outcome data to possibly identify and predict treatment improvement outcomes among high sex/drug-linked clients. The Sexual Health in Recovery Assessment measure in this book is adapted from many of the approaches and questions Dr. Zians included in the original Stepping Stone client survey.

Stepping Stone compared client retention rates during the 3-year period of the study against those in the 3 years prior to the study. During the study, client retention increased from 25% to over 50%. Discharges and unplanned discharges linked with relapse decreased to 1 in 10 from what was believed to be almost 1 in 3.

Most importantly, Stepping Stone found sexual behavioral problems within the treatment center plummet after implementation of the program. I believe that when you provide a specialized environment for sexual health discussions, it eliminates the need for sexual issues to spill out in other rooms or places.

The outcome evaluation substantiated the basic assumptions of this intervention. This work will need to be replicated and studied in a variety of different settings and circumstances to determine the reliability and construct validity of sex/drug-linked relapse prevention as a tool for improving drug and alcohol treatment outcomes. This intervention is not limited to only research-based settings for implementation. The concept is sound, the need is great.

We found no harm in the intervention; clients did not get worse because of a sex-positive treatment program. Certain clients may have "opted out" of considering Stepping Stone when they learned that sexual health intervention was a basic element of treatment for all program residents and clients. However, we found that other clients specifically chose Stepping Stone *because of* the sexual health program. If you are the only program in your community offering this program, or are a therapist who develops a reputation for addressing sex/drug-linked relapse in a constructive way, be prepared to see an increase in clients specifically because of this program. There may be a pent-up, unspoken need to address sex and recovery among men and women in your community.

ADDRESSING RESISTANCE TO CHANGE

Addressing sexual health in recovery was a daunting prospect for many of the staff and clients at Stepping Stone, and it might be for you, too. Many treatment programs are based on sex-negative, avoidant, or fear-based approaches that must be overcome. (I will discuss this more in Chapter 3.) This was true at Stepping Stone as well; prior to sexual health in recovery, the program relied almost exclusively on outdated, impulsive, judgmental, and reactive procedures in addressing resident sexual concerns. With little evidence other than intuitive support from many informed professionals, everyone at Stepping Stone moved forward with the intervention.

As a researcher studying how people successfully change, James Prochaska noticed that a person's reasons for changing a behavior (or belief or idea) always increase as the person moves from precontemplation to contemplation (pages 163-164, *Changing for Good*, Avon Books, 1994). If a drug counselor is to change her approach, she must perceive more positive reasons for providing sexual health in recovery-based treatment than negative objections. If sex/drug-linked relapse prevention is to have a future in drug and alcohol treatment, it will depend upon many individual counselors and program leaders personally discovering for themselves the wide range of positive outcomes that occur when sexuality is seen as an ally in recovery.

Richard Siegel, a national expert on sexuality issues in chemical dependency, describes this in his (as of August 2010) unpublished review of *Sexual Health in Drug and Alcohol Treatment: Group Facilitator's Manual*.

> In my opinion, this may be an easy syllabus to read to a group, but if it's to live up to its powerful potential, this therapeutic curriculum requires a genuine commitment, and a tremendous amount of

preparation and training, from any facilitator willing to take on the role. From my own experience working in a variety of in- and outpatient chemical dependency treatment settings, I'd say that Doug Braun-Harvey's experiences with the staff at Stepping Stone and the initial study groups and programs in San Diego were exceptionally enthusiastic and lucky. I can easily picture far less enthusiasm and willingness to embrace the idea of installing Sexual Health in Drug and Alcohol Treatment programs at other centers. This is why I feel the hardest part of proposing this program will be convincing often rigid culture and systems within traditional chemical dependency treatment of the importance of this (what amounts to a) sea change! (Draft copy of review for *Journal of Sex Education*, written April 14, 2010)

The benefits for changing an often rigid culture and system regarding sex in recovery are powerful; they have great potential to help clients with the universal goal of staying sober and remaining in recovery. For this reason I hope that there will eventually come a tipping point at which implementing sexual health-based approaches expands from individual counselors and leaders to a broader base of treatment centers.

Prochaska's change research found that those who strongly oppose changing long-established approaches may not need to change as much as we may think. Prochaska discovered that in order for people to move from precontemplation to action, it was more important that they *decrease their objections* rather than *increase their reasons* for change. This suggests that addiction professionals do not need to abandon *all* their concerns and objections about this intervention in order to proceed with implementation. What is more essential is increasing their sense of the positive arguments for change. I believe that support for this program may in many cases come directly from the clients. The client's stories will support what many treatment providers already intuitively know: for some clients, sexuality plays a central role in almost every component of their addiction.

How many times have you heard the following from a client in treatment?

- I have never had sober sex.
- How can I date without relapsing?
- Sex is what took me out of my last treatment program. (relapse)
- Drugs lowered my inhibitions.
- I have never had sober sex with my spouse.
- I love raw sex; I could have as much as I wanted when I was high.

- I get high when I thought I needed someone.
- I had sex right before I came here (before entering drug treatment program).
- I am damaged goods: I am HIV positive….I don't have anywhere to talk about it.
- I am afraid I will never have sex again.
- Crystal meth is a "three-way," drugs are the third partner.
- 99% of all my sex has been under the influence.
- I cruise online for sex and drugs.
- I have turn-ons I am afraid to let myself fantasize about unless I am high.
- I can't have an orgasm unless I am high.
- I can't think about having sex in my mind when I am sober.
- I don't know what "normal" sex is.
- When I was young I prostituted for drugs and I am ashamed of my past.
- I am attracted to someone in the program….should I tell them?

What did you notice about your feelings and thoughts as you read these statements? What would it be like for you to listen to a client discuss these concerns? Imagine being able to respond to these concerns and fears in a way that supports the client in his or her recovery. It is my belief that when counselors see their clients' relief and gratitude for finally being able to discuss their sex/drug-linked addiction, the positives for instituting this relapse prevention intervention will begin to quickly and rapidly accumulate.

The change may be slow. Focusing optimism on seeing the benefits of a gradually increasing visibility and relapse prevention for sex/drug-linked addiction patterns rather than relying on an unrealistic widespread sea change in the many objections and fears surrounding sex and recovery is a more hopeful model for going forward.

HIGH SEX/DRUG-LINKED CLIENTS IN RECOVERY

What do we know about the men and women who merge drug and alcohol use with sex? This is still an emerging area of study, but a number of reports suggest that there is a powerful connection that needs to be explored.

In a 2002 study, Rawson, Washton, Domier, and Reiber investigated differences between psychoactive drug users' sexual thoughts, feelings, and behaviors during their previous incidence of using their drug of choice. Their investigation found gender differences both within drug of choice and within the sexual effects related to specific drugs. Their study recognized the lack of valid measures to identify these relationships for discerning clinical interventions to improve treatment.

I observed the sex/drug link anecdotally while conducting supervision of onsite counselors who went to every residential drug treatment program in San Diego County to test for STI and HIV infections. The staff I supervised would conduct a brief pretest interview with the client, followed several weeks later by a posttest interview. (This was prior to the more immediate testing procedures now available.) The counselors were overwhelmed by the intensity of questions about sex, sexual activity in treatment, and a wide array of sexual health concerns. They were also struck by how infrequently the residents reported a significant concern about HIV as opposed to a host of other sexual issues. The HIV testing counselors were the "de facto" sexual health experts. Residents commonly stated they could never discuss their sexual concerns with the counselors and staff at the residential treatment center.

The Clinical Trials Network (CTN) research projects (Calsyn, 2008) identified the need for recovering men and women to learn how to enjoy sex sober. Eighty percent of the men in the CTN methadone study reported having sex under the influence in the last 90 days and 70% of the men in an outpatient rehabilitation program linked drinking with sex in the same time period.

The most significant gap in the research and development of sex/drug-linked treatment improvement is the integration of client sexual health, relapse prevention, and sex/drug-linked addiction patterns in all areas of substance abuse treatment. Compartmentalization of sex/drug-linked relapse prevention within specific demographic groups is important for research, but limits the development of sexual health within a drug and alcohol treatment center. Sexual health-based relapse prevention is a treatment improvement intervention for drug and alcohol treatment. We frankly do not know the typical prevalence of high sex/drug-linked addiction patterns within the wide range of public, private, inpatient, outpatient, drug-specific, poly-drug-focused treatment programs in the United States. Premature movement to focus on existing demographic groups from current research will do a disservice to the drug and alcohol treatment profession.

An invisible subset of alcohol-dependent and/or drug-dependent men and women in treatment remains undetected. These clients may be stigmatized as "treatment failures," "difficult clients," "untreated sex addicts," "deviants," and "sluts" and recognize a clinical population in need of treatment-specific approaches to increase rates of treatment completion and maintenance of recovery. This is why the term "sex/drug-linked addiction" is so important. This term provides language for the clinical relapse factor within drug and alcohol treatment.

CONCLUSION: THE IMPORTANCE OF SEXUAL HEALTH IN RECOVERY

The experience at Stepping Stone has increased my belief that sexual health is an aspiration for almost everyone in recovery. Sex/drug-linked relapse prevention can be effectively implemented by a wide variety of drug and alcohol professionals in an environment of nonjudgmental open-minded curiosity about sexual health in all its facets. The enthusiastic implementation of the relapse prevention program at Stepping Stone significantly challenges the current orthodoxy that drug counselors cannot address issues of sexual health within recovery.

The wonderful staff at Stepping Stone demonstrated to me that there is a tremendous hunger for sexual health recovery tools among drug and alcoholism professionals. Their dedication to learning and changing was an inspiration. As for the clients, the residents of Stepping Stone embraced this program with excitement, relief, and increasing confidence in their ability to stay sober. They finally had a place to talk about sex and drugs! The determination of the men and women whose lives were on the edge of destruction before entering treatment was not to be underestimated. From the first day of the experiment they looked forward to the Discovering Sexual Health group and were so grateful to be in a treatment program in which sexuality was positively addressed rather than feared and avoided.

I

Counselor Readiness

1

What Is "Sexual Health in Recovery"?

Since the founding of Alcoholics Anonymous (AA) and the beginnings of contemporary addiction treatment in the United States, abstinence has been the primary goal of those diagnosed or self-described as alcoholics and/or addicts. Although far from a universal goal in addiction treatment around the world, it remains the typical standard of health and well-being for addiction treatment.

Men and women who choose to face their dependency on drugs and alcohol must adjust to and maintain a lifelong shift to abstinence. This is not easy under any circumstance. Because their brain structure and body chemistry have been altered because of their addictive behavior, ending the use of mood-altering chemicals can cause a state of havoc and withdrawal in many addicts.

Over the years, relapse has been seen as a moral failing, a denial of one's disease, a sign of lack of willpower, a hopeless case, a spiritual void, an oppositional rigidity, a bewildering act of self-destruction, or just plain stupid. Relapse following a commitment to sobriety and recovery can cause deep hurt, betrayal, suffering, legal problems, financial catastrophe, personal demoralization, divorce, alienation from family and friends, homelessness, mental illness, disease, accidents, and death. Faced with such consequences, we must ask: Why would someone do this?

New scientific research is changing our understanding of the nature of addiction. Imaging technology that lets us view the working structures of the brain provides compelling data about changes in the brain circuitry of addicts. We now know that addiction to drugs and alcohol changes the brain structure and chemistry. These changes, combined with the life circumstances and typical behavior patterns of addicts, can be powerfully destructive to body, mind, and spirit. This knowledge has led drug and alcohol treatment professionals to become more compassionate about the occurrence of relapse. Knowing that the brain and the accompanying addict behavior is not going to change overnight upon the removal of drugs and alcohol helps us feel greater empathy for substance abusers who do not find stable abstinence when entering recovery.

Despite the increase in normalization of relapse, the all-too-human response of consternation and frustration is prevalent among addicts, their families and friends, and the professionals who treat them. Even when we know the many valid reasons for relapse, we may remain reactive, judgmental, and hurt when it occurs. It is this emotional response—the impulse to punish, shun, abandon, ridicule, or chastise—that leads addicts to treatment centers, 12-step fellowships, or addiction counselors who can provide a voice of equanimity during the calamity of relapse. However, even the best trained treatment professionals may find their emotional responses difficult to regulate when relapse is associated with sexual behavior.

Sexual Health in Recovery will explore sex/drug-linked behavior and will discuss how substance abusers can maintain abstinence and prevent relapse resulting from sexual behavior fused with alcohol and/or drug use. I define *sex/drug-linked behavior* as the merging of drug- and/or alcohol-dependent behavior and sexual activity. Clients who show high levels of sex/drug-linked behavior need specific relapse prevention skills and interventions that help them prepare for and integrate sexual situations *without* using drugs or alcohol. This will improve treatment outcomes and positively integrate sexuality within all phases of recovery. I developed this term to create a common language among drug and alcohol treatment professionals and sexologists who research, treat, or design clinical treatment programs.

It is difficult to quantify the number or percentage of substance abusers who demonstrate sex/drug-linked behavior patterns because this area is greatly lacking in research. However, in the last decade, some researchers have studied the relationship between sexual behavior, thoughts and feelings, and specific drugs (e.g., see Haynes, Calsyn, & Tross, 2008; Rawson, Washton, Domier, & Reiber, 2002). Methamphetamine use was correlated in almost three out of every four clients asked to discuss their sex/drug-linked behavior (Rawson et al.). This same study found cocaine and alcohol use in almost one out of every three clients. Statistics similar to the Rawson sample were found among a population within a 2004 and 2005 National Institute on Drug Abuse Clinical Trials Network (Haynes et al.).

Haynes et al. (2008) propose the necessity of assessing sex/drug-linked patterns of addiction among clients presenting for treatment as a vital first step toward increasing the likelihood of broaching sexual topics with these men and women in treatment. Some interventions designed to address sexual health, HIV issues, and positive gender role identity have been adapted for use in a handful of treatment programs with research funding from HIV prevention funds. Although not specifically designed to measure and individually clinically treat a wide array of relapse risk factors specific to sex/drug-linked addiction, these pioneers have been vital to introducing this gap in substance abuse treatment.

HIV research has been another source of preliminary data on the prevalence of sex/drug-linked behavior. Studies designed to reduce HIV risk-taking behavior among clients in drug and alcohol treatment programs have provided a secondary gain of increasing the frequency of sexuality-focused discussions between counselors and clients (the HIV risk factor being sex under the influence). Subjects in such research have been more likely to discuss their frequency of sex/drug-linked behavior.

THE LACK OF SEXUAL HEALTH KNOWLEDGE IN THE RECOVERY PROFESSION

In 2005, the U.S. Department of Health and Human Services, Substance Abuse and Mental Health Services Administration's Center for Substance Abuse Treatment (CSAT) invited a wide spectrum of leaders in the treatment and recovery field to create a cohesive set of principles of recovery and a care delivery system for men and women in recovery. This National Summit on Recovery defined recovery as a "process of change through which an individual achieves abstinence and improved health, wellness and quality of life" (CSAT, 2007, p. 9). For people recovering from addiction and alcoholism, recovery is now promoted as a process of both abstinence and improved health. Although this is not a new idea, the federal endorsement of this principle has important implications for policy, programming, and funding.

The 2005 summit also developed 12 guiding principles of recovery. They are the following:

> **There are many pathways to recovery.** Individuals are unique with specific needs, strengths, goals, health attitudes, behaviors and expectations for recovery. Pathways to recovery are highly personal, and generally involve a redefinition of identity in the face of crisis or a process of progressive change. Furthermore, pathways are often social, grounded in cultural beliefs or traditions and involve informal community resources, which provide support for sobriety. The pathway to recovery may include one or more episodes

of psychosocial and/or pharmacological treatment. For some, recovery involves neither treatment nor involvement with mutual aid groups. Recovery is a process of change that permits an individual to make healthy choices and improve the quality of his or her life.

Recovery is self-directed and empowering. While the pathway to recovery may involve one or more periods of time when activities are directed or guided to a substantial degree by others, recovery is fundamentally a self-directed process. The person in recovery is the "agent of recovery" and has the authority to exercise choices and make decisions based on his or her recovery goals that have an impact on the process. The process of recovery leads individuals toward the highest level of autonomy of which they are capable. Through self-empowerment, individuals become optimistic about life goals.

Recovery involves a personal recognition of the need for change and transformation. Individuals must accept that a problem exists and be willing to take steps to address it; these steps usually involve seeking help for a substance use disorder. The process of change can involve physical, emotional, intellectual and spiritual aspects of the person's life.

Recovery is holistic. Recovery is a process through which one gradually achieves greater balance of mind, body and spirit in relation to other aspects of one's life, including family, work and community.

Recovery has cultural dimensions. Each person's recovery process is unique and impacted by cultural beliefs and traditions. A person's cultural experience often shapes the recovery path that is right for him or her.

Recovery exists on a continuum of improved health and wellness. Recovery is not a linear process. It is based on continual growth and improved functioning. It may involve relapse and other setbacks, which are a natural part of the continuum but not inevitable outcomes. Wellness is the result of improved care and balance of mind, body and spirit. It is a product of the recovery process.

Recovery emerges from hope and gratitude. Individuals in or seeking recovery often gain hope from those who share their search for or experience of recovery. They see that people can and do overcome the obstacles that confront them and they cultivate gratitude for the opportunities that each day of recovery offers.

Recovery involves a process of healing and self-redefinition. Recovery is a holistic healing process in which one develops a positive and meaningful sense of identity.

Recovery involves addressing discrimination and transcending shame and stigma. Recovery is a process by which people confront and strive to overcome stigma.

Recovery is supported by peers and allies. A common denominator in the recovery process is the presence and involvement of people who contribute hope and support and suggest strategies and resources for change. Peers, as well as family members and other allies, form vital support networks for people in recovery. Providing service to others and experiencing mutual healing help create a community of support among those in recovery.

Recovery involves (re)joining and (re)building a life in the community. Recovery involves a process of building or rebuilding what a person has lost or never had due to his or her condition and its consequences. Recovery involves creating a life within the limitation imposed by that condition. Recovery is building or rebuilding healthy family, social and personal relationships. Those in recovery often achieve improvements in the quality of their life, such as obtaining education, employment and housing. They also increasingly become involved in constructive roles in the community through helping others, productive acts and other contributions.

Recovery is a reality. It can, will, and does happen. (CSAT, 2007, pp. 5–7)

The inclusion of "relapse and other setbacks" as part of the recovery process represents a significant step forward in addiction treatment. Although not viewed as inevitable, it is important that relapse is now seen as a naturally occurring result of the process of improving one's body, mind, and spirit. This helps to humanize relapse and lapse as part of the recovery process. *Relapse* is distinguished from a *lapse* based on the length and level of acuity of substance abuse following a period of abstinence while in the process of recovery. A lapse is a brief return to use followed by a motivated return to recovery. A relapse is a more prolonged period during which the client returns to previous levels of use that meet the diagnostic criteria for symptoms of substance dependence.

It is noteworthy, however, that sex is *not* overtly referenced anywhere in the 12 principles. In the entire document, there is no mention of human sexuality, sexual health, or sexual behavior. Although great strides have been made in treating women and men suffering from addiction, their sexuality—particularly as a part of the recovery process—is marginalized and even made invisible. You may have experienced this marginalization in your professional experience as well. It is my assertion that sexuality, when not directly and positively addressed in recovery, can contribute to treatment failure and relapse.

Noted author and recovery expert Stephanie Covington wrote:

> Recovery means more than the elimination of one's drug of choice, either through harm reduction or abstinence. Recovery is also about what is added or gained in one's life. To me, recovery means wholeness. It means having one's inner self (thoughts, feelings, values, and beliefs) *connected and congruent* with one's outer self (behavior and relationships). (Braun-Harvey, 2009, p. ix–x)

If your clients' sexual thoughts, feelings, values, and beliefs are not integrated within their recovery, their sexual lives are sidelined out of their relapse prevention recovery work. This book will teach you how to help your clients connect sexual situations with their personal level of relapse risk. I hope the tools and skills in this book increase your confidence and ability to help clients manage their sexual activity and relationships without jeopardizing their recovery.

Sexual Health in Recovery combines the wisdom of recovery and relapse prevention with important findings in sex research and principles of sexual health. In my experience, many addiction professionals are quite well informed about addiction but have no training or experience in sexual literacy and sexual health knowledge. It is time for our first integration step.

A BRIEF HISTORY OF SEXUAL HEALTH

Prior to the 1970s, *sexual health* meant the absence of a sexually transmitted infection. Basically, if you did not have a venereal disease or unintended pregnancy, you had sexual health. Focusing on bacterial and viral infections that result from sexual activity has been a public health concern for millennia. Of course, sexually transmitted infections like gonorrhea, chlamydia, herpes, human papillomavirus (HPV), syphilis, and, more recently, HIV remain constant sexual health concerns. However, the tremendous focus on sexually transmitted infections and unintended pregnancy left far too many other sexual concerns understudied, even among sexologists.

In 1975, the World Health Organization (WHO) published *Education and Treatment of Human Sexuality: The Training of Health Professionals*. In this document, the first definition of sexual health was proposed: "Sexual health is the integration of the somatic, emotional, intellectual, and social aspects of sexual being, in ways that are positively enriching and that enhance personality, communication and love.

Fundamental to this concept are the right to sexual information and the right to pleasure" (WHO, 1975, The Role of Human Sexuality in Health Programmes section, para. 1). Since this early definition, the concept of sexual health has been continually improved and refined by many organizations in various documents (e.g., see Office of the Surgeon General, 2001; Pan American Health Organization & WHO, 2000; WHO, 2002, 2006; World Association for Sexual Health, 1999). These documents articulated and emphasized issues of sexual rights, as well as contemporary constructs of sexuality and sexual health.

In 2001, Surgeon General David Satcher released *The Surgeon General's Call to Action to Promote Sexual Health and Responsible Sexual Behavior.* The *Call to Action* was developed through a collaborative process "which sought the broadest possible input and brought together a wide range of experience, expertise and perspective" (Office of the Surgeon General, 2001, p. ii). Dr. Satcher combined the previously established WHO sexual health definitions with the "responsibilities that individuals and communities have in protecting sexual health" (p. i). This report provides a foundation for envisioning a path to promote sexual health within recovery.

THE SIMILARITIES BETWEEN SEXUAL HEALTH AND RECOVERY

In 2002, the WHO convened to develop a global consensus for a working definition of sexual health.

> Sexual health is a state of physical, emotional, mental, and social well-being related to sexuality; it is not merely the absence of disease, dysfunction, or infirmity. Sexual health requires a positive and respectful approach to sexuality and sexual relationships, as well as the possibility of having pleasurable and safe sexual experiences, free of coercion, discrimination, and violence. For sexual health to be attained and maintained, the sexual rights of all persons must be respected, protected and fulfilled. (WHO, 2006, p. 5)

I am struck at the similarity between the CSAT's definition of recovery and WHO's conception of sexual health. Both see health as a process that brings together our body, feelings, psychology, and relationships into a well-choreographed convergence leading toward health. No one single dimension is solely responsible for health. Just like abstinence is not solely responsible for recovery, neither is avoidance of serious infections or unplanned or unwanted pregnancy the pivotal component of sexual health.

Both focus on a process, not an event. Both require a respectful, thoughtful, and mature health discussion. Both require overcoming stigmas, shame, and difficulty with facing aspects of oneself that may be very uncomfortable to acknowledge or reveal. Both developed out of a process of consensus. Many people with diverse disciplines, ideologies, life experience, and values collaborated to find common ground to move an agenda forward.

The evolving definitions of sexual health and recovery are similar. What, then, is the current state of these two health issues when placed side by side? How do sexuality and abstinence both play a role in maintaining recovery?

STORIES OF SEXUALITY IN RECOVERY

Men and women in recovery know the healing power of telling their stories and listening to the stories of others. They come to believe in the necessity of telling their stories of recovery to professional helpers, sponsors, or strangers and friends sitting in chairs at fellowship meetings. Stories are magic. However, stories about their sexual lives during addiction and in recovery are not welcomed among people in recovery. Stories of sexual concerns, sexual pride, sexual yearnings, sexuality linked with drug or alcohol use or abuse, and sexual histories are not, in my experience, well handled among fellow addicts or addiction professionals.

To understand the current state of affairs of sexual health and recovery, we need to look from both vistas across a wide canyon. I have been to the Grand Canyon. This wonder of nature can be viewed from two central park locations—North Rim and South Rim. If you have been to both, you can attest to the striking difference between the two locations, yet you are looking at the same carved earth. The current state of sexuality and recovery are similar. Recovery professionals bring one perspective; sexual health experts have another. Sexual health in recovery bridges both. To successfully construct this bridge, we must start by examining the ground on which each end is built. To do this, we will return to the magic of personal stories. The following descriptions of people in recovery will demonstrate the profound links between sexuality, addiction, and recovery. These are not based on real clients, but rather composites of the many stories I have listened to as a therapist, trainer, and consultant. We will follow their stories throughout this book.

Sabrina: Using Drugs to Escape Sexual Anxiety

"I am still scared of my own shadow," Sabrina said. Now in recovery for 10 months, Sabrina was feeling the stress of single life in recovery. A debilitating social anxiety kept her from asserting herself in sexual situations. She found herself frozen with anxiety during sex. Drinking and partying was an easy solution; so for years, she combined sex with alcohol, pot, cocaine, and crystal methamphetamine. "Everyone I dated was a partier," she told her treatment counselor. In the last 5 years, she had had six sexually transmitted infections and two pregnancies, both of which ended in spontaneous miscarriage.

Sabrina is much less lonely now, thanks to the meaningful relationships she has developed in recovery and the effective treatment tools she uses to treat her social anxiety. She would like to date again, particularly a man she met in her apartment building. She is determined to find a sober relationship without using drugs to create a false sense of self-confidence. However, her recovery community tells her to avoid entering into a relationship until she has a year clean and sober. "Stay focused on your recovery!" they say. The message is the same from everyone: Wait.

Traditionally, alcohol and drug recovery centers as well as the 12-step community have relegated sexual behavior in early recovery to the back burner—typically because they believe that pursuing sexual relationships too soon in recovery risks relapse. This standard is so universal that individual circumstances are rarely considered. "Three hundred sixty-five days clean and sober" is a cultural norm that is upheld with vigilance and dire warning. "Sex took me out" is a frequently mentioned experience that leads many addicts, Sabrina included, to become wary of sex and sexual desire. Fear of the inevitable link between premature sexual activity and relapse is forged so tightly partly because of the lack of any alternative relapse prevention approaches.

Frank: Using Drugs to Escape Traumatic Memories

"You're out of control" Frank's early recovery friends said. He disagreed. His history of drinking and crystal meth led to entering an intensive treatment program at 37. Unemployed, estranged from his family, single, and poorer than he has ever been in his life, he would be homeless were it not for his willingness to enter a government funded residential treatment program.

Now, 7 months into his treatment and recovery, he wants to begin discussing his current sexual life. He is choosing to not date or have a partnered sex. In recovery, he has come to accept that his memories of being sexually assaulted by his mother's boyfriend when he was 6–9 years old will take more time to heal. Intrusive memories of the violence are triggered during sex. In recovery, he has come to know that he drank before sex to unconsciously block out the anticipation of the trauma recall. Using meth during sex allowed him to have sex without the memories inhibiting him and interfering with his pleasure.

Currently, Frank is enjoying a very active sex life—with himself. "Masturbation is my safe place now." He has discussed his solo sex life with his sponsor and the counselor at his treatment center. Both tend to focus on his masturbation frequency and the fact that he looks at sexual images on his computer as part of his arousal. He has stopped discussing it because of the judgmental and scolding comments. However, this leaves Frank feeling hurt and frustrated by what he sees as a source of pride in his recovery. He has yet to find a person in his support system with positive attitudes about masturbation.

As Frank's experience indicates, sexuality is typically addressed within drug and alcohol treatment centers and fellowship groups as a problem, a worry, a concern, an addiction, or a threat to sobriety. Many will take a *sex negative*, disease or pathogical perspective. In my experience, many addiction professionals will only address sex through a few very limited and negative themes: sex addiction (which is *not* the same as sex/drug-linked behavior, as I will discuss in Chapter 2), sexually transmitted diseases, HIV, pregnancy, and/or the moral dimension of conforming to an arbitrary set of sexual values and behaviors. Counseling sexual conversations typically only occur in response to a relationship crisis, health crisis, or relapse. This was not helpful to Frank, who wanted to talk about his pride in choosing safety and pleasure as a recovery path. Sex-positive conversations—those focused on sexual pleasure, insights about oneself through one's sexuality, and learning about ones body and sexual response in sobriety—are sidetracked and avoided because of the more comfortable and familiar focus on fears about sex.

Trish: Out-of-Control Sexual Behavior

"I just get so horny!" was Trish's response to the program director who was counseling Trish for the third time in 2 weeks. "I'm such a slut, what do you expect?" Trish has been flirting with a particularly attractive new male counselor at her treatment center. She took a cell phone picture of herself lying on her bed and sent it, with a provocative text message, to the surprised counselor's personal cell phone. She had sent these cell phone bombs before, except this time she was not high.

> Trish was ashamed of her behavior and even more intensely ashamed of her attraction to the counselor. It did not even cross her mind to reveal this. It was easier to play the "slut" card. Everyone would believe that.

Without a sexual health group in her treatment program, Trish had no place to ponder the more shameful, hidden, and central motivations for her rule-breaking behaviors. Without sexual health treatment program principles to draw on, the program director is left to focus on boundaries, risk of termination, and the humiliation of her behavior rather than its underlying causes and issues.

The subject of sex is often taboo in alcohol and drug treatment environments. Most professional staff members have a difficult time broaching the subject. They have little to no education in human sexuality or sexual health. When painful and disruptive sexual behaviors intrude on the treatment environment, both client and counselor are unable to look beyond the immediate circumstance to create an opportunity to reveal shameful, painful, and hurtful aspects of sexual behavior and addiction.

Without a sex-positive space for learning and conversing about sex/drug-linked addiction, clients will unconsciously force the issue through their behavior. "If you won't talk to me about this, I will *make* you talk to me!" This unconscious strategy risks treatment termination because of arbitrary, idiosyncratic, and, at times, punitive reactions by undertrained and overstressed counselors.

Stephen: The False Choice Between Recovery and Celibacy

> Growing up in rural Nova Scotia, Stephen discovered his attraction for men through an exploitive, nonconsensual, illegal sexual contact initiated by a man he met in a restroom at a regional cattle exhibition he was attending with his father. It turned out the man lived in the same county as Stephen. He told the boy they could do what they did as often as Stephen wanted as long as his father did not know. The man introduced Stephen to "poppers" (amyl nitrite). Sex and drugs have been linked for Stephen ever since. He has never had sex without being under the influence of drugs or alcohol. He had not even masturbated without poppers since his late teens. Now 32, he has been HIV positive since he was 19 and living with an AIDS diagnosis for the last 9 years. Prior to entering treatment, he was diagnosed with hepatitis C.
>
> Because his treatment center specializes in treating the lesbian, gay, bisexual, and transgender addict, Stephen expected to discuss his sexual history in more detail. He wants to address his fears that choosing sobriety means he can no longer be sexually active. In his mind, abstinence from drugs and alcohol was defacto making a choice for celibacy.

Stephen's motivation for treatment is a common story. The threat of life-threatening medical conditions and the fear of dying makes treating addiction seem like a pretty reasonable trade-off. Stephen does not want to stop being sexual. How does a person maintain abstinence from drugs and alcohol but still pursue a fulfilling sexual life?

Cindy: An Addiction Professional With Sexual Health Secrets

> *"I've been sober for 7 years, married for 20, a drug counselor for 3 years, and I haven't had sex since I got sober,"* Cindy disclosed to her supervisor in a moment of candor. A client had just asked Cindy about what sex was like being sober. Cindy was unprepared to give an answer, so she lied. She told the client that the sex in her marriage was much better when sober and the most important concern was to stay focused on recovery and worry about sex later. It was the pat answer she and other counselors said over and over.
>
> Cindy had been through three treatment programs in 5 years before she found lasting recovery. She had not had sex without being high since she was in high school. Throughout her marriage, sex meant drinking and getting high. Each of her early attempts to "cut back" were done in by this marital pattern. She was terrified to have sex without being high, and she was afraid her husband would stray if she did not have sex with him.
>
> In her first two treatment programs, she disclosed her secretive use to her husband, but not the underlying motive. In her last treatment, she was finally asked about the connection between using and her marriage. Couples counseling provided Cindy with a forum for the honest disclosure of her fear of sober sex with her husband. They left treatment relieved and planned to follow up with couples counseling after 6 months of Cindy's sobriety.
>
> Fortunately, Cindy's supervisor was the perfect person to hear Cindy's confession. She was a confident and sexually alive woman in her early 50s. She had mentored many women in AA about sex in recovery. Cindy was a fortunate exception among drug and alcohol counselors—she happened upon a mentor who was confident and willing to address sexuality in recovery.

Like Cindy, many drug and alcohol counselors in the United States are themselves in recovery from addiction. Some attended professional treatment, therapy, or a residential program to begin sobriety, and for most, if not all, sexuality was not addressed during this treatment. Through this process, a culture evolves: New professionals rely upon their own experiences in treatment, which means that they are not prepared to discuss sexual issues with their own clients. Further, there is little (if any) sexual education required to become a certified drug counselor. Treatment programs have so much to handle that sexual concerns are often seen as a frivolous diversion from the perilous complexity of early recovery and relapse prevention. For all these reasons, addiction professionals are ill equipped and poorly trained when it comes to handling issues of sexuality in treatment.

Cindy's supervisor was the exception: an individual capable of addressing sexual issues for clients and fellow professionals. I have met such individuals and I am encouraged by those drug and alcohol treatment providers who are proud of their skills, commitment, and passion about addressing sexuality in recovery. Unfortunately, when a sex-positive counselor leaves a treatment center, there may be no one to take his or her place. The "status quo" of sexual illiteracy reemerges. This creates a treatment gap. Cindy's conversation with her client reveals the real treatment failure. A caring and skilled counselor is unprepared to address a vital aspect of recovery and a central relapse trigger in a client. The client is so invested in her recovery that she initiates a sexual health conversation with a counselor. By doing so, the client is demonstrating a strong motivation for recovery to an unprepared counselor who has no training or experience to address the issue.

I applaud those readers who, like Cindy, occupy a dual role as both in recovery and addiction professional. You have two vital reasons for understanding sexual health in recovery: both for yourself and for the clients you are deeply passionate about helping.

Marcus: The Counselor and the Client

The moment Marcus saw him in the new client registration area, he freaked out. The new client was the last sex partner Marcus had used crystal with before he got sober 6 years ago. He remembered this man particularly well, because Marcus suspected that the time they were together was the night he had been infected with HIV.

At the time, Marcus was 7 months out of his first treatment program. He had been addicted to crystal and the intensity of crystal-fueled sex, for 3 years prior. Determined to stay sober, for several months, he worked closely with his sponsor, therapist, and gay AA groups to navigate his addiction and sexual identity.

Then he started missing sex. No one said much about this aspect of adjusting to sobriety, so for a while, he tried to meet his sexual needs by visiting online sex sites and watching men have sex at sex clubs.

One night, he was at a club and saw a friend from Narcotics Anonymous (NA) having sex. They made eye contact and Marcus was filled with shame. After that, he stopped going to meetings. What if he ran into another person from a meeting at a sex club? He retreated to online sex sites. Soon he began watching videos of men that were clearly high having sex. He began to recall the intense pleasure of sex and crystal.

One night, he was on Craigslist looking at men's ads for "PnP" (party and play, meaning crystal and sex). That night, he met up with someone high on crystal. He asked him not to use the crystal in front of him. Each time the man went into the bathroom to take another hit of crystal, Marcus had intense feelings race through his body. The urge to use was unlike any relapse trigger he had ever felt before. He had sex, the real sex he wanted. Somehow using a condom was not even on his mind. Marcus left feeling relief that he was able to have sex without using crystal, even though he was worried about having intercourse without using a condom.

Marcus got an emergency test for HIV 3 days later. He tested positive for the presence of HIV in his blood. Soon after, he reentered treatment. Now, 6 years later, he was a counselor. And the person he had sex with, was about to become a client at the drug treatment center he was working at.

We ask much of drug counselors. In how many other fields of professional health care do most of those treating the condition also have the disease? What guidance or training does Marcus have to guide his ethics and conduct?

Anitra and Tiffany: Sexual Behavior in 12-Step Programs

A 2005 HBO documentary called "Rehab" followed young adult women and men for a year following a 1-month stay at a residential treatment center in California. In one scene, two women, Anitra and Tiffany, have snuck out of a treatment program to attend a 12-step meeting. Why must they sneak? The scene immediately shifts to Tiffany hugging Keith, a 33-year-old member of the fellowship. Anitra is seen holding Jerry, another member of the fellowship.

Of her relationship with Jerry, Anitra says, "I think personally, he's good for my recovery. And that goes against everything that everybody says. In early recovery, don't get into relationships because it distracts from yourself." Tiffany concurs. They continue to list their rationalizations and justifications for refuting the one piece of sexual health guidance that seems universal in the recovery community.

Tiffany goes on to describe a story of nonconsensual sex at her dealer's house. "I use to fuck around with my dealer. He would get me so high that I woke up one time and there was three people in the house and they took turns with me." She disclosed that she terminated a pregnancy that resulted from this sexual assault. "I can never forgive myself. I mean, what would my parents think?"

The pain and sorrow of sex/drug-linked behavior can leave scars that require a lifetime to heal. This is an awful truth for many men and women in recovery. However, it is important to note that this vital sexual health conversation between Anitra and Tiffany is not happening in a 12-step meeting, nor at their treatment center. All too frequently, newly recovering women and men must rely on each other for sexual health conversations to avoid the punitive responses of the helpers in "the rooms." In addition, what if the 12-step meeting itself becomes a place where fundamental boundaries of sexual health are crossed?

SEXUALITY IN RECOVERY

Sabrina, Frank, Trish, Stephen, Cindy, Marcus, Anitra, and Tiffany have compelling stories about sex, sobriety, and the many complications that arise when addressing sexual health in recovery. However, their stories are only one side of our proposed bridge between recovery and sexuality. Where are the sexual health advocates, researchers, therapists, and educators? What is going on at the other side of our future bridge?

Unfortunately, despite a few innovative sexual health experts who are examining the link between sexuality and recovery (and who helped contribute to this book), the majority of sexual health, sex research, and sex therapy treatment professionals are often illiterate regarding addiction and recovery. In fact, many books and journals on the subject of sexuality make little to no mention of drug abuse, alcoholism, and the interplay of recovery and sexual health.

I recently gave a workshop on sexual health in recovery to a gathering of sex educators, therapists, and counselors. A preeminent sexological scholar and writer asked, "So, when people go to those meetings, you know, what are they called?" I said "Alcoholics Anonymous" and he said, "Yes," that is what he meant. "What are those meetings like?" I was delighted to have such a respected leader be so upfront about his lack of knowledge about recovery—it was informative. Much like drug and alcohol treatment professionals who often cannot engage in a sexual health conversation, sexologists and therapists may lack a basic vocabulary of recovery. This lack of common language is a significant barrier to begin a dialogue.

I often encounter rather strident opinions among my sexological colleagues that those in the drug and alcohol treatment field and those in the recovery community are hopelessly bound into sex-negative, fear-based attitudes. They often shake their heads when I describe my work. They seem as perplexed about the culture and process of recovery as drug and alcohol providers are avoidant of sexual health.

HIV AND RECOVERY

HIV deserves special mention because it is an issue that has brought drug and alcohol recovery and sexual health experts together. Most people at risk for HIV infection through needle sharing are abusing or addicted to drugs. For that reason, you would be hard pressed to find a drug and alcohol treatment program in the United States that does not test for HIV and provide HIV prevention services.

Many experts in recovery and sexual health find common ground in advocating for sexual health conversations to reduce the spread of HIV and to improve the health of recovering women living with HIV. The focus is often on educating the recovering HIV-infected person about HIV disease, getting proper medical attention, and becoming proficient in risk-reduction sexual practices to prevent infecting a spouse, partner, or casual sex partner. Sex researchers are funded to study correlations between substance abuse and rates of HIV infection.

Men and women who are HIV positive and in recovery may be highly anxious or depressed about not only navigating sex in recovery but, now, also addressing HIV and HIV disclosure issues with their partners. How is this a risk for relapse in recovery? This question is often unanswered.

Although HIV prevention and treatment is of course important, I find it sad that even in drug and alcohol treatment programs, the only explicit attention given to sexuality is focused on HIV education and testing. The focus is on knowing if you are HIV infected. In some treatment settings, HIV infection risk is another justification for the "don't focus too much on sex in the first year of recovery" message.

Sexual health in recovery is about developing positive attitudes about sexuality, sexual pleasure, and sexual relationships while being mindful of relapse triggers and keeping sobriety as central to sexual health. HIV education and prevention for people in recovery should be much more than using fear of infection as another justification for sex avoidance in early recovery. Sexual health in recovery is an opportunity to build a new bridge between HIV and recovery.

SEXUAL BEHAVIOR IN TREATMENT CENTERS

You probably know someone or have heard a story about someone having sex or falling in love with someone at his or her addiction treatment program. Sex with other patients is a significant boundary crossing.

Coercive, nonconsensual sex between patients or between patients and professional staff is a harmful boundary crossing. Keeping these violations secret is corrosive to recovery.

Many treatment centers do not, in my opinion, know how to properly handle these violations. Many drug and alcohol treatment centers operate under significantly outdated, ineffective, and disapproving views about sex. Sex is often addressed only when a client's sexual behavior conflicts with treatment program policies.

I believe a vast majority of the women and men who were asked to leave treatment following the disclosure of a sexual encounter with a resident have unaddressed sex/drug-linked patterns of addiction. I believe a significant portion of men and women engaging in sex with new comers at 12-step meetings suffer from unaddressed sex/drug-linked shame. Professional staff, counselors, and medical care providers who engage in sex with clients have more serious problems. Their conduct is a violation of their trusted role with a vulnerable patient. In many situations, this may also be illegal and should be investigated to determine if their conduct should be prosecuted.

All of these sexual boundary crossings exist within a culture where sexual health related to treatment, recovery, and relapse remains unaddressed. Sexual health in recovery is about providing affirming, factual sexual health information to discuss, explore, and understand how sexual behavior can be an ally for recovery and not only limited to fears of jeopardizing recovery.

In my opinion, this inability of treatment centers to effectively address sexual concerns does a disservice to both the caring counselors and motivated clients. Some treatment providers are frustrated by the knowledge that their clients might have a better chance for recovery if sex/drug-linked behaviors are addressed more directly and thoroughly in treatment. Clients, who have assimilated recovery information and are ready to apply it to their lives, unfortunately remain at risk and often relapse because their treatment provided inadequate skills for navigating sexuality in recovery.

I gave a presentation at a nationally well-respected treatment program. During a break, a shy staff member approached me. She described a popular, respected, and experienced adolescent drug counselor's questionable boundaries with female residents. It was painfully difficult for her to even be seen talking with me. She was afraid to talk about it. I clarified my role as a trainer; I was not in authority within the organization. I could not take action to address her concerns. We discussed what it was like for her to observe the behavior and keep it to herself. She told me what made her come forward and speak with me: "You just seemed like you wouldn't judge me." She felt guilt and shame about not protecting the young residents and afraid for her job if she did. I normalized this bind when anyone is exposed to exploitive, nonconsensual sex in his or her workplace. I acknowledged her commitment to herself, her workplace, and the patients by taking the time to discuss her plight with me.

I have no idea what happened next.

What is important is that sexual health conversations require a perception from all participants that the time spent disclosing and listening will be a space for suspending judgment. Without a set of sexual health principles in place, effective disclosure of sexual boundary concerns, crossings, and violations cannot happen. This creates an atmosphere that is ripe for relapse.

CONCLUSION

Sexual health in recovery is a solution—a way to confront and discuss relationships, sexual feelings, and the deep shame about the ravages of sex combined with addiction. Without a positive solution for action, everyone—those in recovery, those helping recovering people, and those with the dual role of being both—is at sea for addressing sexual health in recovery. In the following chapters, I hope to offer you many practical solutions that you can integrate into your professional practice.

2

Eight Key Concepts of Sexual Health in Recovery

Jim is 2 weeks sober. He has begun his second rehab program in 2 years. He is 33 years old living in a small house in an urban city with 14 other alcoholic and drug-addicted men. He is ashamed and disillusioned that "sex took him out" of his first rehab program. He used cocaine, pot, alcohol, and methamphetamine with women he met on Craigslist.

Jim loves getting high and having sex with new partners. His sexual behavior is always part of his drug and alcohol use. The drugs free him up to experiment with sex acts that he is completely ashamed to discuss with his wife of 6 years. However, Jim does not think he can talk about this with the counselors and staff at his treatment center.

Jim entered treatment for the first time after being robbed at gunpoint by a woman whom he had just had sex with, without a condom. She was a crystal addict and needed the money. He was humiliated and told his wife a story about being robbed on the street in a dangerous part of town when a drug deal went bad. He told his wife that his drug use was out of control. A week later, he left his wife and daughter and flew to a nationally recognized treatment program he had seen on a television commercial.

During the first week, he was given the lab results of his HIV and sexually transmitted infection (STI) status. When the doctor said, "Your lab results came back fine," Jim burst into tears. He was so relieved and so ashamed of his behavior that he decided to "come clean." Jim told the doctor about being robbed by his sex partner and how he had lied to his wife. The doctor listened patiently and said, "There will be plenty of time to talk about that. I am glad you are beginning to get honest. Right now you need to focus on getting sober."

The next day, Jim told his counselor the same story. She told Jim that if he was concerned about his sexual behavior, he could check into Sexaholics Anonymous. She talked about how too often people in recovery focus on sex as a means of diverting attention from their primary addiction. She talked about how secrets, like having sex outside of marriage, would continue to make him sick and lead to relapse.

Jim did not know where or when he would have to tell his wife the truth. He began to fear that when his wife came for "family week" he would be expected to tell her about his recreational sex with anonymous women. He did not want his wife to divorce him. He loves her. He loves his daughter. He decided not to talk about it any more.

Interestingly, the staff did not ask him much more about his sex life until it was time to write his biography. (The biography is a written drug or alcohol history read aloud in group therapy.) He had listened to five other men's biography. Only one man, an HIV-infected gay male sex worker who is a crystal-meth addict, talked in detail about his sex/drug-linked behavior. Jim was not like him.

Jim decided to write the story of the robbery as a "one time thing when he was fooling around online one night." He also said he thought it would be best for his marriage if he did not disclose this during family week. The group gave him various opinions about his choice to not tell her. No one suspected this was just a story.

Two months after leaving treatment, Jim was back on Craigslist. Three days later, he relapsed. A month later, his wife found out he had started using again. He went back to his Narcotics Anonymous (NA) home group and was even more determined to stay clean.

Jim and his wife slowly reintroduced sex into their marriage. They wanted to have another child. Jim began to have erectile difficulties during sex. He went to a doctor and was given tadalafil (Cialis). His sexual functioning improved enough to complete intercourse with his wife, but his pleasure and excitement about sex was very low. It just seemed dull.

He tried to talk about his boring sex life with friends and his sponsor. He got dismissive comments like "At least you're getting some," or "Don't expect it to be the same as when you were high."

Jim's story is one of multiple missed opportunities to introduce sexual health approaches to improve treatment and prevent relapse. Jim is a fortunate man. He has access to high-quality drug and alcohol treatment professionals in inpatient and residential treatment programs. He intuitively disclosed symptoms of sex/drug-linked relapse risk in both of his rehabilitation programs. Doctors, counselors, and multiple 12-step fellowship members have engaged him in addressing his recovery. Jim's relapse luckily did not result in cataclysmic consequences. However, he remains uninformed about a central pattern in his addiction. The link between his drug use and his sexual behavior and unresolved sexual conflicts remains unseen by Jim and his professional and personal support system.

This chapter will review eight key concepts for sexual health in recovery. These eight principles integrate key findings from the fields of sexual research, addiction treatment, harm reduction, and relapse prevention to create a framework for creating a sexual health in recovery program.

Some of these concepts may be new; others may be very familiar. It will depend on your primary training. If you are an addiction specialist, abstinence-based treatment and relapse prevention will be quite familiar to you. If you are a sex therapist or sex educator, you will readily recognize the sex-positive principles. Those who are both treatment providers and recovering themselves may doubly identify with the stories of drug and alcohol dependency linked with sexuality, relationships, and attractions.

The eight key concepts of sexual health are as follows. Sexual health in recovery is:

1. essential for identifying sex/drug-linked patterns of abuse,
2. sex positive,
3. based on harm-reduction principles,
4. abstinence based,
5. evidence based,
6. a shame-reduction intervention,
7. a relapse prevention intervention, and
8. a bridge for sexuality as an ally in recovery

We will examine each of these concepts throughout the rest of the chapter.

CONCEPT 1: SEXUAL HEALTH IN RECOVERY IS ESSENTIAL FOR IDENTIFYING SEX/DRUG-LINKED PATTERNS OF ABUSE

As the story of Jim demonstrates, people have better treatment outcomes when the linkage between their sexual behavior and drug use is directly addressed in all phases of recovery. Sexual health in recovery requires honest and informed conversations about the relationship between addiction and sex. I believe that the individual motivations for combining sex with drug and/or alcohol use are varied and often misguided attempts to solve a sexual problem.

There are five general motivations that explain a large portion of sex/drug-linked behaviors. In no particular order, they are as follows:

- sexual functioning
- sexual arousal or desire
- sexual turn-ons
- emotional regulation
- emotional expression

Sexual Functioning

Worrying about one's sexual response is one of the most common sexual concerns and one that almost everyone, recovering or not, has some experience with. The list is long and varied: "Can I make an erection last longer?" "Will I be ready for intercourse?" Will I orgasm when I want to?" "Will my partner respond and get aroused?" "Will I have a good orgasm?" "Will my partner have a good orgasm?" "Will I stay focused enough to enjoy having sex?"

For people in recovery, the answers to these questions may have an additional dimension. They may have coped with these typical sexual concerns by using. It is common in early sexual exploration with partners to combine sex with drinking or getting high. For some people, they do not know how their body functions or responds to sexual situations without being high.

Women and men in recovery who have little to no sober experience with their sexual functioning may find themselves avoidant of sex, anxious about sexual functioning, or disappointed in their level of sexual pleasure. Drug and alcohol treatment providers may have little to no training in addressing these concerns. The subject may never be discussed in group or individual counseling sessions. At best, like in Jim's experience, the topic may have been given a cursory listen with the conclusion that more important matters are the priority in early recovery.

Sexual Arousal or Desire

Who hasn't imagined that a certain drug combination will lead to just the right level of arousal and desire for a really pleasurable sexual experience? Drugs and alcohol are heavily promoted as aphrodisiacs. Wanting more of a good thing is a common motivation for introducing drugs into sex.

On the other end of the spectrum, many women and men may have used drugs to adjust their low or nonexistent sexual desire. Using drugs to put oneself in the mood for sex is an ancient tradition. The lack of sexual arousal or desire remains a complex sexual problem that today's sex therapists and researchers still do not fully understand.

Sometimes, a person in recovery may not be aware of the link between drug use and low sexual desire. A recovering alcoholic, for example, may be unaware of a history of low desire that preceded her alcoholism. She may be disappointed to find that recovery has not been an antidote for her general disinterest in sex. Sexual health in recovery provides a space for this link between sexual desire or arousal and motivations for using to be discussed. In this instance, addressing the low level of desire may be a key component in the process for recovery.

Sexual Turn-Ons

We all have that "special place" we go in our mind during sex that takes us to our most intensely felt sexual pleasure, our most meaningful or ecstatic state, and our peak turn-on. This is often accompanied by orgasm and sexual release. Our sexual turn-ons give us access to a vital aspect of sexual health—the ability to experience orgasm. An important relapse prevention sex/drug link exists when a history of drug use is linked with this turn-on. A person's inability to experience this turn-on due to abstinence presents a serious relapse risk.

Imagine losing this turn-on. Imagine losing access to the sensations or fantasies that give you the most pleasure. This would be upsetting to many people. In fact, it is a sign of sexual health when someone *is* upset about missing out on his or her most desired source of sexual pleasure.

In this situation, the sex/drug linkage may arise from a history of using drugs or alcohol to perform a specific sex act or to reduce embarrassment about sexual interests that are "strange" or "perverted." A person may have a specific unconventional turn-on that is central to his or her sexual pleasure but that he or she is conflicted or ashamed of. Drugs and drinking resolve this conflict enough for him or her to pursue the turn-on and experience the sex act.

This sex/drug-linked situation may have been motivated by shame about sexual desires that are disapproved by society, family, religion, or oneself. The turn-on may be as common as desiring specific sexual acts like oral sex, anal sex, or sexual positions that challenge expected behavior based on gender or power dynamics in the relationship.

The sex/drug link between a person's turn-on and getting high is an important relapse prevention to address early in recovery. For some men and women, the soothing familiarity of the erotic turn-on may be so linked with using that the pleasure of the arousal is linked with thoughts and memories of using. Education, awareness, and preparation for this relapse risk are important recovery sexual health skills.

Emotional Regulation

Sexual activity changes our feelings. To feel sexual arousal, we must transition from our current emotional state to the feelings, thoughts, and behaviors that move us toward sexual pleasure. This is one of the joys of sex. It is a different emotional place. When the ability for sex to transport us to a different emotional state has been consistently linked with using drugs or drinking, an additional sex/drug-linked recovery skill is indicated. Some in early recovery may feel much more interested in sex, perhaps through masturbation or with their current partner. Others may find themselves experiencing infatuations, attractions, or sexual fantasies. Others may dread the thought of sex.

Treatment professionals warn that sex and relationships are an intense emotional and relational stressor that can easily trigger relapse. This warning stems from a long history of treatment failures linked with sex and relationships. Decades of witnessing these relapses have led to a universal approach in which nearly all treatment professionals use fear-based messages that warn: "Sex will take you out."

The recovery community addresses this sex/drug-linked pattern through the message of staying out of new relationships in the first year of recovery. This prevention practice in drug and alcohol treatment is on common ground with sexual health principles. Both educate recovering addicts about the link between sex, relationships, and using.

However, sexual health in recovery moves beyond the duty to warn by providing skills that allow clients to think through *which* sexual situations may be risky for relapse. One of the most significant challenges of implementing sexual health in recovery will be addressing objections of drug treatment experts to approach this common sex/drug-linked relapse risk with sex-positive prevention rather than fear and avoidance of sexuality.

Using sex to get out of a negative or overwhelming feeling and to experience sexual pleasure or excitement instead will remain a central relapse concern. Expanding current approaches to this significant recovery problem is the goal of sexual health in recovery.

Emotional Expression

Sexuality is not only a means of escaping unwanted feelings. Sexual connection allows us to express feelings of love, affection, and commitment. Sexual health recognizes sex as central to the human experience of pleasure, meaning, relationship, and the all-too-rare moments of falling in love. People want to feel this. And of course, drugs and alcohol are means of eliminating barriers to experiencing the complexities of love. How many scenes in movies, television, theater, and novels have incorporated drinking or using drugs within romantic scenes to convey vulnerable feelings of interest, desire, falling in love, or long-withheld expressions of desire?

Using drugs and alcohol to express love to a partner or to receive expressions of love from a partner is common among men and women with high sex/drug-linked patterns of addiction. Their minds and bodies may be unaccustomed to the sensations, thoughts, and feelings that are stimulated by sober closeness and affection. Understanding the link between drugs and the emotions of love and relationships is vital to increasing clarity about sex/drug-linked addiction patterns and their influence on recovery.

CONCEPT 2: SEXUAL HEALTH IN RECOVERY IS SEX POSITIVE

A core element of sexual health in sobriety is a sex-positive attitude about sex and recovery. A sex-positive approach to recovery is being deeply committed to believing in one's ability to maintain recovery *and* have an active, pleasurable, and emotionally meaningful sexual life. Sex-positive recovery is a process in which negative judgments about sexuality (as a destructive force leading to high risk for relapse) are suspended to allow for a more balanced contemplation. Sex-positive recovery welcomes exploration of sex in recovery beyond the one-sided focus on the dangers of sexuality, crushes, sexual activity, and falling in love as a key relapse risk. Drug and alcohol treatment professionals will become more effective with clients, regardless of the client's sex/drug-linked addiction pattern, when they evaluate their personal sex-positive and sex-negative attitudes, beliefs, and values.

To fully grasp the meaning of sex positive, we must spend a few minutes understanding sex negative. First, the terms *sex negative* and *sex positive*, as I use them, are adjectives. They describe something. They are not put-downs or moral judgments. We are all a combination of sex negative and sex positive.

Sex negativity includes unspoken sexual judgments, emotional reactions, and a hierarchical designation of certain sexual behaviors as *normal* (nonpathological) and the rest as *deviant, perverted* or *inferior* (pathological) based on degree of variance from societal norms.

Sexual health requires that we understand our own individual spectrum of positive and negative attitudes about sex. Sexual health increases when we become conscious about our own biases regarding certain aspects of sex. For example, we may feel that certain sexual acts or behaviors are inferior, immoral, destructive, a violation of a religious creed, or do not comply with the majority culture's views of human sexuality. Highly sex-negative attitudes are reflected in a preoccupation with the destructive elements of sexuality and the marginalization of the pleasure and diverse ways in which men and women find meaning in their sexual desires.

On the other end of the spectrum are highly sex-positive attitudes—which have their own limitations. Some people may retain sex-positive attitudes that marginalize basic agreements of safety, consent, shared values, honesty, and the essential mutuality of sexual connection. This is also a distortion. Sex positivity is a balancing force to sex negativity. Sexual health is the balance between the two.

Sexual health in recovery advocates that we honestly evaluate the lack of balance within the recovery movement and attempt to redress this balance by integrating the positive potential of sex to prevent relapse and improve recovery among men and women whose sexuality and drug use has been fused.

Here, I propose five sex-positive skills for drug and alcohol counselors. Each is a client-centered skill. It will increase the counselor characteristics that research indicates to be associated with successful outcomes. We know that the way a drug and alcohol treatment professional interacts with clients is as important (if not more important) as the specific theory, treatment approach, or clinical techniques of that therapist. These five basic sex-positive counselor skills can counteract the more traditional sex-negative attitudes and help you address the wide range of sexual diversity among men and women in treatment.

Skill 1: Suspending Judgment

A significant sexual health barrier in drug and alcohol treatment is the high frequency of clients who withhold sexual health worries and problems because they fear their own judgments as well as the judgmental responses from professional helpers, sponsors, fellow clients, spouses, family, or church. Drug treatment counselors, group therapists, doctors, nurses, administrators, educators, paraprofessionals, and volunteers must know how to suspend their sexual judgmental thoughts and responses to inculcate a relationship that welcomes sexual health conversations.

Drug and alcohol treatment professionals do not magically know how to suspend sexual judgments. It is a rare skill among treatment providers. Perhaps you encountered a counselor in your own recovery with a knack for setting aside her personal opinions about a sexual matter and just listened. Or you may know a professional in your current setting who is the "sex magnet." Clients readily and easily open up to him or her about their sexual concerns. Perhaps you occupy this role! Typically, these counselors have an uncanny or well-practiced ability to suspend their judgments and stay focused and present on the client.

I find it quite common among mental health professionals who gather together for education and training to express a wide range of sex-negative attitudes and beliefs without the usual norm of self-observation, scrutiny, and curiosity that is typically used when discussing a diagnosis, treatment approach, or clinical formulation of a case. Sex negativity among counselors is expressed when they exhibit an inability to regulate their immediate emotional reactivity.

It is not the counselor's judgmental thought that is the consequence of immediate significance within the relationship with the client. The relationship will be disrupted by the unexamined judgmental response and accompanying instantaneous expression elicited by the counselor's dysregulated moment of judgment. The unexamined or unguarded moment is the barrier to continued sexual health discussions. Avoiding this sex-negative impulse takes practice.

Sex therapists, sex educators, and sexual health care providers practice this skill daily. This skill is so central to the delivery of sexual health services that the American Association of Sexuality Educators, Counselors and Therapists (AASECT), which is the nationally recognized body that certifies sex therapists, requires an extensive process-oriented group experience to assist sex experts to understand how their sexual attitudes and values affect them personally and professionally. No matter the level of experience, every certified sex therapist must complete a Sexual Attitude Reassessment (SAR) seminar every 5 years to maintain certification. No one outgrows the need to reaquaint oneself with his or her evolving sexual values and attitudes across the life span. SARs are offered through various organizations and conferences throughout the year. A schedule can be found at the AASECT Web site (www.aasect.org).

Counselors who develop their ability to temporarily suspend judgments about sex will find a space to delve deeper into the source that fuels their quick reaction. Only through this self-exploration will counselors come to understand what motivates these reactions. Suspending judgment is crucial to creating an environment that supports the possibility of addressing sex/drug-linked behavior. Between counselor and client, there will come a moment in sexual health discussions where the counselor, client, or both misconstrue or misread one another, question something, or engage in vehement criticism. It is only human to reflexively feel tense, heated, impatient, and irritated. By suspending judgment, one can rein one's self in at the most pitched emotional moment and avoid acting or commenting out of emotional reactions, especially if strong feelings of anxiety and anger are involved. Counselors are best able to suspend judgment about matters of sexuality when they can investigate their own emotional reaction. A valuable counseling tool for suspending judgment is to be curious about these moments of intensity as they arise. You can ask yourself:

- "Why am I having such a strong reaction to this particular sexual story, situation, or circumstance?"
- "What aspect of my life contributes to this reaction?"
- "Is the intensity of this feeling limited only to the details the client just shared, or is something else going on?"

As you can see, suspending judgment requires the ability to self-observe and self-reflect in a moment of emotional reactivity connected with sex. Counselors who are confident in their ability to examine their reactions to the sexual situations of their clients possess a key skill set for providing sexual health relapse prevention dialogue.

Another significant positive outcome of suspending judgment during emotionally stimulating sexual health conversation is modeling this skill for the client. I have come to believe that the counselor's nonjudgmental action is an essential learning moment in which men and women in recovery can learn about their *own* judgments. When the counselor does not insert his or her own sexual opinions and reactions, it allows the spotlight to be placed on the client's belief and attitude. Repetition is key. Clients will need to experience these potentially polarizing moments of judgment in the same suspended manner many times before they will be able to anticipate and welcome the suspension. I have often heard clients immediately dismiss my suspension of judgment as "phony." In some cases, they confuse suspending judgment with having *no* judgment. Of course we have judgments; we simply suspend them in the moment to shed light on clients' judgments about their sexual behavior or attitudes.

It is vital to have a few handy counselor responses at these times:

- "Is it hard for you to believe that I am more interested in your judgments about what you just said than being distracted by my opinions?"
- "I am really listening to you right now, I am not really all that interested in my reactions, I want to give you a chance to explore your reactions to what you just said."

In other words, let clients know you have a regulator on your judgments and you are using it to be present with them. Too often, therapists will deny, minimize, or deflect attention directed by the client toward the therapist's judgmental thoughts. Rather than act as if they do not happen, model a process that demonstrates you can manage these experiences of your own reactions well enough to stay focused on the client for just now.

Suspending judgment interferes with the most common reaction to matters of sexual health: vehement criticism. Criticism is an expected reaction to disclosure of painful, hurtful, injurious, unconventional, illegal, unusual, detailed, explicit, factual, titillating, arousing, lusty, loving, erotic, enticing, pleasurable, private, personal, sweet, endearing, shameful, embarrassing, confusing, curious, or mundane matters of sex. Suspending judgment is one of the *least* expected responses to talking about sex! When counselors stop and regulate their immediate reactions to sexual conversations, they reduce the client's fear of attack, derision, or moralizing. There will be many opportunities to repeat this skill with your clients. They will be expecting your judgment. They will need to see you self-regulate your judgments not only at the beginning of the relationship but throughout your relationship with them. The more counselors expand their capacity for suspending judgment during sexual health conversations, the more likely clients in recovery will begin to discuss their innermost thoughts and feelings about their sexual lives and the more likely they will remain sober in treatment and on the road to recovery.

Skill 2: Affirming Sexual Pleasure

The rewarding experience of sex is pleasure. Sexual pleasure is associated with satisfying the biological drive for sex. The mind has many pleasure centers designed to be stimulated and allow for sensations of happiness, euphoria, excitation, enjoyment, and orgasm. The brain is the pleasure center. Humans have a natural tendency to want more pleasure. If a little feels good, more will feel even better; thus, the historically omnipresent search to combine mind-altering and pleasure-enhancing chemicals or plants with sexual behavior. When this results in dependency and addiction, a sex/drug link emerges. How then is the positive effect of sexual pleasure affirmed by men and women in recovery when their pursuit of sexual satisfaction may be fused with drugs?

Affirming sexual pleasure is central to sex-positive attitudes and conversations. As discussed earlier, sex positive is the counterbalance to the more commonly accepted focus on the perils of sex. Sex positive approaches sexuality as a balance between pleasure and safety. Affirming sexual pleasure is the counterbalance to education about the negative consequences of sexual pleasure. Sexual pleasure is a positive force in our world. It may seem obvious, yet not often enough defended. How many of us have been in sexual health conversations where we must first establish our credibility by affirming the dangers of sex first? How many times has the imprimatur to discuss sexual pleasure been hampered by the necessity to establish our credentials as an authority on the hazards of sex? Reviewing the risks of sex prior to discussing sexual pleasure seems to be the required sequence of sexual dialogue, especially in United States.

What often happens in sexual pleasure discussions is the requirement to address the "fear factor" before discussing the science. This is the cultural context that men and women in recovery face when addressing sexual pleasure in recovery. The fear of relapse is such an important focus, yet what has been lacking is a balance of discussion about the pleasure of sex. What happens to the human drive for sexual pleasure within the context of recovery and abstaining from drugs and alcohol? It is the responsibility of drug and alcohol treatment professionals to provide a safe and informed forum for addressing this sexual health challenge.

To affirm sexual pleasure is to affirm the central and inherent human desire for one of life's most rewarding experiences. Sex-positive recovery is the inclusion of sexual pleasure in evaluating motivations for sex in recovery. Sex-positive recovery affirms not only the harmful consequences of sex but also takes the responsibility to challenge sex-negative drug treatment approaches that emphasize the fears of merging sexual activity with sobriety. Affirming sexual pleasure educates men and women in recovery about the role sexual pleasure has in physical and emotional health. Sober playful sexual exploration—solo or with a partner—is a powerful ally for connection in recovery. These messages of sexual health are impossible for drug counselors to credibly convey without affirming the inherent nature of sexual pleasure.

Skill 3: Understanding That Sexuality Is a Central and Basic Need

Human sexuality is fundamentally linked with human existence. This is basic. Sexuality shapes our thinking, behavior, and relationships. Of course, recovery is about reshaping our thinking, actions, and interpersonal lives. Sex influences the recovery process. It is germane to the general practice of drug and alcohol counseling to begin considering sexual health beyond exploitive, abusive, relapse fears, and conforming to cultural or societal norms as the central focus of sexuality in recovery. Sexual health in recovery, at its foundation, moves sexuality from a rare moment of focus in counseling to an important relevant position in counseling, treatment planning, and relapse prevention.

Skill 4: Understanding How a Client's Behavior Might Indicate an Attempt to Address a Sexual Worry or Concern

Drug and alcohol counselors are trained to address the cognitive distortions inherent in the mind of a person addicted to drugs and alcohol. This is important work. When sex/drug-linked patterns are the focus of addiction, the automatic response will be to focus on basic addiction management tools. This response often places sexuality as the adversary to abstinence.

A client may discuss how going online to dating sites triggers euphoric recall of sex/drug-linked use. A counselor may quite rightly focus on the relapse's pull of the addicted mind. What may be unseen is the honorable intent by the client to address a sexual worry or concern. Let's use a case example:

> Lisa is 28, is single, and lives in a large urban city. She has been clean and sober for more than 4 months. She has not had an orgasm since she was sober. She is afraid to masturbate for fear of reliving her previous relationship with her crystal meth–addicted boyfriend. She has avoided sexuality in recovery. She has not discussed this with anyone in her recovery process. Lisa really wants to recover; she also wants to begin to understand her sexuality in recovery. One night she decided to do a Google search with the words "women and sex." She soon found herself in a live chat room talking with men and women. The talk moved to what people like to do sexually, what kind of person they are attracted to, what their favorite sex memories are. Lisa began to remember her sexual history and how she could not separate sex from using and getting high. She decided to talk with her therapist about this at her next session. Her well-trained recovery specialist counselor listened to Lisa's story. She inquired about Lisa's thoughts about using. How did she cope with the euphoric recall? Is she concerned about relapse? What was it like to remember the relationship? What the counselor did not ask about or explore was the sex-positive component: What was it like for Lisa to begin to welcome her sexuality back into her life without getting high? What is happening now with Lisa that she is beginning to consider her sexual and relationship desires in recovery? This could be an opportunity for the counselor to affirm Lisa's movement to sexual health. Does Lisa have a sexual concern that she wants to discuss? Is she worried about her sexual response, sexual arousal, and sexual fantasies linked or separated from drugs?

When a drug treatment professional takes the time to wonder how a sex/drug-linked situation may also be an honorable attempt to address a sexual concern, then a sex-positive perspective has been included in the therapy. This is not an either–or approach. Sex-positive drug and alcohol treatment moves beyond an asexual approach to recovery without exclusive focus on the threat of relapse or hypersexuality-overwhelming ability to regulate relapse risk. By focusing on the positive aspect of integrating sexuality within recovery, it removes the imbalanced polarities of avoidance or fear as the primary voice within sexual health conversations.

Skill 5: Focus on Client Motivation

> Constructive behavior change seems to arise when the person connects [change] with something of intrinsic value, something important, something cherished. Intrinsic motivation for change arises in an accepting, empowering atmosphere that makes it safe for the person to explore the possibly painful present in relation to what is wanted and valued. (Miller & Rollnick, 2002, p. 12)

Sexual health firmly rooted in sex-positive attitudes creates an environment for motivating change. The fundamental centrality of sex to humanity (as just discussed) suggests a central concept of how people change. Sex will motivate people to change. This is not the key concept for sex-positive recovery, however. More to the point is for counselors to learn each client's individual motivations for sex and recovery. The key treatment provider skill is to focus on what change or adjustment in recovery is relevant to each individual client. What sexual change does he or she perceive as relevant or linked with something significant or even cherished to himself or herself?

Sexual health counselors who wish to focus on a client's motivation for a specific sex/drug-linked behavior would be wise to understand and use motivational interviewing (MI). Developed more than 20 years ago, MI is

> a directive, client-centered counseling style for eliciting behavior change by helping clients to explore and resolve ambivalence. Compared with nondirective counseling, it is more focused and goal-directed. The examination and resolution of ambivalence is its central purpose, and the counselor is intentionally directive in pursuing this goal. (Rollnick & Miller, 1995, Definition section, para. 1)

MI techniques are quite different from shaming and humiliating confrontational tactics (which had been used in many drug and alcohol treatment programs). MI approaches can be used to combine a counselors desire to understand individual client motivations with a method for enabling professionals to utilize these motivations within their clinical work. Addressing sex/drug-linked relapse risk may evolve into a significant recovery motivation when sexual health is clearly seen by the client as connected with an essential motivation for choosing recovery over addiction.

The current state of drug and alcohol treatment and counseling relies too heavily on the false perception of an inherent conflict between sexuality and recovery. This artificial polarity (recovery/asexuality or relapse/sexuality) is resolved by many drug and alcohol counselors in the direction of marginalizing sexual desire in the name of abstinence and recovery.

Missing from this solution is the client's motivation. This either–or counselor's mindset precludes attending to the specific discrepancy between clients' motivation for recovery and their ambivalence regarding sexual behavior. Studies on how people change suggest that this forced choice approach can paradoxically strengthen the very client behavior that is intended to change (Miller & Rollnick, 2002).

The sex-positive recovery skill is for the counselor to facilitate a process that leads to clients voicing their argument for change (Miller & Rollnick, 2002). A sex-positive approach to relapse prevention is to support men and women in recovery to identify their personal values for sexual health in recovery. Sex-positive change talk focuses clients on incongruencies between their sexual health goals and aspirations in recovery and current behavior. This discrepancy, which is based within the client's value system, is the condition that stimulates motivation for changing sex/drug-linked impulses and behaviors. This approach places confidence in the transformative potential of a client's deeply held sexual values and attitudes as an important source for resolving ambivalent feelings and sex/drug-linked patterns in recovery. Sex-positive recovery believes in the restorative potential of honestly and painfully unfolding personal discrepancies in an individual's vision for sexual health.

In a sex-negative environment, sexual values, ethics, and boundaries are not seen as profoundly important enough to motivate significant change. This may be a particularly pernicious perception within drug and alcohol recovery. How could the very behavior that is so self-destructively linked with the ravages of addiction become an intrinsically useful motivation for healing? A key concept of MI is also a central sex-positive notion. When a sexual behavior comes into conflict with a deeply held sexual health value, the sex-positive therapist throws his or her lot in with changing the relapse behavior, not the deeply held value.

> Marcus, father of twin 9-year-old girls, is a 42-year-old African American. He is married to his second wife, Tara, the mother of his children. Marcus has been in and out of recovery for many years. He recently completed an extensive evening adult outpatient treatment program to once again begin his abstinent recovery from pot, alcohol, and cocaine. He was arrested in an undercover police operation when he was at his dealer's house during a raid. He remembers the terror he felt in jail and the despair at the thought of not being able to raise his children or the thought of his wife leaving him.
>
> Marcus began to connect his relapse with paying for sex. He had been paying for sex since he enlisted in the Navy. During shore leave, he would get very drunk and seek out cocaine-laced sex with women sex workers. Marcus remembers these intense sexual encounters in fantasy during masturbation and to reach orgasm during intercourse with his wife. Marcus had not told his wife about his sexual history when using. It had never come up in previous treatment programs either.
>
> The day he was arrested, he was picking up his supply himself because his dealer's house was close by the location he was going to meet a woman for a paid sex encounter. It was in jail that he allowed himself to see, for the first time in his life, that his sexual life with sex workers violated a more fundamental principle. Marcus wanted to be a father that raises his children with their mother. He was less certain about monogamy in his marriage. However, it never occurred to him that monogamy might be a reasonable compromise to reach the enormously important life goal of maintaining a family in which to raise his children.
>
> A skilled drug counselor would provide a space for Marcus to verbalize and declare this value without inserting her own reaction, and would instead believe in the motivating force of Marcus's deeply held aspiration as the source to fuel change. The counselor must make a leap that the conflict between Marcus's values and his sexual behavior will matter deeply to him.

Sex-positive recovery is enhanced by the basic premise of MI: The sexual health goals of the client are explored and clarified for resolving ambivalent feelings that emerge when a wide difference between behavior and personal beliefs becomes unacceptable. This moment is the opportunity to rely on sexual health values to direct a person toward changing his or her sexual behavior linked with high-relapse risk to align himself or herself with her deeply held convictions and ideals.

Sex positive is a complex series of behaviors, attitudes, and skills that require a personal growth plan. Most of us have not had the privilege of growing up in a sex-positive or even sex-neutral environment. We may carry automatic thoughts that one's sexual values are rarely a positive force for change, particularly for the nature of change inherent in the recovery process. As I discussed in Chapter 1, the recovery-oriented system of care principles created by the Center for Substance Abuse Treatment (CSAT; 2007, p. 9) delineated 12 guiding principles of recovery. Strikingly absent from all 12 was any reference to human sexuality, sexual health, or sexual behavior. This is a significant omission given the fundamental place sexuality occupies within humans. I think, it also reflects a lack of faith in men and women to value their sexual lives and behavior as a significant center for personal values; values essential enough to rely upon as motivation for recovery.

CONCEPT 3: SEXUAL HEALTH IN RECOVERY IS BASED ON HARM-REDUCTION PRINCIPLES

Sexual health in recovery is a harm-reduction technique for improving abstinence-based recovery. This may seem like a contradictory statement. Harm reduction does not originate from the abstinence theoretical orientation and is, thus, often viewed as contrary to traditional addiction disease models.

Sexual health in recovery is a client-centered intervention where the personal sexual needs and patterns of the client are reflected and in which relapse prevention tools are best implemented to achieve abstinence. Thus, the sex-linked behavior is not seen as an addictive process. The behavior is not associated with changes in brain functioning that are measured among men and women with co-occurring chemical dependency and out-of-control sexual behavior. The sexual behavior is not viewed on a spectrum of loss of control of sexual behavior. It is discussed in terms of its linkage with addictive substance abuse. An addiction to drugs and/or alcohol that is strongly linked with sexual behavior does not co-opt a person's agency over his or her sexual behavior; but unconscious, unaddressed sex/drug-linked behavior is a significant source of harm (i.e., relapse) when not adequately identified and planned for as part of sobriety and abstinence. Changing sexual behavior patterns are discussed in relation to reducing the harm of relapse rather than a lifelong process of abstaining from specific sexual behaviors.

The harm-reduction component is especially important for counselors and clients to understand, in relation to sex addiction, compulsive sexual behavior or what I prefer to call *out-of-control sexual behavior*. A common sex-negative characteristic among professional drug counselors is to use terms like "sex addiction" or "sex out of control" to begin discussing sexual issues in recovery. It is not uncommon to have very experienced counselors discuss sex/drug-linked behavior with statements such as the following:

- "His sex addiction is getting in the way of his recovery."
- "Her sex addiction is a big relapse risk."
- "He acts out his sex addiction to avoid recovery."
- "You (speaking to a client) need to check into sex addiction recovery if you plan to stay sober."
- "If you go to SLAA (Sex and Love Addicts Anonymous), you can meet other women like you who can't stay sober because of relationships."

As I was researching my original studies on sex/drug-linked sexual behavior, the only place I found sex mentioned in association with recovery was within sex addiction research. The experts I spoke with 10 years ago initially assumed I was discussing co-occurring sex addiction. Today, few addiction treatment professionals seem able to envision an approach to sexuality within recovery that does not assume the sexual behavior is pathological.

The ability to distinguish sexual patterns as a harm-reduction intervention and drug and alcohol abuse as addiction treatment creates a space to focus on sexual feelings, sexual thoughts, and sexual behavior delinked from a progressive disease, which when unchecked, can lead to terrible health outcomes including death. Sexual health in recovery provides an important option for many people in recovery whose sexual behavior is not indicative of out-of-control sexual behavior but is rather an adaptation to the progressive, chronic, and degenerative progression of drug and alcohol addiction.

In the recovery field, harm reduction is an alternative, nonabstinent-based approach for patterns of drug use, abuse, and addiction. This is *not* the context in which harm reduction is conceptualized in sexual health in recovery. Abstinence from using drugs and alcohol is the basis for sexual health-focused relapse prevention. Sex/drug-linked behavioral patterns represent the harm as they may increase relapse risk. Reducing sex/drug-linked relapse risk is the harm reduction. Sex is not the problem; sex/drug-linked addiction is the focus. Women and men in recovery have sexual needs. Their sexual needs are not exclusively

Chapter 2 Eight Key Concepts of Sexual Health in Recovery

linked with addiction and recovery. When drug treatment professionals expand their focus to include sexuality and sexual needs in recovery, they are providing a harm-reduction experience by flexibly understanding the role of sex in the development of addiction and the acceptance of sexual needs within the process of recovery.

Addressing sex/drug-linked behavior may be a crucial step in reducing drug-related harm. For some clients, unless the sex/drug link is directly acknowledged and given primary importance, drug treatment can easily be dismissed as irrelevant and misguided.

Jared was young, was living far from his family and hometown in the Midwest, and, for the first time, was fully exploring his attractions to men. Jared has the kind of looks men his age are really drawn to. Meeting men, often for casual sex, and not "falling in love" was easy. Then he met Tom. Jared had never fallen in love with a man before. His small town world and religious life precluded any possibility for pursuing love with men. Jared had no idea, until Tom, what kind of mental and physical preoccupation the body will feel when it is bitten by love.

Tom was 28. He has lived in a large metropolitan city his entire life. He came out to his family in high school. He has been dating and falling in and out of love with men since he was 16. Tom has smoked pot since he was in high school. He has regularly linked getting high with getting off. At 25, Tom was introduced to crystal methamphetamine by his partner. Tom began to combine crystal with other drugs for even more sexual enhancement. When the relationship ended, Tom did not end his relationship with drugs and sex. Enter Jared.

They both fell in love very quickly. Their sexual and physical attraction was mutually intense, exhilarating, and wildly unexpected. At first, Tom did not combine drugs and sex with Jared. After about 5 months, though, Tom was not as preoccupied with Jared as intensely. Tom remembered the intensity with his former lover (and managed to forget that it did not last). He thought that perhaps getting a bit high with sex might bring the spark back.

It was not a big step for Tom to introduce the idea to Jared. They began to use crystal before sex. It was a sex blast like no other for Jared. Jared's progression from use to abuse and dependence are similar to many sex/drug-linked addictions. Three years later, now 27, Jared is sitting in a drug treatment group session. He is afraid of being sober and trying to be in a relationship. He thinks sobriety will mean never really being in love. He worries his crystal-meth brain is forever ruined to fall in love. Jared is an example of the need to separate the harm reduction of sexual health in recovery from the addiction to drugs.

Relapse prevention teaches Jared recovery skills for dating and experiencing attractions while identifying triggers for drug relapse. Harm reduction accepts Jared for his current psychological relationship and sexual development. In treatment, Jared needs to learn to respect the increased risk of relapse due to his history of sex/drug-linked behavior—not only in sexual relationships but also when he falls in love. He has not experienced the transition from intense new love to a more stable love bond that comes with establishing an enduring partnership. Sexual health in recovery is the ability of recovery professionals to assist their clients by advocating for sexuality within recovery while maintaining abstinence.

CONCEPT 4: SEXUAL HEALTH IN RECOVERY IS ABSTINENCE BASED

Most drug and alcohol treatment professionals in the United States establish a boundary of abstinence, stopping the use of drugs and alcohol. The fundamental initial phase of recovery and sexual health in recovery is achieving a sustained total abstinence from mood-altering drugs.

For some women and men, entering into abstinence and recovery is achieved with minimal effort and little (if any) professional help. They may also have high sex/drug-linked addiction patterns and find integrating abstinence from drugs as a welcome relief from sexuality, and enjoy the recovery process within their sexual lives. Such clients are likely in the minority, yet they serve as an important reminder to treatment professionals that treatment is really for those who are far more ambivalent about recovery.

There is a wide range of approaches to processing and resolving clients' ambivalent feelings about abstinence. Sexual health approaches for recovery can help clients address ambivalence about abstinence due to the sex/drug linkage. "I want to stop using, but I am not sure what that will mean to me sexually." Resolving ambivalence about abstinence without addressing pros and cons of sexual sobriety and sexual relationships is an often overlooked or marginalized component in addiction treatment. Sexual health in recovery supports abstinent-based treatment without relying on abstinent-based principles for sex.

CONCEPT 5: SEXUAL HEALTH IN RECOVERY IS EVIDENCE BASED

The Substance Abuse and Mental Health Services Administration's Center for Substance Abuse Prevention (CSAP) published *Identifying and Selecting Evidence-Based Interventions* to guide state and community planners to identify and select evidence-based interventions to reduce local substance abuse problems (CSAP, 2009).

The methods and techniques discussed in sexual health in recovery have been tested with clients in a treatment facility over a 3-year period. In 2002, a team of drug treatment specialists, sexual health experts, and research and outcome evaluation professionals worked together to create what would become the *Discovering Sexual Health Program*. We hypothesized that when drug and alcohol treatment provides sexual health–based relapse prevention skills in a sex-positive recovery-oriented system of care, client retention will increase and sex/drug-linked relapse behavior will decrease.

We received funding to test our hypothesis at Stepping Stone of San Diego, a San Diego County Alcohol and Drug Services–funded program. Stepping Stone is a 28-bed residential program. It specializes in treating gay men, lesbians, bisexuals, and transgendered men and women. About 25% of the clients at Stepping Stone identify as heterosexual.

Prior to our intervention, the program relied almost exclusively on outdated, impulsive, judgmental, and reactive procedures in addressing resident sexual concerns. With little evidence other than intuitive support from many informed professionals, everyone at Stepping Stone agreed to try the intervention.

However, there were many obstacles in moving Stepping Stone from its traditional approaches to sex and recovery. Our first obstacle was that no one had done this before. We had no evidence other than the demoralized consequences from watching too many men and women who fail treatment be asked to leave or just never return, and to know that their premature end to treatment was linked with sex and drugs.

The counselors and managers received training in sexuality, the sexual health curriculum, the goals of the program, and policies and procedures that supported a sex-positive treatment environment. This process from 2002 is expanded and outlined in the remaining chapters of this book.

Stepping Stone compared client retention rates in the 3 years prior to the study against the 3 years of the intervention. During that period, client retention increased from 25% to more than 50%. Discharges and unplanned discharges linked with relapse decreased to 1 in 10 from what was believed to be almost 1 in 3.

Jim Zians, PhD, led the team in designing an assessment measure to identify clients with high sex/drug-linked addiction as well as to measure client retention. Dr. Zians assembled a wide range of psychological measures to glean potential correlated psychological factors specific to high sex/drug-linked clients. If we could identify what most distinguishes the high sex/drug-linked clients, we could perhaps identify which component of the intervention was most correlated with change. We wanted the client assessment and outcome evaluation measures to detect possible methods, procedures, or processes correlated with our goals for client retention and relapse prevention among high sex/drug-linked men and women in recovery. The most exciting possibility would be to use our outcome data to possibly identify and predict treatment improvement outcomes among high sex/drug-linked clients.

The infancy of sex/drug-linked relapse prevention theory requires development of adequate instruments to measure levels of sex/drug-linked behavior, key change variables specific to individuals with high sex/drug-linked patterns of addiction, and outcome measures that compare changes in relapse rates and treatment completion in comparative studies. The 2003–2006 San Diego pilot study is only a beginning of evidence-based studies. The "Sexual Health in Recovery Assessment" I present in this book (see Chapter 6) is adapted from the pilot study and is only a rudimentary initial step toward developing a measure that withstands rigorous scientific examination.

The items were developed by utilizing existing sexological, drug and alcohol, HIV, and MI scales and adapting language to sex/drug-linked relapse. Do these items have clear and strong links with the topics and theories of each domain identified as the psychological constructs that contribute to sex/drug-linked addiction? I hope they do. Do we have scientific research that has sufficiently answered this question? No. It is a start. I welcome scrutiny. If sex/drug-linked relapse prevention is to advance as a viable treatment construct, science is needed. The American Psychological Association has established that "sound measures must demonstrate content-validity, criterion validity, construct validity, and internal consistency" (Germain, 2006). The "Sexual Health in Recovery Assessment" awaits this process. At this time, it is to be used only as a clinical tool for counselors to identify general levels of individual client sex/drug-linked addiction patterns and to organize each client sex/drug-linked picture within overall treatment planning. It is not a measure for scientific research.

It will take funding and collaborative determination (not unlike the initial team at Stepping Stone) to develop a measure that reliably and validly corresponds with the concept of sex/drug-linked addiction and relapse prevention. I can only hope that this initial foray catalyzes drug and alcohol professionals, sexologists, researchers, clinicians, funding sources, and the recovery community to develop valid and reliable sexual health in recovery assessment measures and clinical intervention tools that pass muster when held up to rigorous scientific inquiry.

The outcome evidence from the Stepping Stone study will be reviewed throughout this book. Given the challenging nature of sexuality in most professional counselor's work as well as the many sources of misinformation and folklore that fills in the gaps of sexual health knowledge, it is vital to sexual health in recovery to stand on the evidence of measures and outcomes designed to evaluate the consequences of this program.

CONCEPT 6: SEXUAL HEALTH IN RECOVERY IS A SHAME-REDUCTION INTERVENTION

One correlation measure for sexual health in recovery in the Stepping Stone assessment, shame, was so robust that it plays a prominent role in sexual health in recovery. The preliminary outcomes from this first pilot study lead to the untested hypothesis that sexual health in recovery is a shame-reduction intervention. As mentioned earlier, Zians developed a client assessment survey for Stepping Stone. The survey included measures of many different psychological constructs. Several measures were adapted to survey targeted behaviors and attitudes specific to treatment outcomes related to sex/drug-linked patterns of use. The survey also measured sexual health attitudes and behaviors, especially those connected with the client's anticipation of treatment completion given his or her history of sex/drug-linked behavior.

The most salient measure turned out to be an assessment of *shame and stigma* associated with sex/drug-linked history and current behavior. Stepping Stone residents assessed to be at highest risk for sex/drug-linked relapse entered treatment with levels about *double* the measured levels of shame when compared with the lower risk sex/drug-linked clients.

Three months later at the next assessment, after completing nearly 12 sexual health psychoeducational groups and the other program components, the measured levels of shame among the same high sex/drug-linked clients had decreased to the levels seen among the low sex/drug-linked clients. This was the only measure that was statistically significantly changed within the high sex/drug-linked group. Of course, this is one outcome in one study. However, it is consistent with the role of shame in other areas of severe and negative consequences for sexual activity (HIV, unplanned pregnancy, termination of pregnancy, STIs, out-of-control sexual behavior). Sexual health in recovery is a potentially new source for shame reduction among significant subsets of men and women entering treatment and beginning recovery. Woven within the basic understanding of sexual health in recovery is to reduce shame, stigma, and the distortions that go with these feelings to empower clients and professionals to engage in reasonable, informed, and client-centered approaches to reducing the risk of relapse linked with sexual shame.

CONCEPT 7: SEXUAL HEALTH IN RECOVERY IS A RELAPSE PREVENTION INTERVENTION

The core goal for sexual health in recovery is relapse prevention. Sexual health in recovery teaches professionals and their clients to prevent and manage relapse patterns that may emerge from sex/drug-linked feelings and behaviors. Sexual health in recovery, offered in tandem with a psychoeducational group program, combines cognitive interventions and recovery skill practice lessons to decrease the risk of sex/drug-linked relapse.

This book incorporates a large swath of sexual health and relapse prevention information. It combines sex-positive language with cognitive–behavioral components of relapse prevention. As you read it, you will learn sexual health relapse prevention approaches that focus on sexual health as a lifestyle value within recovery. Just as relapse prevention is more than specific actions needed at the moment of decision within a high-risk situation, sexual health in recovery teaches counselors to provide a sexual health zone for evaluation of values, principles, life goals, and sexual pleasure. This will allow your clients to build a self-management system for regulating sexuality within boundaries of sexual health—not only to prevent relapse but also to enhance recovery. Sexual health is at its heart an additional recovery tool to prevent progressing from abstinence to a state of relapse and suffering.

CONCEPT 8: SEXUAL HEALTH IN RECOVERY IS A BRIDGE FOR SEXUALITY AS AN ALLY IN RECOVERY

There are many allies for those in recovery. First are loving families, spouses, children, grandparents, friends, neighbors, and colleagues. Beyond the immediate circle of support, such as members of 12-step programs, highly trained professionals in drug and alcohol treatment, researchers, public policy makers, and employers who support their workers in receiving addiction treatment, is but a few of many other allies for recovery.

Sex researchers, sex educators, and sexual health professionals are not often thought of as allies for recovery.

For many sexual health experts, the concept of aligning sexual health principles with improving treatment outcomes makes sense, but they are usually unfamiliar with the culture of recovery to conceptualize how this would be enacted.

An ally is capable of providing not just cooperation but also assistance. It is not enough for drug and alcohol professionals to work together with sexual health advocates to create the common aim of improving recovery. Sexual health in recovery is a series of actions between informed professionals in sexual health and addiction treatment to collaborate in helping men and women in recovery. The alliance at Stepping Stone linked sexual health and recovery as necessary counterparts aligning to decrease treatment failure and relapse due to unaddressed sexual behavior.

Sexual health should be viewed as an ally in recovery. It should not be viewed as an adversary, a feared threat to stability in the fragile months of early recovery, an irritating intruder within recovery, a marginalized diversion, a detail that is best addressed after a year in recovery, an area not within the purview of certified drug and alcoholism counselors, a significant problem for patient management and safety in treatment centers, or a topic shunted aside until a significant crisis or relapse inserts itself in the treatment process. When raised by a client in recovery, it should not be met with indifference, anxiety, ignorance, or judgment from a helper.

The most challenging element of sexual health in recovery is the proposition of instituting matters of sexual health within the foundational elements of recovery. There, it can be a vital source for improving treatment outcomes and reducing relapse among men and women who are at greater risk to respond poorly to treatment.

CONCLUSION

If you have read this far, you may be interested in developing an alliance with sexual health and recovery. I hope you have read something that excites and inspires you to learn more. The elements of sexual health in recovery are manifold. The objections to sexual health as a tool for improving treatment are also numerous. This book is not only for those who are ready to learn and implement sexual health approaches for relapse prevention. There are many who may have read this far and are skeptical at best. Ambivalence about sexual health in recovery is expected.

Some of you may not even be ambivalent; you may already be formulating your conclusions that refute this hypothesis. I encourage you to read more. If for no other reason, it may give you even clearer conclusions to support your position. If you find yourself intrigued, interested, yet filled with questions, the next chapter is for you.

Before preparing to implement and provide sexual health in recovery assessment and interventions, I want to take time to speak to the reader who is still unsure of the benefits of a sexual health in recovery approach. Some of you may be torn among traditional approaches to sexuality in recovery and yet wanting to learn more. Some of you may be thinking, finally, this has been needed for so long, but is this the approach to sex/drug-linked relapse that I can support? As I say to my clients who fluctuate between interest and repellence in looking at their own vision for sexual health, ambivalence is good. It is necessary. It is part of change. It is important. It demands respect. Without resolving our simultaneously wanting and not wanting to address sexuality as an ally for recovery, there is no hope for sustainable positive change within the current practices of sex and recovery.

3

Are You Ambivalent About Sexual Health in Recovery?

Contemplation is thinking about change. Contemplating before taking action is an essential process for moving forward. Think of an 11-month-old baby standing next to a chair leg, using every bit of the sturdiness of the furniture to remain standing. You can see the expression on the child's face change as he begins to consider the possibility of letting go of the chair—relying on his own balance. The baby does not know what will happen, yet the internal drive to *see* what happens is a compelling sensation. The brain wants to know; the person is not so sure.

We stand back in amazement. Do we let this child fall? Do we intervene and hold our child who may not be quite ready to stand? How do we tolerate this time of incremental change? What happens inside us as we observe someone else attempt to change? This moment is central to professional counselors working with someone in a change process.

In this chapter, we will think about taking away what is familiar and leaping into the distress and exhilaration of letting go. Understanding our ambivalence is much more important than whether we are ambivalent. Ambivalence is normal. What, in this moment, is the nature of my ambivalence is the useful question that will be the focus of our sexual health conversation.

Too often, professionals are given little time to consider their reactions to new information. There is often an expectation to make a more immediate conclusion: thumbs up or thumbs down. Motivational interviewing (MI) approaches for facilitating change have clearly demonstrated the centrality of contemplating a variance in routine as essential to build a lasting change. In introducing sexual health in recovery, I as well, want to include a space for contemplation. I have found that, when it comes to matters of sexuality, adults need time to objectively and honestly evaluate their personal reactions to new information. I do not want to assume that if you have read this far, you are ready for action, ready to learn about how to provide sexual health–based relapse prevention counseling. This chapter is meant to provide a space to not prematurely jump ahead.

Readiness to learn and implement sexual health approaches within recovery is a gradual blending of current approaches to recovery with sexual science. This chapter will help you evaluate your readiness for this change. Readiness exists along a continuum from not at all ready or perhaps even opposed to various degrees of uncertainty to the other end of the spectrum: ready, willing, and open to change. Many readers may be quite certain of the importance of sexual health in recovery for improving treatment. Others may not feel confident in their ability to move immediately into sexual health conversations to decrease relapse rates among sex/drug-linked addicts.

Regardless of your current readiness to change, I encourage you to read this chapter, if not to explore your own ambivalence, then to understand the range of ambivalence you may encounter among your colleagues. Sexual health in recovery is a team effort. You will need collaborators, associates, and peers to cooperatively invest in this change. Your stage of readiness is one component. Understanding the range of various circumstances and events that form the environment of readiness for each of your colleagues will be important in developing a treatment program ready to prepare for sexual health.

AMBIVALENCE

In Chapter 1 we met Sabrina, whose social anxiety left her afraid of her own shadow. Her history of sexually transmitted infections, pregnancy, and drug addiction were her legacy from an untreated anxiety disorder and a consequence of sex/drug-linked behaviors. Drugs and alcohol were her treatment for sufficiently diminishing anxiety to engage in sexual relationships.

For Sabrina, sex is important. It remains important in recovery. Often, this valuing of sexuality combined with a barrier to sex (in Sabrina's case, untreated anxiety) may lead men and women to use drugs and alcohol as a solution to this dilemma. In recovery, Sabrina needs to resolve her desire for sexuality and relationships with her anxiety, which interferes with sexual response and functioning. Her ambivalence about sexual health in recovery might well be expressed in wanting either to diminish or devalue her sexual life (for fear of relapse) or to minimize the link between sex and drugs because she fears that recovery will limit her sexual and love relationships.

A counselor working with Sabrina's ambivalence might affirm the importance of sexuality and mirror this aspect of herself. The counselor might provide Sabrina a space to understand the decisions she made to navigate untreated anxiety, how anxiety interfered with her sexual development, and how she came to use drugs and alcohol to "solve" this problem. Sexual health in recovery recognizes the importance of Sabrina's sexual health and will focus on increasing her confidence in combining meaningful pleasurable sexual relations with recovery.

Motivation and Ambivalence

Sexual health is an important topic in recovery for people like Sabrina who need to parse out the interwoven motivations for sex and getting high. As a helping professional, you might ask yourself how worthwhile this is for you in your work. Will a counselor working with Sabrina make a difference in her recovery and reduce her risk for relapse through this approach? Is this a constructive way to improve Sabrina's treatment and recovery?

Drug and alcohol treatment providers are universally invested in the recovery of their clients. This is doubtless one of the most important reasons for doing the work, to facilitate recovery. I believe that this deep, abiding, personal passion for recovery is a significant gift within drug and alcohol treatment providers. Their unwavering commitment is an anchor for contemplating men and women to rely upon.

Self-Efficacy and Ambivalence

In Chapter 1 we also met Frank, a 31-year-old recovering crystal-meth addict who is currently maintaining a solo sex life without pursuing relationships. What ambivalence might Frank be experiencing? What might Frank be unsure or unready to address in recovery? How might Frank benefit from sexual health relapse prevention? Frank has made an important choice for sex in early recovery. He is not ambivalent about sobriety. His boundary about masturbation as his sexual life for now is well thought out and stems from a clear understanding of being a high sex/drug-linked person in recovery. Frank is just not sure he can do it.

Frank's ambivalence requires a counselor to address a different relapse risk factor: self-efficacy. Frank needs help increasing his ability to maintain his sexual health in recovery plan given the pervasive sex negativity surrounding masturbation. Self-efficacy is "the degree to which an individual feels confident and capable of performing a certain behavior in a specific situational context" (Marlatt & Donovan, 2008, p. 8). Self-efficacy is a central tenant of cognitive behavioral models for relapse prevention, including sexual health in recovery. These models help clients evaluate the level of risk in breaking abstinence in response to facing or avoiding a particular sexual situation. Self-efficacy increases client confidence in dealing with a wide array of responses within the recovery community when it comes to talking about sex.

Frank will be better prepared for his relapse prevention plan when he increases his confidence that he can maintain his sexual health in recovery and stay sober. He wants both.

Frank has a sexual health boundary concern. Sexual health boundaries in recovery address ambivalence and self-efficacy by teaching the importance of boundaries combined with repetitive skills for increasing a client's confidence in setting boundaries.

Resolving Ambivalence

The tools needed to learn and develop sexual health in recovery relapse counseling are consistent with a key element of MI: resolving ambivalence (first, by focusing on counselor's ambivalence using sex/drug-linked relapse approaches, then addressing client ambivalence). An ambivalent counselor may be unsure about his or her interest, confidence, and readiness to address sexual health. Many counselors may simply not think they can do this.

You may be more certain of the importance of sex/drug-linked relapse prevention than you are confident you can actually do it. "We chose the term *confidence* instead of *ability* because it focuses on the person's underlying psychological state, and avoids the mistake of assuming that talking about this topic is merely a matter of focusing on 'technical' coping skills" (Rollnick, Mason, & Butler, 1999, p. 22). To address this uncertainty, I encourage you *not* to think about sexual health as an accumulation of skills, but rather to learn and understand your mental attitudes and emotions about sex.

The Continuum of Ambivalence

In their book *Health Behavior Change: A Guide for Practitioners*, Rollnick et al. (1999) reviewed the literature on health psychology and behavior change. The authors studied the process of practitioner behavior

Chapter 3 Are You Ambivalent About Sexual Health in Recovery?

change and they proposed a series of general guidelines for patient-centered directive approaches on which counselors needed to contemplate. Like the authors, I too believe that counselors need a space to reflect on their perceived level of confidence and the level of importance of integrating the sexual health relapse prevention into current counseling practices.

Over the last 20 years, readiness to change has become an important area of research. How people move toward change is a vital area of counselor knowledge within drug and alcohol treatment. Just as understanding *client* ambivalence is central to treatment improvement, I believe understanding *counselor* ambivalence is necessary for readying many drug and alcohol counselors to consider sexual health in recovery.

Rollnick et al. (1999) found that two key questions could explain why one person might be completely ready to change whereas another may find himself or herself not at all ready. They found that perceived level of importance ("How worthwhile is this change?") and self-efficacy ("How confident am I that I can do this?") significantly contributed to the level of readiness to change. My experience at Stepping Stone, the program where sexual health in recovery was first tested, supports these findings. When the staff understood the potentially important treatment improvement outcomes for their clients combined with confidence in coping with the many psychological, emotional, and attitudinal states of mind provoked by the sexual health in recovery program, Stepping Stone counselors expressed a high degree of readiness, enthusiasm, and skill in instituting these changes.

Ambivalence is a necessary part of change. We accurately anticipated a wide range of readiness for change among the counselors and regularly provided a space and time to gather and talk. Our goal was to provide a process for addressing everyone's objections, reluctance, fears, and concerns before and during the change. What was most significant was the determination by the leadership to address sex/drug-linked treatment. The discussion groups were not designed to lead to not changing. The process allowed staff members who could not envision themselves providing this intervention to decide to consider if staying at Stepping Stone was going to work for them.

At Stepping Stone, we encountered a wide range of opinions about the necessity of placing so much emphasis on sex/drug-linked addiction patterns within the overall treatment program. Some of the staff members were clearly ready and were convinced that proactively addressing sex/drug-linked behavior for everyone in treatment would directly lead to decreased premature treatment terminations and decrease in relapse linked with sex. Others were less certain. They needed more information and a space to process their emotions about sex and recovery. An important, though smaller, group was not ready for the change. They saw little value in the program or its potential for accomplishing good outcomes. In fact, some feared that introducing sexual health interventions would make things worse; that the treatment center would become preoccupied with increasingly unmanageable sexual behavior among residents. I believe a similar continuum of readiness will be found in most treatment centers among drug and alcohol counselors.

Addressing Your Own Ambivalence About Sexual Health in Recovery

Take a moment to contemplate your thoughts and attitudes about sexual health in recovery. In particular, consider these two questions:

- "How important is sexual health in recovery?"
- "How confident am I that I can do this?"

See if you can place every reservation you have within these two spheres of contemplation. Uncertainty is not an easy emotional place to stay for very long. Focusing your ambivalence around these two questions may make this an interesting and revealing process, rather than one that evokes dread and anxiety.

The remainder of this chapter will focus on the many ways the drug and alcohol profession is quietly struggling with these two questions. We will consider how counselors' confidence in their ability to learn sexual health relapse prevention skills and conduct meaningful sexual health conversations with clients and colleagues is a central component of readiness. We will look at the historical confidence of drug and alcohol counselors and treatment programming to cope with sex/drug-linked circumstances. We will look at some particular theories that the field has settled upon that have all, but eliminated, any chance of addressing relapse and sex in recovery. Lastly, we will look at how the relationship between sexual health efficacy and sexual health outcome expectations in drug and alcohol treatment contribute to counselor's readiness for this change. We will explore why the wide range of ability and willingness to change sexual health attitudes and treatment approaches is an outcome of incongruent and misaligned relationships between the why and how of change.

Chapter 3 Are You Ambivalent About Sexual Health in Recovery?

THE IMPORTANCE OF ADDRESSING SEXUAL HEALTH IN RECOVERY

Why is sexual health in recovery important? In the previous chapter, we discussed some of the positive outcome data from Stepping Stone. It is not enough to answer why sexual health in recovery is important based solely on this singular pilot project outcome data. However, the program at Stepping Stone points to the importance of changing current approaches to sex in substance abuse treatment.

This intervention will be important (if not absolutely necessary) for a wide variety of clients who:

- are chronic relapsers;
- have a history of treatment noncompletion;
- have sex/drug-linked behaviors that are not being addressed in treatment;
- are concerned about their likelihood of sustaining recovery because of their sexual behavior in recovery;
- are dissatisfied with current level of sexual activity, relations, and pleasure in recovery;
- feel that sexuality is a "missing gap" in their recovery and want to fill it;
- want to learn how to help others in recovery with high sex/drug-linked relapse risk;
- want to differentiate between out-of-control sexual behavior and sex/drug-linked relapse; and
- want to learn principles of sexual health within the context of recovery and are open to sexual health conversations and contemplation.

There are some clients who will not consider these issues important or meaningful to their own recovery, or who simply may not yet be ready to address them. This intervention is *not* for:

- people who are too uncomfortable or may have moral and ethical conflicts with the concepts of sexual health within recovery;
- people who are not interested or curious about their sexual health as it relates to recovery;
- people who do not currently experience any level of concern in how sexual health may be part of maintaining ongoing recovery;
- people who have religious or cultural objections to the detail of sexual content or sexual health principles put forward in this book;
- people whose stability in mental health or sobriety is so shaky that other emotional or behavioral concerns take priority;

- people who have been fortunate to have a treatment program, professional helpers, sponsors, or colleagues in recovery who have been valuable and open resources for addressing sexual health and establishing sexual health in recovery; and
- people who may see sexual health as an irrelevant diversion from the primary and traditional principles of treatment and recovery.

ADDRESSING COUNSELORS IN PRECONTEMPLATION

In *Addiction and Change: How Addictions Develop and Addicted People Recover*, Carlo DiClemente (2003) defines the characteristics of precontemplation for recovery (p. 114). I see many similarities in his description of the precontemplative activities that addicted individuals employ to "neutralize any momentum that builds toward considering change" and the common objections of drug and alcohol treatment professionals toward considering changing treatment approaches for sex/drug-linked addiction. DiClemente summarizes five activities that enable precontemplative addicts to impede momentum to contemplate change. He labels these activities as reluctance, rebellion, resignation, rationalization, and reveling (DiClemente, pp. 115–116).

Many drug and alcohol counselors favor the status quo of their particular approaches to sex in recovery. More importantly, they have a cluster of objections to considering change that outweigh any of the possible benefits of altering current approaches to relapse and sex. Common counselor strategies to avoid this change bear a close resemblance to those used by substance abusers as impediments to considering change.

Reluctance

A common counselor response is one of unwillingness to contemplate sexual health in recovery at this time or the near future. (DiClemente recommends considering 6 months as a "near future" time frame for adults.) As the saying goes, "timing is everything." This may not be the time for you to consider adding or expanding sexual health information in your repertoire of treatment. You may have many other more pressing concerns in your current work. Just because this book has been published does not mean this is your time for integrating the information into your treatment approaches. Reluctance is more about a hesitation, a form of inertia where the consequences of staying with what I know are fine with me. There just isn't a huge feeling either way in response to the opportunity.

Chapter 3 Are You Ambivalent About Sexual Health in Recovery?

The reluctant counselor sees sex/drug-linked relapse prevention as not sufficiently problematic within their own skill set or among the clients they treat.

Reluctance may stem from an assumption of "If I read this information, I have to change." Perhaps that is not the case. This book may be a valuable tool to more clearly outline your current attitudes and beliefs about addressing sex. So rather than read this book from the perspective of change, it may be an opportunity to formulate your current thinking about sex, drugs, relapse, recovery, and treatment.

What if you just gave yourself permission to do nothing more than gather information through observation of others? Noticing the many different techniques that colleagues, trainers, supervisors, clients, and the recovery community in general currently have for addressing sex and relapse may be an interesting addition to your day. Let others model and teach you how they are doing this work (or not doing this work). You may notice how little sex and sexual issues are actually talked about in treatment. There may be times when you sense that you, a client, or a group may *wish* for sexual issues to come up in conversation and yet they are not mentioned. Let that be enough. Do not do anything but make a note of it. Do not even feel obligated to bring it up with anyone. If reluctance is your primary response at this point, I encourage you to develop your skills of observation.

This technique might improve your counseling skills. As you observe how sex is addressed or sidestepped in drug treatment, you will hone your skills in noticing the common defenses people use to avoid sex and remain precontemplative about sexual matters in recovery. Becoming aware of the mental defenses that divert us from sex talk is a good exercise for improving our skills in working with precontemplative defenses common among substance abusers.

A common defense I have noticed among precontemplative drug and alcohol counselors is turning the problem of poor treatment outcomes and sex/drug-linked relapses outward onto the clients. Given the limited opportunities for treatment professionals to engage in informed discussion about sexuality and its role in recovery, they may misdirect frustration and concern about sex and recovery solely onto the clients. This takes various forms of faultfinding, blaming, despairing, labeling, and excoriating men and women in recovery for their "antirecovery" sexual lives. In normalizing these counselor behaviors, I hope to move beyond criticism and blame to an understanding of the usual ways in which people handle new information they are reluctant to consider.

I call the reluctance stage "collective counselor sex-negativity." As discussed in Chapter 2, sex negativity is made up of a cluster of various attitudes and behaviors that focus concerns primarily on the harmful, negative, or self-destructive aspects of sexuality and sexual relationships in recovery. When sexuality is almost exclusively discussed in drug and alcohol treatment in terms of the negative or harmful aspects of sex, collective sex-negativity may have set in. Here are some examples.

Coercion, fear, and threats: The most severe threat is treatment termination due to sexual behavior. In many treatment centers (residential or outpatient), clients are removed from treatment or must discontinue treatment as a result of violating the sexual rules and guidelines of the treatment center. Sometimes, the sexual behavior is the exclusive reason for terminating treatment. No drug or alcohol use was involved. Other times, the sexual behavior violation is merged with using. The counseling intervention is to threaten termination to coerce sexually active clients to change or stop their problematic sexual behavior at the treatment center. Examples of sexual behavior that may result in terminating a client from treatment include:

- engaging in a relationship with another patient,
- having sex with another patient,
- having sex with a member of a 12-step meeting group while a patient is on a treatment program, and
- having sex with a staff member or volunteer.

Unfortunately, most treatment centers rely exclusively on environmental barriers to reduce the likelihood of this behavior, for example, single-sex sleeping areas (which assume that men will not have sex with men or women with women). There may be rules about physical contact, language, sexualized talk, and so forth, which are geared toward desexualizing and decreasing sexual tension within the treatment setting. Counselors who rely upon clients' fears of treatment termination and environmental boundaries omit a significant additional source for good sexual boundaries in treatment. Sexual health in recovery is a proactive sexual health treatment and counseling approach that anticipates and provide tools for managing sexual attractions, impulses, and behaviors during treatment.

Counselor sex-negativity may be observed in frequent warnings about the risks of relapse as a consequence of sex or new relationships in recovery. Counselors may discuss sex from the perspective of the threat to abstinence and recovery posed by sexual activity. Sex as a destructive force in recovery, especially in early recovery, is a message to listen for as you allow yourself to remain a reluctant, yet an aware, drug counselor.

Rebellion

In my work as an advocate for sexual health in drug and alcohol treatment, I see "rebels" as passionate addiction counselors who highly value making their own way. They may, paradoxically, be some of the counselors already attempting to address sexual issues with their clients. What I find important to these rebels is that they typically define themselves as the exception. Usually isolated, lone warriors, or highly principled individuals who value being a force for change, these rebel drug and alcohol counselors find a passionate cause in addressing sexuality in drug treatment. Some see the struggle as an opportunity to liberate clients from forces that restrict, deny, repress, or demand sexual conformity. The recovery community is not immune or separated from the larger cultural, religious, political, social, and moral dimensions of sexuality. In drug and alcohol treatment, there is no single consensus determining who controls the messages about sexuality, sexual values, and/or sexual practices as they relate to recovery. Sexual values and attitudes may vary enormously in different regions of the country, among different cultural groups, age groups, gender, sexual orientations, and gender identity groups.

The dilemma for the rebel precontemplator is to relinquish the role of the "special" sex counselor. Sexual health in recovery involves bringing together a team of treatment center professionals. At its core, sexual health relapse prevention is a collaboration among drug treatment services, counselors, sexologists, sexual health experts, physicians, therapists, social workers, nurses, psychiatrists, psychologists, researchers, program directors, administrators, board members, funding sources, as well as the men and women in treatment. Rebels are comfortable in a place of contested positions. Rebels have difficulty seeing conflict as a multidimensional complex relationship. They are more familiar with seeing right or wrong positions and perceiving those in the "wrong" position as forces focused exclusively against change.

Rebels can move out of the precontemplative position by stepping back from their autonomous position and reflecting on their motivations for addressing sexuality.

- What have you gained by being the forerunner of sexual health–based relapse prevention?
- What have you liked about being the clarion call for sex/drug-linked relapse concerns when others avoided or dismissed these client concerns?
- What role, if any, do you want to play in bringing sexual health approaches to drug and alcohol treatment?

- With whom do you want to collaborate in addressing client sex-related relapse more openly and proactively? Do you want to help others increase their competencies in this area?
- What is the best reason you have for working toward integrating sexual health into the larger community of drug and alcohol counselors?
- How do you feel about relinquishing your domain to share sexual health interventions among a wide array of treatment professionals?

Resignation

A more profound level of counselor reluctance can be found among a subgroup of drug treatment professionals who rely upon a defense commonly found among addicts. I call it "a retreat into hopelessness or helplessness." It is a form of demoralization common among addicts and seemingly acceptable among some drug and alcohol counselors when it comes to sex/drug-linked patterns of addiction. The resigned counselor assumes sex/drug-linked behavior is overwhelmingly impossible to address. They comment on having tried "everything" and nothing seems to work for them. These well-intentioned counselors have resigned themselves that there is nothing new or effective that can be done to address clients who insist on going against their recommendations about sex and recovery. Change is not an option. It's just too late.

Some of the resigners may be very experienced long-time drug counselors who do not have the enthusiasm or investment in changing treatment approaches to sex/drug-linked relapse risk. They may see this as a new issue for younger and less experienced counselors. The idea of sex education and becoming current with sexual knowledge may, in itself, feel overwhelming. Perhaps they grew up during times when sexuality was less openly discussed within the recovery movement in an era where sexual matters were strongly considered private and deeply shameful to openly discuss.

Just as in addicts, resignation within counselors leads them to see their *inability to change* as an exemption from any *responsibility for change*. "Whether this is an excuse or a reason, these feelings of resignation allow the Precontemplator to continue to engage, either comfortably or with significant discomfort" (DiClemente, 2003, p. 118).

Resignation is not a result of studied investigation into the sexual health and recovery approach. Studied investigation and research about sex/drug-linked behavior and effective relapse prevention approaches is in early stages of germination. Resignation is an automatic response, a flee to hopelessness prior to investigation. This pattern is a common defense with many in the precontemplation stage. It is an all-too-human response for many adults not ready or willing to consider a change. Unfortunately, drug and alcohol counselors who choose resignation may easily transmit this emotion among colleagues and, most importantly, to their clients.

In addiction treatment, hope is a foundation for early commitment to recovery. Counselors who retreat to hopeless attitudes toward clients with sex/drug-linked behaviors may unconsciously convey their hopelessness to clients and their families. With no vision for recovery and sexual health, the possibility for recovery among very high sex/drug-linked addicts is a dead end for everyone involved. This was the very demoralized state that existed among the counselors at Stepping Stone before instituting the Discovering Sexual Health program.

An enormous influx of crystal-meth addicts had overwhelmed the untrained and unprepared staff with increasingly high percentage of clients with very high levels of crystal-meth use merged with sexual behavior. The staff resorted to treatment termination as the primary intervention for multiple sexual behavior boundary crossings among the men and women in treatment. Resignation, giving up on these clients, and relying upon treatment termination were techniques used more frequently than at any other time in the history of the program. In a few instances, this policy meant finding out that a client who had been terminated for a sexual boundary violation (absent a drinking or using relapse) had died from an overdose weeks or months later. This was painfully difficult for Stepping Stone.

If you find yourself identifying with resignation in addressing sex/drug-linked relapse issues, the first step is to acknowledge this. Do not see it as a source of self-admonishment but rather as an honest moment with yourself. Consider the path that has lead you to this position. Empathy and compassion for yourself is central to observing and being honest with yourself about your resignation. How often and with whom have you spoken about your helplessness in response to concerns, disappointments, disillusionment, frustration, apathy, avoidance, disgruntlement, or despair in addressing sexuality with your clients? When has a colleague come to you to discuss his or her own feelings and concerns about his or her ability to effectively respond and guide clients who may want help with sex/drug-linked addiction?

As I have traveled the country talking about sexual health relapse prevention, I find one or two "sex experts" within most treatment settings. Their enthusiasm and confidence in proactively addressing sexual matters with clients is a ray of hope. Until the development of this program, they have relied on their talents for creativity in integrating sexuality into recovery. Most treatment centers delegate clients' sex relapse concerns to these chosen few. This sex-expert delegation allows the reluctant and resigned counselors to maintain their precontemplative state of change. It may also assuage their discomfort with not being a sex/drug-linked resource for their clients.

For the resigned counselor who had made it this far in this book I suggest a few options. First, stop reading any further. Think about your professional support circle. Perhaps you have a trusted colleague or a clinical supervisor, a therapist, a sponsor, a spouse, a former teacher, or professor. Take a moment to ponder whom you might sit down with and disclose your level of hopeless or helpless feelings about how you currently counsel clients with high sex/drug-linked behaviors. Expect nothing more of yourself until you have taken the time to have this conversation. Reading more will run the risk of increasing your reluctance, overwhelming you into more intractable rigidity.

I invite you not to even think about change. Rather I invite you to connect. Choose to remove yourself from the isolation or the inflexibility of quiet hopelessness. Remember, you are a helping professional. When clients can convince us that their situation is hopeless, then they and we are mired in perpetual precontemplation. Our addicted clients remind us every day that the beginning of recovery is not a commitment to change; it is a commitment to honestly connect.

Rationalization

Some of you may have been anticipating this precontemplative defense. The rationalizer may be the articulate thinking counselor. The rationalizing drug counselor's acumen for language is hands above most others. They are good critical thinkers. As DiClemente (2003) writes, "They appear to have all the answers, in contrast to the resigned Precontemplator, who has none" (p. 119). When it comes to sex/drug-linked relapse prevention, I believe rationalizing that current approaches are sufficient is the most common precontemplative defense. A very common concern among precontemplative rationalizers is a deeply held belief that changing current approaches to sex and recovery will cause harm, havoc, or mayhem.

At Stepping Stone there was a very clear rationalization for not changing: Counselors and staff feared that the program would make things worse. Often, rationalizers can offer clear and confident reasons for avoiding danger.

- "If we talk about sex too much, it will make clients' sexual impulses and desires get out of control."
- "Clients will just have sex on their mind all the time."
- "We will trigger them to use."
- "Lots of men and women have gotten sober through our program, why change this now?"
- "What does Doug Braun-Harvey know about treating addiction?"
- "I have not heard anyone ask us to change the way we address sex and recovery."

Rationalizing counselors have strong convictions about recovery. They help their clients face the monster of addiction with full force and determination. Their loyalty to helping people recover is to be commended and admired.

If you are a rationalizer, I invite you to harness this strength to continue reading. When you find something you object to, think it through. Take the time to consider your thinking and evaluate how you have come to a different conclusion about sex/drug-linked relapse. This is an important contribution: We need all the critical thinking we can find to address this aspect of addiction treatment. This book is not about prescribing one singular path for addressing relapse linked with sex. My hope is to begin a much-needed conversation from many perspectives. This book just happens to be the beginning of what I hope is a much longer process of more program ideas, more research, more outcome evaluations, and more voices from drug treatment and sexology working together to effectively address sex, drinking, and drugs. So, read on. Notice what you think. It matters.

Reveling

Let's face it, there are many talented and enormously gifted drug and alcohol counselors and therapists. You have probably worked alongside men and women who have an amazing ability to connect, relate, and effectively engage a wide range of addicts at the most cantankerous levels of denial. These men and women are assets to every treatment center and counseling program. They are very good at what they do. They enjoy their work. We usually enjoy their personal and professional colleagueship. They are well respected and may have decades of experience behind them. They rarely experience significant disappointment in their work. Admired, relied upon, and sought out for their wisdom and leadership, they may have little incentive to consider an evaluation of their current approaches to sex/drug-linked addiction. Confidence, combined with a high level of self-efficacy (not only can I do this . . . I excel at doing this) may influence their initial receptivity to integrating sexual health relapse prevention approaches. When someone is having a really good time, feeling highly rewarded, and effective in their work, they may respond to sexual health relapse content with ridicule and disbelief that their current approach may need to be reevaluated.

If you identify yourself among the talented elite and are thinking something along the lines of "This is really a worthless addition to drug and alcohol treatment," "This just doesn't seem deserving of my time or attention," or "Who is this guy, what does he know?" (a disrespect for the value of the information based on who is the messenger) you are not alone. There are probably many other highly skilled professionals who may be having similar thoughts. This is a common human response to information that just does not fit on our radar screen as immediately useful.

Reveling in your confidence will not be a motivation for reading further. However, your leadership and respect among your colleagues may be a very useful asset to others. You could become an advocate for more open discussion of sexuality and relapse prevention by more directly, frequently, and specifically discussing your approaches to sex and recovery and how you have come to find them to be highly effective and useful in your work. You may have underestimated how important it is for you to model openness and confidence in working with client sexuality in recovery to other less confident and experienced professionals. It may be a very caring and generous moment to mentor and guide your colleagues in honest and straightforward discussions of sexuality. This could be another area to see yourself as a leader. This leadership does not necessarily require you to embrace the sexual health approach outlined in this book, but you can be a significant influence on many others to understand the importance of sexuality within all stages of recovery.

It may also be valuable to articulate both the short-term and long-term benefits of your approaches to sexuality in treatment. In your many years of addressing sexuality in treatment, what has been the most important information you have found to be consistently useful to clients? What has been your clinical focus to address sexuality early in treatment? What have been the consistent benefits you have seen with your approach? What long-term benefits have you come to believe are the outgrowth of your approaches to sex and addiction?

Again, your ability to clearly describe your work is not about creating debate or requiring agreement with only one approach to sex and recovery. Your voice will be an important contributor to the critical thinking necessary for less experienced professionals to form and develop their own understanding and goals for working with client sexuality. Your role as a leader and influential professional is not to take sides or present your thoughts about sex and recovery as an "expert," but rather to provide leadership in creating a space for a discussion. People will listen to you. You may be an important source of helping other counselors reevaluate (or evaluate for the first time) how they want to address sex/drug-linked behavior as a counselor. You can increase your fellow counselors' understanding of the importance of addressing sexuality in addiction treatment without imposing your approach as the only correct or responsible course of treatment.

Inquiring among other professionals about how they currently address sex in treatment to prevent relapse will have an added cache because the question is coming from you. Use this moment to steer clear of prematurely moving to a decisive pronouncement of what you think or your negative opinions about sexual health in recovery as an alternative strategy. You do not need to immediately make an opinion about the "correct" way to address sex in recovery but your enthusiasm, confidence, and engaging excitement for talking about sex and recovery can be a wonderful catalyst for other counselors to find their own source of confident ability to discuss and address sexuality within their work as a drug treatment professional.

Taken together, these five counselor precontemplation stage defenses contribute to much of the current lack of inertia in drug treatment to look closely at new ways to address sexuality and recovery. Most importantly, these defenses conspire to keep sexuality as a less important and often marginalized component of drug counseling only to be addressed when circumstances are such that it can no longer be avoided. These defenses also ensure that responsibilities for handling sex/drug-linked relapse issues are left to a few specialists who are comfortable, able, and willing to carry the load for the rest of the profession. As I speak with treatment providers around the country (and the world), I hear evidence that this piecemeal approach continues to condemn a subgroup of addicts with high sex/drug-linked addiction to lower client retention, poorer treatment outcomes, and increasingly high levels of despair about finding lasting recovery, and let us not forget that some die. We can no longer afford to settle for a less effective approach for these clients.

Changing health behaviors is not only understanding the importance of change. If information were enough, change would happen at a very different pace. For drug and alcoholism counselors, becoming convinced that sex- and drug-relapse issues are important to successful treatment is not a hard sell. Precontemplative counselors often report the problem and most do not deny drug and alcohol treatment's poor track record in effectively addressing sexuality in treatment. Everyone can agree to some degree that sex and recovery is important to address. The precontemplative defenses are much more vociferous when it comes to counselors' confidence and self-efficacy to address the issue.

ADDRESSING COUNSELOR CONFIDENCE

Counselor confidence is central to the work of providing a healing relationship to our clients. In her foreword to my first book, *Sexual Health in Drug and Alcohol Treatment: Group Facilitator's Manual*, Stephanie Covington described addiction counselors, not the clients, as unready to develop treatment approaches addressing sexuality as a core issue in addiction recovery (Braun-Harvey, 2009). As we have seen, some of this neglect is due to varying levels of importance placed on sexuality among drug counselors. I believe a more central barrier to counselor readiness for changing approaches to sex in recovery is the drug and alcohol treatment profession.

Sexual health training is virtually absent in drug and alcohol treatment programs and counselor education training programs. For example, in the state where I work, the California Association of Alcoholism and Drug Abuse Counselors (CAADAC) lists 12 core functions within the basic training curriculum for certification in California as a drug and alcoholism counselor. These core functions include:

(1) Screening, (2) Intake, (3) Orientation, (4) Assessment, (5) Treatment Planning, (6) Counseling (individual, group, and significant others), (7) Case Management, (8) Crisis Intervention, (9) Client Education, (10) Referral, (11) Reports and Recordkeeping, and (12) Consultation (with other professionals in regard to client treatment and services). (California Certification Board of Alcohol and Drug Counselors, 2008, p. 5)

Sexuality is mentioned regarding culturally relevant sexual orientation counselor education, and the guidelines mandate "education on health and high-risk behaviors associated with substance use, including transmission and prevention of HIV/AIDS, tuberculosis, sexually transmitted infections, hepatitis, and other infectious diseases" (p. 21).

(This reflects the common sex-negative approach of only discussing sexuality in terms of disease prevention, which I discussed in more detail in Chapter 2.)

The Certified Drug and Alcohol Counselor assessment criteria are defined as "the procedures by which a counselor/program identifies and evaluates an individual's strengths, weaknesses, problems and needs for the development of a treatment plan" (p. 21). The guidelines cite "areas of client history gathered, such as substance abuse history, social history, legal history, medical history, family history, educational history, vocational, psychiatric history, relationship history, etc. Specific facts from the history are not required to demonstrate competence in this Global Criterion" (p. 21).

Are sexuality and sexual relationships assumed to be addressed within the more general and vague term "relationship history"? Subsuming sexuality within the vague context of a "relationship" is pervasive among counselors and therapists who are not provided with sexuality and sexual training. Sexuality is much more than partnered relationships (in particular, consider the implications for single addicts, who are encouraged not to enter into new relationships for the first year of recovery). In short, in California and most other regions, drug and alcohol counselors are left to fend for themselves in learning basic human sexuality education.

What do low levels of counselor education and confidence in addressing sexual matters in recovery look and sound like? Drug and alcohol counselors with little confidence in themselves or hope of effectively addressing sex/drug-linked behavior often remain at a precontemplative stage of change. I have spoken with many drug and alcohol counselors who find themselves frustrated and discouraged by the sexual issues they see among their clients. Their stories reveal a wide array of coping strategies common among counselors who are frequently faced with sex/drug-linked addiction and left with little or no direction, training, or hope to address them. The following stories reflect some of the attitudes I have seen and heard among counselors regarding their levels of confidence and self-efficacy.

Changing or Avoiding the Subject

Remember Cindy from Chapter 1. She has been a drug counselor for the past 3 years, sober for more than 7 years, and married for 20 years. She has been sexually abstinent throughout sobriety. Cindy had lied to a client about her own sexual life in sobriety and felt shame and conflict for her defensiveness. Her story is a common one; counselors frequently have impulsive and sudden responses to an unexpected client question about sex that create distance and significant barriers to sexual health conversations between helper and client.

A common rejecting counselor behavior is to change the subject or quickly end a sexually focused client concern. The counselor may be subtle or quite direct to move the focus of the conversation away from sex. Consider the following scenario:

> *Fred is a well-liked drug counselor who facilitates several group sessions a week at a community clinic drug treatment center. Group members attend the evening outpatient program while living at home. At a recent group session, Victor and Angela were reporting concerns about wanting to stay sober. This was a big change from the week before when both acted as strong support for another group member, Tom, who was considering leaving treatment. Tom had not returned this week. Word on the street was that this client had used.*
>
> **Victor:** *Tom went out, I could have told you he wasn't going to make it.*
>
> **Angela:** *Exactly, he was on the prowl the whole time he was here, he made me uncomfortable. One time in group, he winked at me. I didn't like it.*
>
> **Victor:** *He told me he had a thing for you.*
>
> **Fred:** *How do other group members feel talking about Tom and his relapse?*

Fred's conception of his role as group leader was to focus on Tom's relapse. Fred wanted the group members to discuss their own fears and tools for managing relapse risk. Fred had always thought that focusing on attractions, flirtation, and seductive behavior was a dead end. As he listened to Victor and Angela, he was looking for an opportunity to bring the discussion back to relapse and away from what he perceives to be a diversion from the central work of the group.

Denying Treatment

Some counselors may take a position that chronically relapsing men or women with a significant history of sex/drug-linked addiction are not "appropriate" for their treatment center. High sex/drug-linked addicts with a history of treatment failure may be treated as "too toxic" or "have not bottomed out enough" to be considered as patients. This philosophy may be more common within centers supported by government programs or tax dollars. The waiting time is long, treatment spaces are precious, and admission professionals may be leery of letting a chronic treatment failure into their program. They may

Chapter 3 Are You Ambivalent About Sexual Health in Recovery?

be just too much of a risk when other men and women pose a less worrisome and optimistic treatment outcome. Consider the dialogue that will follow.

> *Sarah has been to four other county-funded drug treatment programs in the last 3 years. She is somewhat of a familiar figure among the staff because of her repeated attempts to get sober. In fact, Nancy, the admissions counselor, has seen Sarah in Alcoholics Anonymous (AA) meetings. She has heard Sarah introduce herself at meetings with 22 days, 41 days, 3 months sober . . . and then back to day one. In meetings, Sarah often talks about how she gets high to have sex. Nancy notices the steely glances from some of the long-term sober members. She also observes some of the men looking a little too long and hard at Sarah. Nancy wonders if Sarah ever notices how uncomfortable the group seems when she talks about dating, sex, and trying to stay sober.*
>
> *Now Nancy is talking with Sarah about trying treatment again.*

Nancy: *So Sarah, what do you think will be different this time? You have been to three different treatment programs.*

Sarah: *I am just so sick and tired of going back out. I just can't seem to put a good program together.*

Nancy: *What happened at your last treatment center? It says here (looking at Sarah's application form) that the last two treatment centers asked you to leave.*

Sarah: *I know, I just met these two guys and we really hit it off. They were so mad at me for having sex with that last guy James, they were really mean to me. One of the counselors said that I was making it unsafe for everyone at the treatment center because all the other people where too focused on whether James and I had sex. I was so mad and upset I just said "fuck it" and walked out.*

Nancy: *Sarah, we are just not sure this won't happen here. What is going to be different this time? We have the same rules, no sex with clients. We will kick you out if you do that.*

Sarah: *I know, I promise to control myself this time. I really want to get clean. I am tired of sleeping on friends' couches. I still have my job, but unless I get sober, I think I will lose that too.*

Nancy: *When was the last time you used?*

Sarah: *Two months.*

Nancy: *Was it with James?*

Sarah: *Well, yeah, we still see each other. He is trying to get clean again too. I figure if I can make it work this time, we may be able to make something together.*

> *Nancy:* Sarah, I am just not sure this is the right place for you. We just can't take the risk of you behaving this way here. Perhaps you may try an all women's treatment center. We just don't want to have to worry about you having another relationship with someone who is here trying to get sober.

A treatment center that is unprepared to deal with chronic sex/drug-linked relapse may be quite restrictive on admission to treatment. They may set up behavior contracts or agreements with clients about sexual behavior or relationships with other clients as a prerequisite to entering treatment. Other programs may simply decide they do not want to deal with the many complications of regulating potential sexual behavior concerns. Unfortunately, they may communicate a message of blaming the client or of suggesting that the sex/drug-linked relapse pattern is the client's problem, a symptom that is not the responsibility of drug treatment programs to solve. Sexual relapse patterns may be seen as outside the purview of "this treatment program." All too often, the sole solution is single-gender treatment programs (as if the solution to sexual issues in treatment is to put people who are not sexually drawn to each other in treatment to desexualize the treatment environment). This allows for other treatment centers to refuse treatment or to refer out as a means to decrease the disruption of the sexual behavior within their own treatment facility.

Focusing on Recovery, Not Sexuality

Counselors tend to focus clients not only on what seems to be the most important treatment priority but also on the areas in which they have the most confidence. Drug counselors are the experts in recovery. Many do not see themselves as possessing even basic sexual information necessary to address client sexual concerns. Thus, counselors may reflexively guide clients toward recovery-focused concerns (especially in the first year of recovery) and place sexuality on the sidelines. What ensues is a process not unlike herding cats (cats being the high sex/drug-linked clients). Men and women whose chemical dependency is merged with sexual activity will want counselors to focus on sex, whereas the counselors use the equivalent of a water spray bottle in directing the client away from overfocusing on sexuality. Each believes their intentions are correct, neither has reached consensus with each other (try negotiating with a feline) about discussing recovery skills focused on sex/drug-linked relapse.

Chapter 3 Are You Ambivalent About Sexual Health in Recovery?

Deshaun is finally entering rehab. He is a 38-year-old, single African American man. Deshaun has been coming to terms with his identity as a man who not only has sex with men but has for the first time fallen in love with another man. His partner, Myles, is 33 years old, HIV positive, and a director of an HIV service center. Myles gave Deshaun two choices: "Keep using and I will not stay with you, get sober and we can make a life together."

Deshaun smoked pot every day. He had never had sex with anyone without pot. In the last few years, he began to experiment with crystal meth. Myles did not know Deshaun was meeting other men for sex combined with crystal. When a drug connection showed up at Myles, HIV service center threatening harm to him if Deshaun didn't "pay up," Myles confronted Deshaun. He entered treatment the next week. Deshaun had not been in counseling or mental health care before. He was unfamiliar with talking openly about himself, his life, and especially his sexual life. He was hesitant but knew from his relationship with Myles that talking about matters of sex was commonplace at the HIV center. Myles encouraged him to be as honest as he could be. He loved Deshaun and wanted his treatment to work.

Kurt was completing his education at a local prominent drug and alcohol counseling school when he took on Deshaun as a client. Kurt was known for his easy rapport with clients, willingness to learn, and seeking guidance from supervision. Kurt will make a fine drug and alcoholism counselor. In recovery himself, Kurt is single, the third generation son of Irish immigrants. He is not currently in any significant dating relationship. In the past, his substance abuse was rarely combined with his sexual life with women. He is a very low sex/drug-linked person in recovery.

Kurt has been Deshaun's counselor for 3 weeks. Deshaun has earned his first weekend visit home since entering residential treatment. Myles has been talking about how much he is looking forward to having sex. Deshaun misses having sex, but he has no idea what sex will be like when sober. Deshaun has less arousal and difficulty climaxing without remembering "crystal sex." Four days before the weekend pass, he decides to bring his concern up with Kurt.

Deshaun: *You ever talk about guy stuff?*

Kurt: *What do you mean by "guy stuff"?*

Deshaun: *Well, you know, man, this is hard, ummmm, well, I am going home this weekend. Myles wants to get it on and I'm not so sure.*

Kurt: *You mean Myles wants to have sex and you don't?*

Deshaun: *Yeah, I guess that's it, well, no not really, I mean I miss him, I really want to do it too, I've kinda been practicing if you know what I mean. But I just don't know. I mean, well, did you ever have sex without being high?*

Kurt: *Mmmm, well, I don't know, well, I, ummm, well, I am not sure we should be talking about my sex life, but well, what are you worried about?*

Deshaun: Well, I just don't want to have it be bad.

Kurt: Look, if you're this worried about sex, maybe you should just worry about staying sober over the weekend. A lot of guys get so focused on sex they forget to keep their mind on staying clean. First things first, if you know what I mean. That worked for me. I just kept my focus on staying clean, staying away from using, going to meetings. Maybe you should just let Myles know you want to keep your focus on staying sober for now. Do you think you can let him know that? Recovery is hard work, you have worked so hard to be in your treatment up to this point, you don't want to get your mind away from working your program, going to meetings, and just being at home sober.

Deshaun: Yeah, I guess you're right. I may need a few days to think about talking with Myles about it, but you're right, I should just keep my mind on staying sober.

The counselor who is unprepared for a sexual health conversation, regardless of his level of training or experience, is often guided by the principle of addressing denial, minimization, rationalization, deflection, and other defenses that sustain active addiction. Too often, a client's legitimate sexual health relapse concern is seen by well-meaning drug and alcoholism treatment professionals as a defense mechanism meant to deflect from the central issue of recovery.

Kurt responded using his own experience with recovery combined with what he had been taught in school and by his treatment center supervisors: Keep the client focused on recovery, relapse prevention, and staying abstinent. Kurt saw Deshaun's focus on sex with his partner as a side issue deflecting from the primary issue of staying sober on his first visit home. Neither of these men considered the desire for partnered sex and the ability to negotiate this as a relapse prevention skill.

Sexual health relapse prevention provides an avenue for both to be addressed. Sexual health–based dating and relationship in recovery skills provide counselors and clients a guide for integrating sex within relationships and marriage by evaluating sexual health recovery activities and skills prior to initiating sex. Deshaun's concern about sobriety is linked with his concern about sex with his partner and an attempt to address a central concern for relapse. Unfortunately, his treatment program and recovery community do not invite discussion about introducing sober sex with an existing couple. Kurt's lack of education and training in sex and sobriety leads to counseling that moves the client away from a sexual focus (which is assumed to be a movement back to recovery). Both men are committed to recovery and relapse prevention. They lack a common language to address both of their concerns. Without the confidence to discuss sex/drug-linked behavior, counselor and client will easily retreat to the area of common confidence: focusing on drugs and putting the sexual concerns to the side. Both will be relieved in the moment, both will believe they are doing the right recovery action. Relapse may not be prevented.

Counselor Advocacy Responses

For drug and alcoholism counselors, the worst love stories of all time are rehab romances. They are universally critiqued for the doom they bring to recovery and maintaining abstinence. They are forbidden in most treatment settings. Husband and wives who are both addicts are rarely (if ever) treated simultaneously at the same treatment center. The unique trust and vulnerability inherent in addiction treatment is sabotaged by crushes, infatuation, romance, or sex between clients and residents in treatment centers. This is an issue not debated by sexual health in drug and alcohol treatment.

When counselors lack confidence in how to address these issues, or rely upon standard treatment procedures, a vital sexual health relapse prevention message is missed. Often, the counselor, treatment center, and the general recovery community are focused on condemnation of love feelings, crushes, attractions, and especially engaging in sexual contact. Counselors and the recovery community condemn, moralize, lecture, criticize, judge, ridicule, shame, and even command men and women to cease the relationship. Their motives are sincere: The relationship is a serious risk to treatment. Ignore the warning at your own risk.

Counselors have an important relapse prevention and sexual health education moment when feelings of attraction emerge between clients. Unfortunately, this opportunity is often lost amidst the emotionally reactive program staff. Relationships between clients are a source of much gossip among other clients (and staff). Staff members may see themselves as vigilant watchdogs protecting the treatment center from inappropriate sexual behavior. And because most centers emphasize potential termination from treatment as a consequence for sexual rule breaking, treatment centers can be risky places to openly discuss complex concerns related to sex, attractions, abstinence, and recovery. The bind for many treatment centers is to maintain a safe treatment environment while creating opportunities for open discussion of relapse and recovery concerns related to sexuality and relationships.

> In the HBO documentary Rehab, resident Josh finds a new girlfriend (Corrine) at the camp. Corrine is an 18-year-old recovering alcoholic in treatment at the same residential program as Josh. Josh's 16-year-old former girlfriend (Brandi) is 6 months pregnant, in recovery, and not a resident of the program. Josh and Brandi are working with a program counselor to plan for the birth of the child and Josh's role in the baby's life. The scene opens with Corrine and Josh walking closely, smiling, and looking into each other's eyes adoringly.
>
> **Corrine:** Well I guess my biggest concern is that you will want to go back to Brandi for the baby, to make that a better situation.
>
> **Josh:** Well I guess you know what my first concern is . . . is like your first relationship, afraid I will scare you away with all my shit 'cause I've had some pretty hard relationships with some pretty screwed up girls, don't know how you're going to take it, I love you.
>
> **Corrine:** Me too.
>
> They look into each other's eyes, smile, Josh gently rubs her arm, Corrine leans toward Josh and they lightly kiss.

When I show this scene to drug and alcohol counselors attending my sexual health trainings, the comments come fast and furious:

- "That guy is on his way out!"
- "How can they let that happen?"
- "That is bad news."
- "Man, it happens all the time."
- "This is what happens when you don't have strict rules."
- "Men and women should not be in treatment together!"
- "She's a fool."
- "He is just using her."

The emotional reactions of the workshop attendees often mirror the reactions among counseling staff members at treatment centers. Drug counselors often move to a warning position, a parental authority role, and take an immediate stance of doom for the client and his recovery. Counselors may abandon precontemplative or contemplative stages of change strategies and revert to confrontational counseling styles and behaviors that intensify client resistance. Miller and Rollnick (2002) describe these "I know best, listen to me" counselor interactions as *counselor advocacy responses* (Miller & Rollnick, p. 50) that are contrary to MI counseling. Even counselors who have many skills in MI may automatically and routinely retreat into advocacy responses when the topic is attractions, relationships, or sexual behavior at a treatment center.

Chapter 3   Are You Ambivalent About Sexual Health in Recovery?

There are six types of counselor advocacy responses (Miller & Rollnick, 2002, p. 50). How might each of these reflect the responses of counselors confronting sexual relationships or attractions between treatment program clients? We will examine each in turn.

Arguing: Counselors may quickly express their disagreement with the client wanting to pursue or consider a relationship with another client.

- "You're asking for trouble."
- "What have we told you about relationships in early recovery?"
- "I'm glad you came to me so we can nip this in the bud before it really gets you in trouble."
- "How many men are going to have to take you out before you will stop doing this to yourself?"

Arguing is a common counseling pattern arising from a strong emotional reaction by the counselor. Without a clear plan on how to respond to sexual relapse concerns, the unprepared counselor may be at risk to rely upon common societal, family, and social patterns of discussing sexual concerns. Everyone seems to have an opinion about matters of sex. Persuading someone to agree with our opinion about a specific sexual behavioral norm is a highly prevalent approach to sexual health conversations. These approaches are often all that counselors have learned in their training. Without a sexual health motivational stage of readiness approach, it is no wonder even MI-trained counselors revert to dogmatism and oversimplification.

The expert: Counselors may jump to a parental, authoritarian, lecturing style of interaction. Counselors may have pat scripts that are recited over and over to address attractions or sexual relationships between clients.

- "You shouldn't be entering into a relationship in the first year of recovery."
- "Did you think about your sobriety when you had sex with him?"
- "Do you think she really cares about you or your sobriety?"
- "You are both addicts in treatment, this just cannot continue."

Often these counselor pronouncements, opinions, and warnings are presented in a style that is like a parent speaking to an ignorant misbehaving child.

When client infatuations arise in the treatment process, counselor and client may struggle over whose recovery agenda is to be fulfilled. Counselors may blame the other member of the pair for the irrational behavior of the client. Counselors may attribute the sexual relationship to character defects typical of addicts or refer to their years of sobriety or expertise in treating addictions as fodder for their correct position.

For men and women experiencing attractions toward another person in recovery, the newfound attraction competes with the inconvenient and unwanted circumstance of being in early recovery from a sex/drug-linked addiction. "Expert" counselors will often assume that this new passionate infatuation can only be stemming from the blind self-deception of addiction headed to relapse.

Shaming: Shaming, criticizing, or moralizing about correct sexual conduct can also be a precontemplative counseling response. The use of the jarring shock of shame in response to a sexual concern or worry seems to be guided by the idea of shaking someone out of his or her haze.

- "Oh my god, what were you thinking?"
- "You risked everything in your sobriety for a blow job!"
- "She is nothing, what are you doing with her?"
- "That is such a typical addict."
- "Do you even care about getting sober?"

Counselors themselves may experience sudden shame after saying something critical and blaming of a client. These counselors may have little training, experience, or confidence in using MI approaches to sex/drug-linked relapse. The initial pilot program client assessment identified elevated shame levels as the unique characteristic that was statistically significantly higher among high sex/drug-linked clients compared with low sex/drug-linked clients. This shaming counselor behavior may be the most perniciously harmful counselor advocacy response among men and women who already possess a very strong inner dialogue condemning them for sexual behavior linked with their drug and alcohol dependency.

Labeling: Sexual rule breaking, sexual relationships, errors, or mistakes in sexual behavior with and among the recovery community, high frequency of sexual activity, or unusual/unconventional sexual

Chapter 3 Are You Ambivalent About Sexual Health in Recovery?

thoughts and fantasies may be quickly characterized by a specific name, diagnosis, addiction, or vague stereotype.

- "That's your sex addiction."
- "Because you were molested, you are more likely to be into that kinky stuff."
- "That is immoral, it is a character defect, when you get more sobriety, that will change."
- "You just need to stop being sexual for a while and those perverted thoughts will start to go away."
- "You may be a sex and love addict."
- "You are just substituting one addiction for another."
- "If you don't get this sex addiction under control you're going to get kicked out of here."
- "Oh, she was acting out again. I told her not to wear that low cut blouse to group 2 days ago."
- "He is constantly being reminded by the staff about his sexual acting out."

It is a common shortcut among health care professionals with minimal or insufficient sexual training to feel obligated to provide clients with a label (often an inaccurate one) to explain the current problematic sexual behavior. As if naming the behavior will rededicate the client to abstinence and stave off a much-feared sex/drug-linked relapse. Two common labels I frequently see and used within this context are "sex addiction" and "acting out" (to refer to a sexual behavior, sex act, sexual conversation, sexual rule breaking, or even interest in talking about sex). "Acting out" seems to be a catchphrase that allows counselors to avoid sex-specific language and descriptions of sexual behavior or to make a veiled negative judgment about the clients' sexuality packaged as a professional-sounding counselor observation. Both a premature labeling of "sex addiction" and the overgeneralized language of "acting out" work to create a defensive oppositionalism between counselor and client. This language also creates a shaming and judgmental tone for sexual health discussions that will quickly sour clients' interest in continuing to openly discuss sexual concerns.

Sexual health relapse prevention focuses on what the client and counselor *does*. It is a *behavior* focused endeavor rather than a *label*-focused endeavor. Sexual health in drug and alcohol treatment is first and foremost focused on empowering both counselor and client to better understand sex/drug-linked addiction and to provide prevention skills that can be repeated within the process of recovery.

Being in a hurry: This is a common precontemplative counselor approach to sexual matters in treatment. Let's face it, drug counseling is difficult work. There are multiple issues facing any given interaction with a client, group, family, couple, or treatment center milieu. Drug counselors are expected to multitask on the job, every day. When time is short, it may seem easy to set aside sexual issues given the many competing priorities (especially those priorities that the counselor feels knowledgeable about, competent, experienced, and may have been personally very important to their own recovery). This is human nature. Given the ambivalence most addicts in treatment have toward discussing sexuality, especially highly shamed-filled sex, the hurried counselor response ("I don't have time for this") is a deadening roadblock to clients moving beyond precontemplative readiness for change.

Preeminence: Sexual health relapse prevention is a collaboration between counselor and client. To identify and address each client's sex/drug-linked relapse risk requires an agreement between both client and counselor to keep open, curious, nonjudgmental, and empathic communication regarding planning and executing relapse prevention connected with sex. Counselors who enjoy a preeminent position within a treatment center, their professional community, or among the recovery community may be tempted to resort to a paternalistic approach to sex and relapse. After all, they have achieved a high degree of respect and wisdom in their careers, leading many people in recovery to readily follow their perspectives and advice.

Given the cutting-edge nature of sex/drug-linked relapse prevention, even the preeminent counselors may find themselves less informed than is typical in their counselor role. When presented with client sex/drug-linked treatment concerns, even a well-trained MI addiction counselor may respond with an "I know better" or "I know what is best" approach. In response to this paternalistic stance, clients with sex/drug-linked addiction may either comply or resist. Either way, the relapse risk associated with sex/drug-linked addiction moves from the center of attention as both counselor and client marginalize relapse and sexuality as a central component for maintaining abstinence.

CONCLUSION

Drug and alcohol counselors who are ambivalent (at best) regarding the importance of sex/drug-linked relapse prevention may make up a large percentage of professional treatment providers. Sexuality is most often initially addressed with some trepidation. This is human. Rather than start this book by assuming counselors will be immediately ready to implement sexual health relapse prevention counseling, I wanted to welcome the ambivalent and the uncertain contemplators. If addiction treatment is to prepare for sex/drug-linked assessment and treatment, we must listen, respect, and understand the many hesitations, questions, concerns, objections, and challenges raised by drug and alcoholism counselors, nurses, physicians, therapists, psychologists, administrators, funding sources, public policy makers, government agencies, and treatment programs.

As we have seen, merely agreeing that sex/drug-linked relapse is an important area for treatment improvement is not enough to be ready for change. Most people in drug and alcohol treatment are not ready for this change because of the lack of sexual education and training combined with a wide range of values, beliefs, attitudes, scientific knowledge, and individual psychology within and among the entire drug treatment field. Opinions about sexual health in drug and alcohol treatment vary widely among addiction treatment professionals, between men and women, as well as diverse societal, religious, cultural, familial, developmental, class, ethnic, sexual orientation, and regions of the country.

Sexual health approaches for drug and alcohol counseling are designed to improve the current central agenda for treating addictions. We all want to help our clients enter into recovery earlier, remain longer, and sustain a commitment to recovery as a central life work in treating their alcoholism or drug dependency. Defenses around sexuality arise when the motivation for sexual health conversations is perceived as an attempt to change a sexual value of another person. Sexual health relapse-prevention drug counseling is an invitation to look at your current approaches to sex/drug-linked addiction. The goal is to improve client ability to remain in recovery, to reduce relapse that is associated with sexuality in recovery, and to provide useful lifetime skills for integrating a life of sexual health within recovery.

Sexual health drug counseling asks treatment professionals to observe and evaluate their confidence in industry and individual counseling standards for addressing sex/drug-linked relapse and to consider if making relapse-prevention counseling linked with sexuality is an important means for improving treatment outcomes and reducing risk for relapse among men and women in treatment.

II

Sexual Health in Recovery Assessment

4

Preparing for Sexual Health in Recovery

Preparing to address sex/drug-linked addiction patterns in treatment and counseling is the essential step from ambivalence to implementation. "Planning and a sense of purpose and commitment are essential for effective action, although not always valued by addicted individuals" (DiClemente, 2003, p. 154). Combining sexual health information, research, treatment strategies, and relapse prevention skills is new to the community of recovery professionals and clients. Integrating sexual science with addiction treatment has often been considered, yet rarely implemented. Many drug and alcohol counselors, as well as sex therapists, tell me that sexual health relapse prevention seems like "common sense." The concept of decreasing relapse rates by proactively addressing sexuality in recovery is a welcome discussion within the recovery community. Yet many professionals are hamstrung by a lack of preparation. With no path for preparing to change, wise intentions have remained just that—intentions.

In this chapter, I will suggest various incremental steps to help counselors and addiction professionals move from ambivalent contemplation to implementation of sex/drug-linked relapse prevention and sexual health in recovery programming. I will also provide three skill sets for preparations for change that can be implemented within a wide range of treatment settings.

First, I will outline a series of questions for treatment program sexual self-reflection and self-observation. These questions focus treatment centers and professionals to consider why, what, and how sex/drug-linked addiction and relapse prevention is a desired change within a specific treatment program.

Second, I will expand upon sex-positive counseling skills (as introduced in Chapter 2) as a method to evaluate the level of readiness of a treatment program level of readiness for sexual health–based treatment.

Finally, I will review steps to assess current sexual health–based treatment program policies and current effectiveness in addressing sex/drug-linked addiction.

Preparing for change is a time for important questions. The questions treatment programs and professionals need to address in preparation for sexual health–based treatment echo the many concerns the team at Stepping Stone discussed in their readiness preparation to implement sex/drug-linked addiction.

WHY ASSESS AND TREAT SEX/DRUG-LINKED ADDICTION?

I have addressed this question quite extensively in the previous chapters and hopefully, by now, you realize the answer: We assess and treat sex/drug-linked addition because, either individually or collectively, we have watched too many people relapse because their addictive behavior was insufficiently addressed. This is easy to diagnose after a relapse; at that point, a professional can clearly see how a person's sexual life or sexual history was connected to treatment failure or how his or her behavior resulted in an inability to remain sober. Unfortunately, many sex/drug-linked conversations only occur within treatment centers or with counselors following a client sex/drug-linked relapse. Treatment programs need to engage clients in sex/drug-linked relapse *prevention* rather than reaction.

At Stepping Stone, professionals grew tired of seeing men and women leave treatment or get discharged from treatment because of sexual behavior, relationships, or program violations. Was there a way to assess the level of sex/drug-linked relapse risk at the beginning of treatment? Would giving a client information about his or her individual risk level of sex/drug-linked relapse decrease the likelihood of a relapse? Could clients use this information about their sex/drug-linked relapse risk to increase their motivation for recovery? We were determined to find out.

We soon discovered that to accurately evaluate the benefit of assessing clients' sex/drug-linked relapse risk levels we had to have a staff of counselors capable of addressing sexuality with men and women in recovery.

WHAT IS MY ABILITY TO HONESTLY SELF-REFLECT UPON SEX AND RECOVERY?

Evelyn has been counseling addicts in early recovery for more than 6 years. She is well respected among her peers. Clients are drawn to her easygoing style and warm demeanor. She presents a nonjudgmental sensibility that quietly communicates "I have been there, I understand." She trusts, knowing when to let clients ponder and reflect upon their situation. Her 6 years in counseling addicts has convinced her that silence can be golden when it is attuned with a client's readiness to honestly self-reflect and contemplate their behavior, attitudes, or emotions.

However, Evelyn was becoming increasingly aware of how this quiet space for client reflection was impossible for her to maintain when the subject was sex. She feels her easygoing nature dissipate into an increasing state of hesitancy and tension. She does not feel as confident and clear. She often abandons her trust in client self-reflection. More often than not, she finds herself offering rather strong opinions about sex and recovery. She interrupts clients to interject program slogans. "If you don't want to slip, stay away from slippery places." "We'll love you until you learn to love yourself." "Your mind is like a bad neighborhood: it's not safe to go there alone." This was not like her when she was counseling. She was not satisfied with how she was dealing with sexual topics with her clients. She did not know what to do about this. She went to the director of her program to express her frustration.

Let us stop here for a moment. Can you imagine taking the time to reflect upon how you currently address sexuality in your work as a counselor? Can you identify common patterns of interaction with clients regarding sexual content that may overly rely upon advice, slogans, or glib responses? Do you have a place to discuss how you feel when a client's sexual life or sex/drug-linked addiction history is the focus of counseling? How confident are you in your ability to regulate your reactions to sexual content?

A counselor's ability to honestly self-reflect about his or her responses to sexual health discussions develops from pursuing vulnerable and honest consultation with trusted mentors. We become more confident in our ability to talk about sex by having conversations about sexuality. Sexual confidence in counseling grows through sexual conversations, discussions, education, and interactions. Reading this book is not enough. Sexual health treatment and individual counseling skills emerge from some process of self-evaluation, combined with conversation and interaction with sex and drug addiction therapists. When our own sexual stories are listened to and processed, we develop and hone skills for listening to clients' sexual lives.

Listening to counselors' sexual stories brings us back to Evelyn. The fact that Evelyn is proactively going to a mentor to hear her out is commendable. Unfortunately, many counselors in Evelyn's position are disappointed by evasive, defensive, or helpless supervisor responses.

> Richard has been the director of counseling at Evelyn's treatment program for many years. He is a stalwart among the local recovery community and a leader among drug treatment professionals in his state. Richard is widely sought after by many treatment programs to lecture and consult. Evelyn felt fortunate to have such an esteemed boss.
>
> Evelyn described her disappointment to Richard, who was unprepared for her story. He listened. He did not feel compelled to respond quickly to her concern. He was surprised by her candor and her assertive request to improve this component of her work. Richard felt embarrassed and uncomfortable with the sexual content. His tension surprised him. He did not want Evelyn to notice. His reluctance to be transparent with Evelyn was unsettling to him. He wanted to give her easy answers. It seems as if Richard now occupied the space that Evelyn usually did with her clients. Each was managing his or her counselor/supervisor anxiety for addressing sexuality with avoiding a more transparent discussion and wanting to move quickly into oversimplified advice.

The interaction between Evelyn and her client, as well as the immediate tension for Richard with Evelyn, reflect the need for non-anxious drug and alcohol counselors who can model moving through the anxiety of a sexual health conversation. For those who work with men and women with high levels of sex/drug-linked relapse risk, this is an essential counseling skill.

Stephen Levine and colleagues (2003), in the book *Handbook of Sexuality for the Mental Health Professionals*, write the following:

> Patients are shy about revealing their sexual concerns. It feels so private, so awkward, so potentially embarrassing that many are reduced to paralyzing inarticulateness. They dread being asked, but they long to be asked. They know for sure that they need to be asked if it is ever to come out. Too often, therapists find themselves reluctant to initiate an inquiry. They rationalize, "If my patient doesn't bring up sex, it must not be an issue and I should not be asking about it." At best, this can lead to a missed opportunity to be helpful; at worst, it can lead to the wrong therapy plan. (p. 4)

Evelyn, her client, and Richard were all looking for someone to address sexuality in recovery. They wanted the correct therapy plan. They realized that their own discomfort and lack of education or training was a problem. They were in the necessary contemplative position of needing a helping relationship to sort out their thoughts and emotions.

Sexual health relapse prevention skills among drug and alcohol counselors, supervisors, and treatment programs will develop when professionals become more willing and comfortable with challenging sexual silence in drug and alcohol recovery. A recent study of 175 clinical members of the American Association for Marriage and Family Therapy indicated that sexuality education and supervision experiences are the cornerstone for a base-level counselor comfort with sexual discussions, as well as the key variable for predicting counselors' willingness for initiating sexuality-related discussions with their clients (Harris & Hays, 2008).

Unfortunately, there are currently no assessments or scales developed to measure drug and alcohol counselors' current levels of sexuality education, clinical experience with sexuality issues, sexual knowledge, comfort when discussing sexuality-related issues, and/or initiation of sexuality discussions with clients. I have adapted *The Family Therapist Comfort With and Willingness to Discuss Client Sexuality* questionnaire (Harris & Hays, 2008) for this purpose (see Figure 4.1). A downloadable form is also available on my Web site at www.BridgingSexualHealth.com.

The survey is divided into several sections. The first section reviews counselor frequency of assessing and initiating sexuality conversations on various sex/drug-linked relapse risk factors. This is followed by a series of statements about sexual comfort, knowledge, and history related to your work as a drug and alcohol counselor. The next two sections rate your base sexual knowledge and comfort levels in professional situations discussing sexuality issues. The last section is a compilation of counselor sex/drug-linked relapse prevention drug and alcohol counseling skills.

Each section is an opportunity for honest self-reflection. Notice your emotions, reactions, thoughts, perceptions, and attitudes as you complete the form. Your emotions and feelings are an important impetus for evaluating your readiness to address sexual health in recovery.

After completing the survey, take some time to discuss your feelings with a colleague, friend, or mentor. There is no need to disclose the content of your answers. Focus the initial discussion on your reactions about completing the survey. As counselors, we are often encouraged to prematurely move toward a rational, thinking-based interaction with our peers. In this case, I suggest starting with your emotions. There will be plenty of time to consider your thoughts and opinions. Taking the time to honor emotions is a sexual health skill imbedded in many of the relapse prevention tools you will teach clients.

Among the hundreds of counselors I have given this assessment, one of the most common reactions is "I never thought of some of this

FIGURE 4.1 The Drug and Alcohol Counselor Comfort and Willingness to Discuss Client Sexuality Questionnaire

---

General Instructions

Please circle the following responses or fill in the blank with the appropriate information about you.

Sexuality Discussions With Clients Scale

Every therapist has a system for assessing and initiating discussions about specific client problems. Please answer how much the following statements reflect your practice habits regarding the assessment and initiation of discussions on sexuality-related issues.

I **assess** for and **initiate therapeutic conversations** on:

	Never		Sometimes			Very Often	
Sexually transmitted diseases/infections	1	2	3	4	5	6	7
Sexual dysfunction	1	2	3	4	5	6	7
Client satisfaction with their sexual life	1	2	3	4	5	6	7
Client sexual interaction pattern	1	2	3	4	5	6	7
Reproduction	1	2	3	4	5	6	7
Contraception	1	2	3	4	5	6	7
Sexual orientation	1	2	3	4	5	6	7
Sexual relationship enhancement	1	2	3	4	5	6	7
Nonconsensual sex as victim	1	2	3	4	5	6	7
Nonconsensual sex as perpetrator	1	2	3	4	5	6	7
The impact of drugs and alcohol on sexual health	1	2	3	4	5	6	7
The impact of mental illness on sexual health	1	2	3	4	5	6	7
The impact of medical problems on sexual health	1	2	3	4	5	6	7
How sexuality was expressed/discussed in family of origin	1	2	3	4	5	6	7
STI/HIV protection	1	2	3	4	5	6	7
Client satisfaction with his/her body	1	2	3	4	5	6	7
The impact of the presenting problem on client sexual health	1	2	3	4	5	6	7
Cultural sexual values	1	2	3	4	5	6	7
Religious sexual values	1	2	3	4	5	6	7

(continued)

FIGURE 4.1 The Drug and Alcohol Counselor Comfort and Willingness to Discuss Client Sexuality Questionnaire *Continued*

	Strongly Disagree						Strongly Agree
I only assess and initiate conversations on sexuality-related issues when the client states that it is a concern.	1	2	3	4	5	6	7

Sexual Comfort Scale
Please indicate how **comfortable** you are or would be discussing sexuality issues with the following groups:

	Very Uncomfortable		Somewhat Comfortable			Very Comfortable	
Students/Trainees	1	2	3	4	5	6	7
Supervisors	1	2	3	4	5	6	7
Colleagues	1	2	3	4	5	6	7
Male Clients	1	2	3	4	5	6	7
Female Clients	1	2	3	4	5	6	7
Sexual Minority Clients	1	2	3	4	5	6	7
Client Ethnicity Difference from my own	1	2	3	4	5	6	7
Elderly Clients	1	2	3	4	5	6	7
Teenaged Clients	1	2	3	4	5	6	7
Preteenaged Clients	1	2	3	4	5	6	7
Physically Disabled Clients	1	2	3	4	5	6	7
Mentally Disabled Clients	1	2	3	4	5	6	7

Please indicate how comfortable you are or would be discussing sexuality issues in the following modalities:

	Very Uncomfortable		Somewhat Comfortable			Very Comfortable	
Individual	1	2	3	4	5	6	7
Group	1	2	3	4	5	6	7
Couple	1	2	3	4	5	6	7
Family	1	2	3	4	5	6	7
Supervision	1	2	3	4	5	6	7

(continued)

FIGURE 4.1 The Drug and Alcohol Counselor Comfort and Willingness to Discuss Client Sexuality Questionnaire *Continued*

Please indicate your reactions to the following statements using the following scale:

	Strongly Disagree					Strongly Agree	
I respond openly and confidently when my sexual values are challenged.	1	2	3	4	5	6	7
I communicate effectively about sexuality.	1	2	3	4	5	6	7
I use sexual vocabulary, which is appropriate to the situation.	1	2	3	4	5	6	7
I am sensitive to and respectful of others' feelings and anxieties toward sexual matters.	1	2	3	4	5	6	7
I encourage clients to explore their own sexual issues.	1	2	3	4	5	6	7
I encourage clients to explore their own sexual values.	1	2	3	4	5	6	7
I am not concerned about how I influence client sexuality.	1	2	3	4	5	6	7
I am confident in my knowledge about sexuality.	1	2	3	4	5	6	7
I appear poised in session when addressing sexual matters.	1	2	3	4	5	6	7
I find myself lacking respect for and feeling intolerant of others' sexual values and practices.	1	2	3	4	5	6	7

Note: The instrument presented in this figure was from "Family Therapist Comfort With and Willingness to Discuss Client Sexuality" by S. M. Harris and K. W. Hayes, 2008, *Journal of Marital and Family Therapy*, 34(2), 239–250. Copyright 2008 by *Journal of Marital and Family Therapy*. Adapted with permission.

before." You may feel sad, excited, pleased, disappointed, relieved, embarrassed, angry, concerned, defeated, overwhelmed, or even inspired at various moments during this survey. Enjoying the range of emotions inherent in any sexuality conversation is a confidence builder for counselors to initiate sex- and relapse-focused recovery counseling.

HOW WELL DOES MY TREATMENT SETTING ADDRESS SEX/DRUG-LINKED ADDICTION?

Assessing the environment in which you provide drug and alcoholism counseling is a significant factor in movement toward sexual health in recovery. As I've mentioned in previous chapters, alcohol and drug recovery centers have traditionally relegated addressing sexual behavior in early recovery to the "back burner" or have believed that to address sexuality too soon in recovery risks a client's relapse. Addiction professionals often discuss sexual concerns from a sex-negative or harm context. Therefore, a client's sexual and relationship life are often limited to a focus on co-occurring sex addiction, nonconsensual sex, sexual trauma, sexually transmitted infections, pregnancy, and/or the moral dimensions of conforming to a specific set of sexual values and behaviors. Additionally, the topic of sex is often "taboo" in the alcohol and drug treatment environment. Members of the staff have a difficult time broaching the subject of sex. Individual counselor sexual attitude and behavior self-assessment is only valuable if undertaken in a treatment environment that is open to undertaking its own personal inventory.

My experience at Stepping Stone (the treatment center where sexual health in recovery was first evaluated) provides valuable information about the necessary fundamental components for a drug treatment program to prepare and implement a sexual health in recovery program. Drug and alcohol treatment centers like Stepping Stone are not the only environments for sex/drug-linked relapse prevention services. The thousands of outpatient and agency-based drug counseling centers are another important environment for sexual health–based drug treatment, not to mention the multitude of sober living centers, 12-step recovery communities, psychotherapist offices, detoxification centers, co-occuring treatment programs, and professionally facilitated drug treatment groups. Whatever the setting, a certain percentage of clients will present with a high degree of sex/drug-linked behaviors. The question is how can a given drug treatment program or counselor assess the environmental readiness for sexual health relapse prevention?

All settings and providers of addiction treatment can implement sexual health material in an existing treatment program. It will, however, require a commitment to acquiring skills in sexual health–based treatment approaches as well as addressing program policies and entrenched patterns of ignoring or denying sex/drug-linked relapse risks.

Assessment for sexual health–based treatment readiness begins at the top. The first step in appraising readiness involves getting key leaders (such as the director of a treatment center, a drug counselor in private practice, a program director of a state or county drug and alcohol treatment program, a public policy leader interested in improving treatment outcomes, etc.) to articulate that integrating sexual health content into recovery is an essential value. I suggest two areas for these leaders to focus their attention: First, satisfaction with client retention and, second, level of satisfaction with current treatment approaches to sex/drug-linked addiction. Who in the treatment program measures (whether through opinion, assumption, perception, or quantified statistics) that the current level of client retention is within an acceptable range? If you are a counselor providing your own outpatient services, you may ask yourself if you are satisfied with your current levels of client retention.

The issue of poor client retention rates is of great concern to the substance abuse field. Treatment completion rates from inpatient to outpatient vary from low to moderate. For many in the drug treatment profession, this is not ideal since length of stay is consistently associated with better client outcomes (Amodeo, Chassler, Oettinger, Labiosa, & Lundgren, 2008). Factors associated with treatment failure, drop-out, and low retention vary from poor initial prognosis due to multiple legal, psychiatric, social, and medical problems, low client motivation, poorly matched level of treatment or life circumstances with treatment program, and low counselor–client therapeutic alliance (Amodeo et al., 2008).

The Stepping Stone program evaluation is the only current information to evaluate client-retention rates associated with sex/drug-linked addiction patterns. Client retention at Stepping Stone doubled as compared with the 3 years prior to the implementation of the sexual health relapse prevention program.

For some programs, client-retention rates are the essential measure of good treatment. For others, it may be the role of offering innovative and leading-edge treatment approaches. Perhaps you treat substance-abusing, college-age adults who may represent a high link with sex and drugs. You may provide services to a client base that experiences significant legal, personal, and health consequences from drug use linked with sexual behavior. These men and women may test positive for HIV, hepatitis C, or experience multiple unintended pregnancies. They may have engaged in sex work, sexual assault, nonconsensual sex, public sex, or traded sex for drugs. Some treatment seekers have repeated treatment attempts only to relapse due to sexual activity linked with drug use and no preparation or addressing of this link in any of their previous treatment program.

Drug counselors and treatment programs open to assessing the prevalence of client sex/drug-linked addiction patterns within their treatment settings may be surprised to find a greater-than-expected number of sex/drug-linked abusers who have been largely marginalized or invisible. It takes a commitment to asking these questions to find out your own current sex/drug-linked program or counseling practice demographics.

You may look at your initial screening information forms or interview screening procedures for selecting clients in your treatment program. Including a few self-report questions about sex/drug link in your forms may be all it takes (see Figure 4.2 for such a self-report).

If you are a change-maker in your current role as a drug treatment professional, take a moment to imagine what it might be like to talk with your staff about beginning to include these questions in the initial intake with each and every client (whether inpatient, day treatment, evening outpatient, outpatient, recovery home, or outpatient group/individual counseling). This procedure would begin to address the difficulty that counselors have in initiating sexual discussions. Asking about a link between sex and drug use as part of the overall addiction assessment would begin to normalize sexuality discussions as part of treatment. Often the question can create an opportunity for clients to begin contemplating the connection between drugs and sex. Clients may be relieved to have the subject brought up. They may be more optimistic about entering yet another treatment program if, upon the first encounter, your center is doing something different, something sex positive, something proactive. Might this encounter influence client decision about entering treatment? Our experience at Stepping Stone is a big "yes." Stepping Stone developed a reputation as the go-to treatment center if you want to address sex and recovery. This became a highly regarded asset within the recovery and treatment community in San Diego.

FIGURE 4.2 Initial Screening Process Self-Report

Look at your initial screening information forms or interview screening procedures for selecting clients in your treatment program. Include a few self-report questions about sex/drug link in your forms. Sample questions may be:

	Almost Constantly	Constantly	Frequently	Sometimes	Rarely	Never
■ I worry that sex is not as satisfying sober as it is when I am high on drugs/alcohol.						
■ I worry that my drug- and alcohol-using behavior is too highly linked to sexual relationship(s), sexual pleasure, and/or my sexual behavior.						
■ I worry my sexual relationship(s), sexual pleasure, and or my sexual behavior is so linked with my drug and alcohol use that I cannot imagine sex without being high.						
■ I worry that some aspect of my sexual life may make it difficult to complete this treatment program.						

ASSESSING TREATMENT CENTER ENVIRONMENT READINESS

An environmental assessment does not have to be elaborate. What is important is to create a situation where emotions, ideas, and values of your treatment program provide an environment that allows clients to heal unaddressed, ignored, or unspoken sex/drug-linked pattern of use. A beginning step to gauge your facility's level of readiness may be to take each of the five sex-positive counselor skills discussed in Chapter 2 and expand them as a frame of reference for your overall treatment program or individual counseling practice.

Suspending Judgments

What are common judgments that treatment center staff express among themselves when discussing clients? I find it is the unguarded moments, the behind closed door discussions among peers, where treatment program, sex-negative judgments can find fertile ground. At Stepping Stone, we addressed these (often subconscious) habits by normalizing judgments about sex. We did not expect staff and counselors to somehow be immune from the larger cultural and societal sex negativity that is commonplace in the United States. Welcoming the disclosure of a wide array of opinions, attitudes, and values was essential from the beginning.

I discussed labeling behavior in the previous chapter. During your initial assessment of the environment, listen for the current sexual labels, sex phrases, and sexual metaphors used at your treatment program, in your outpatient groups, and/or in your individual counseling sessions. (By this I mean, listen to what the professional staff are saying. We will deal with client language later.) Take a week. Listen to all the various ways you and your colleagues refer to sexual issues, relationship issues, and sex/drug-linked behaviors when discussing clients out of earshot of the clients. This language is an accurate indicator of the unspoken, habitual, and ensconced sexual policies and attitudes. It will reflect the sex-positive, sex-neutral, and/or sex-negative group think patterns within your setting.

You might hear some of these themes or statements, many of which indicate a hidden judgment:

- "Watch him, he is up to no good today."
- "She took so long in the shower she was late for dinner." (Meant as a veiled reference to masturbation.)

- "I had to send her back to her room twice to change her clothes." (A reference to clothing considered inappropriate by the staff.)
- "He flirts with everyone."
- "I had to separate the two of them in group."
- "She had so much makeup on, I couldn't believe it."
- "I think he picked someone up at his AA meeting over the weekend. When I asked him he just denied it."

. . . and on it goes. It can be quite an eye-opening experience to see how frequently drug counselors talk about sex/drug-linked relapse risk factors and sexual health issues without even realizing it! As you assess the environment, think about what it might be like to rephrase each of these statements as a sex/drug-linked clinical observation. What if "Watch him, he is up to no good today" became "You know, he is a high sex/drug-linked relapse risk client, he may benefit from talking about his sexual boundaries to remind him of his sex/drug-linked relapse risk when he is challenging or crossing boundaries."

Affirming Sexual Pleasure

The concept of pleasure presents an interesting conundrum to drug and alcohol programs. Often the search for pleasure, altered states, and a retreat from the toils of life's traumas is deeply intertwined with alcoholism and drug addiction. Unfortunately, for many people, a brief yet pleasurable experience of being drunk or high can eventually become a nightmare of unquenchable demand. The pleasure of sex and intimate relationships becomes bound up within the unwanted yet very real drug dependency. It can be difficult for treatment programs and counselors to affirm sexual pleasure while still acknowledging the risks for the high sex/drug-linked client.

Early in my consultation with Stepping Stone, a counselor requested my advice on how to respond to a sexual situation. A resident had found a roommate's sex toy and had reported this to the counselor. For years, the policy at Stepping Stone was to confiscate sexual aids—and follow up with the resident in a (often humiliating) discussion about how such materials were not allowed at the residence.

I asked the staff to consider the ramifications of this policy. Clients of Stepping Stone often live in the center for 6–9 months. "Is the expectation that Stepping Stone is an orgasm-free zone?" I noted that clients were not given any positive sexual health messages about masturbation; it was only addressed when a boundary crossing, such as the possession of sexual aids, occurred.

How could the response at Stepping Stone be handled in a way that affirms sexual pleasure? Affirming sexual pleasure is a framework that views sexual fantasies and desires as important and essential aspects of sexual expression. How can a treatment facility establish client guidelines and boundaries about responsible privacy with their sex toy while also affirming sexual pleasure as an intervention to sexual health relapse prevention? In this instance, the counselor clarified for the resident that masturbation is an expected part of sexual activity at Stepping Stone. (Many of the residents are single or away from their partners.) The counselor affirmed that as long as masturbation is handled with good boundaries it was considered part of sexual health in recovery for many men and women at Stepping Stone.

Lastly, the counselor asked the resident who reported the sex toy about his personal concerns. An interesting conversation ensued about how the resident thought masturbation was disgusting. The counselor listened, but did not give an opinion. He affirmed the client's ability to express his values and reflected upon how difficult it must be to share a room with someone with such different values about masturbation than his own. The counselor encouraged the roommate to continue to address sexual concerns as part of his commitment to recovery.

An exercise for assessing your treatment center's current attitudes toward client sexual pleasure might be to take a moment and think about your reaction to the situation you just read. How might your treatment setting have handled such an issue? Would all the counselors have handled it in a sex-neutral or sex-positive manner? Why or why not?

Understanding That Sexuality Is a Central and Basic Need

Sexual behavior, sexual relations, partnered sex, and solo sex come and go throughout the life cycle, but the centrality of sexuality to being human is constant. Sexuality encompasses all the ways people have sexual contact as well as the medical and psychological aspects of sexual activity.

As I mentioned in Chapter 1, sexuality is strikingly absent from the guiding principles of recovery and elements of recovery-oriented systems of care developed through the Center for Substance Abuse Treatment (CSAT). On a more local level, I suggest an exercise for observing the centrality of sexuality to your clients within your specific treatment setting. Take a week to listen for those times when sex is indirectly or metaphorically discussed in clinical conversations. What words, phrases, and clinical observations are used to discuss client sexuality? How much is client sexuality discussed in vague or slang terms? Is sexuality discussed within the context of recovery? Resist the urge to immediately comment or give feedback about what you hear. It is important to remain an observer and listener about your treatment program patterns in discussing sex. However, you may choose to take your observations to a colleague or supervisor who has already identified himself or herself as an ally for addressing sex/drug-linked relapse prevention.

Understand How a Client's Behavior Might Indicate an Attempt to Address a Sexual Worry or Concern

I know you have many, many things to keep in mind as an addiction professional and that the task of sorting out priorities at any given moment with a client is both an art and a science. I find that my work as a therapist is to listen for the unspoken. Sometimes the only way to hear the unexpressed concern of a client is to pose the unasked client question in my own mind: not ask it, but listen for clues to the answer in my own mind as I attend to the client.

Sexual concerns are not easy to bring up in the best of circumstances. I have discussed how counselors often ignore or avoid client sexual health in recovery concerns. I have described how frequently sexual concerns surface at a treatment program arise when no longer avoidable. In an earlier chapter, I described a scene from the documentary *Rehab* in which a client, Tiffany, discloses that she had been paid for sex to have money for drugs, her family now knew this and she was shattered with shame. This conversation did not take place with a counselor but with a fellow recovering addict. Interestingly, this addict did *not* encourage her to talk with her counselor, despite the clear risk for relapse. The treatment center may not have established an environment in which client behavioral or emotional crises were connected with unaddressed sexual health concerns. If Tiffany had disclosed this painful revelation in a counseling session, the focus could initially be on helping Tiffany stay sober despite her shame and issues with her family.

I think Tiffany's plight is all too common. We live a culture that relies on crisis in our sexual lives to have a space to discuss matters of sex. Preventative adult sexual health conversations unaccompanied by the immediacy of the urgent moment are rarely modeled in families or friendships. Drug treatment centers often reflect this cultural norm. Sexual health in drug and alcohol treatment encourages men and women in recovery to anticipate sexual worries or concerns and provide a series of skill sets to process sex-related relapse concerns.

Treatment centers may consider developing a central statement or guiding principle that everyone relies on when uncertain about taking proactive sexual health relapse prevention as an alternative to waiting for a sexual crisis.

For example, Stepping Stone had no such statement that could provide a framework for all the complex sexual behaviors and concerns that emerge among adults living together in a treatment program. I suggested they needed to develop what I called a *statement of affirming sexuality*. This statement would describe what the treatment program *affirms* about sexuality, rather than what it prohibits. This would be a statement that outlined the most basic sexual health principles at the treatment center. I suggested it needed to be one sentence. They laughed, but I was serious. They wanted me to write it for them. I refused; sexual health principles must stem from a process of discussion, not a directive from a sexual health consultant.

Ultimately, this is what they came up with: "Stepping Stone affirms residents and participants sexual behavior that is consensual, legal, and supports abstinence and recovery from drug/alcohol addiction." This statement became the ultimate arbitrator for difficult sexual safety or rule breaking client behavior.

Is this sexual issue about nonconsent? No nonconsensual sexual behavior would be tolerated.

Is the sexual behavior illegal? The treatment center must support sexual laws and regulations of the state. Does the sexual behavior put the client or anyone else at the program at risk for arrest? Does the sexual behavior violate conditions of probation?

Does the sexual behavior support abstinence from drugs and alcohol? This is an important focus of much of sex/drug-linked relapse prevention counseling and treatment.

Does the sexual behavior support recovery goals? This is where sexual behavior may contradict treatment program policies. This conflict between a client's sexual behavior and a program's sexual behavior policies is too often resolved through secrecy between the client and the treatment center staff.

Treatment centers that establish a statement of affirming sexuality will have an important guide for thinking and talking about sexual health policies and procedures. The statement is a proactive message to encourage honesty and openness about matters of sexual safety and relapse. It can be a vital tool for critical thinking about the spectrum of client sexual behavior boundary violations, boundary crossings, or boundary concerns.

A statement of affirming sexuality guides treatment centers to consider problematic client (or staff) sexual behavior as a misguided attempt to address a sexual worry or concern. Focusing first on the most basic sexual health concerns at the treatment center provides an opportunity for dialogue and learning as well as enforcement of boundaries. How might a client's sexual behavior (that is so concerning it is a focus of a treatment center staff or program) possibly be an unseen attempt to solve a sexual concern that the person is avoiding because it has not reached the crescendo of an immediate crisis? A treatment center can formulate responses to sexual concerns by affirming sexuality as well as basic principles of safety and sobriety. The statement of affirming sexuality supports drug and alcohol treatment program curiosity and suspension of judgment by first focusing on consent, the law, abstinence, and recovery goals. Treatment centers that are clear in affirming sexuality in recovery, balanced with fundamental principles of sexual health, open a new understanding for a very familiar symptom, client's sexual behavior concerns within a treatment program.

Focus on Treatment Center Motivation

> The skill required when talking with patients about *why, how, what* and *when* of behavior change is not a matter of applying strategies *on* them, but of structuring a conversation in a useful way which encourage the patient to take as much of the lead as possible. (Rollnick, Mason, & Butler, 1999, p. 103)

When clients transgress, counseling staff may infer that they have a low level of motivation for sobriety. This assumption may prevent a useful conversation between treatment staff and clients. Behavior change is based on change talk that strongly supports the recovering client to take responsibility for movement toward change and recovery. Sexual health–based relapse prevention counseling integrates this behavior change counseling skill by placing the focus of conflict, concern, worry, dilemma, or contradiction between recovery and sexuality on the client. Once the framework for the treatment frame of the statement of affirming sexuality has been established, what the treatment center is concerned about is less important. What is the client's self-discrepancy and motivation?

In Tiffany's situation, the treatment center needed to provide an environment for her to contemplate with a professional helper about staying sober *and* experiencing this shameful secret and boundary violation (her diary had been read by her mother). Motivational interviewing counseling approaches are continually challenging treatment centers to keep their counselors and treatment program interventions focused on the client's discrepancy between two conflicting motivations and to provide an arena for joint decision making as a result of moving through ambivalence to prepare for action.

A suggested exercise for treatment center personnel is to notice a particular sequence of interaction between counselors when they discuss clients. These conversations happen so fast that you have to be quick to notice them. They are the typical conversations counselors have with each other as part of the day-to-day work in an addiction treatment center.

A counselor has just had an interaction with a client. She is clearly frustrated. She is thinking that she was not effective. A coworker asks, "How did it go with Patricia?" She lets out an exasperated sigh and says, "She is just not listening." In this case, many counselors might focus on the client's resistance instead of the counselor interaction. It is this almost automatic tendency to assume low client motivation (resistance) that often elicits counselor frustration. When the subject is sex, this pattern is even more likely due to both the counselor and client's lack of readiness in addressing sex/drug-linked concerns.

A motivational exercise for treatment center staff and program leadership is to begin asking colleagues, coworkers, and other drug and alcohol treatment providers about how satisfied or unsatisfied they are with their current approaches to identifying and treating clients with high sex/drug-linked addiction patterns. This takes the focus off the client motivation and begins placing interest and curiosity on the treatment program motivation. The central mission of sexual health in recovery is to improve overall satisfaction with addressing sex/drug-linked addiction patterns among both treatment professionals and their clients.

Treatment center staff who embark on this exercise need not focus on the responses they hear. The purpose of this exercise is to ask the question. Treatment centers that are motivated to improve treatment outcomes for sex/drug-linked clients need to talk early and often with other treatment centers about sex/drug-linked addiction patterns. The conversation will clarify individual staff discrepancy and motivations for change.

I have asked this question to hundreds of addiction treatment professionals. Engaging in the discussion has honed my critical thinking and ability to understand my motivation for this work. I have less and less ambivalence about the efficacy and validity of this intervention. It is the generosity of the many men and women with whom I have invited into this sexual health conversation that has solidified my motivation and commitment to integrating sexual health–based relapse prevention within drug and alcohol treatment.

SEXUAL HEALTH–BASED PROGRAM POLICIES

Sexual health–based drug and alcohol treatment program policies are an important component of assessing the environmental readiness for sexual health in recovery programming. Can you name three policies, program procedures, treatment guidelines, or counseling approaches that directly address sexual behavior among the recovering men and women you treat? Too frequently, the answer to this question takes little thought:

- No new relationships in the first year of recovery.
- No sex with people at the treatment center.
- Women sleep in one section of the program, men in the other.
- No lingering hugs or touching without permission.
- No provocative clothing (like revealing low-cut tops or jeans down to their knees).
- Clients will be terminated if they engage in sexual activity while in treatment.

What other sexual policies are in place in your treatment setting? Can you think of ways they might be revised to reflect a more sex-positive attitude? For example, earlier in the chapter, I mentioned the policy at Stepping Stone that required that all sexual aids be confiscated. Much has changed at Stepping Stone since those early days.

HOW CAN A TREATMENT CENTER EVALUATE ITS CURRENT LEVEL OF EFFECTIVENESS IN ADDRESSING SEX/DRUG-LINKED ADDICTION?

I encourage you to take the time to implement the previous treatment environment preparation assessment exercises before moving onto this step, because this next evaluation will be difficult for anyone who provides health care. It requires treatment centers to look at when the environment fails, not when it is successful. To adequately prepare for implementing sex/drug-linked relapse, prevention services program leadership must first evaluate its current ability to address sexuality in recovery. This can occur by asking staff, clients, and program administrators various questions:

- Are you aware of sex/drug-linked addiction treatment patterns among men and women in your treatment center?
- Are there clients who may have a strong sex/drug link within our center or program?
- If so, how are we identifying them?
- Are you satisfied with how you personally, and the center/program as a whole, currently addresses these clients?
- Can we do better?

This overall sex/drug-linked programmatic assessment should be conducted by the treatment program leadership, the people in charge of the center, the change-makers who make final policy and program decisions. It is difficult to get useful, candid, and specific information linking poor client retention or treatment failure with the level of client's sex/drug link if the people asking the questions are not the agents of change for the institution.

Treatment failure, as represented by clients who leave treatment prematurely, clients who use during treatment, and/or clients whose behavior (violent or sexual) causes them to be discharged exist in all drug treatment programs. The key to preparing the treatment environment for sexual health in recovery programming is to connect these adverse treatment outcomes with unaddressed sex/drug-linked client concerns within the treatment program.

This process should encourage everyone involved to objectively appraise the current situation without focus on solutions or action. It should not focus on any one particular treatment service or intervention, nor is it meant to identify services that may be failing. It is not a time to list all the negative ways the program currently deals with sexuality. (This assessment can also be a time to consider what the program does *well* regarding sex and recovery.) Open-ended questions, such as the ones listed earlier, will be more effective than a prepared list of concerns predetermined by the program administrators.

Perhaps a voluntary meeting among program staff who are interested in discussing current approaches to sexuality in the treatment program might be a good starting point. The task of the group might be to develop some open-ended questions to be distributed anonymously among staff and clients. Everyone who participates in the questionnaire should receive a summary of the results. The summary may include some objective feedback from the committee such as, "In general, it looks as if our current approaches to sex and recovery are inadequate according to the feedback from the participants in the survey."

In the first year at Stepping Stone, everyone completed such a survey. It included five open-ended questions:

1. What client behaviors would you like a sexual relapse prevention program to address?
2. What is the program currently doing well to help clients deal with sexual behavior?
3. What is the program doing not well/very poorly to help clients deal with sexual behavior?
4. What do you like best and least about instituting a sexual health relapse prevention program?
5. What program policies or sexual issues do you want to make sure are included in developing and implementing the program?

Taking stock of current approaches to sex/drug-linked counseling techniques will lead to conversations that assess the treatment program interest and readiness to contemplate sex in recovery.

CONCLUSION

I encourage the leaders and change-makers at treatment programs of all kinds to reach out to their counselors and clients and initiate a dialogue. Discussing sexuality is not an easy conversation to initiate for most people. A fundamental sexual health behavior is to initiate discussion about sexual concerns within the treatment environment from the very beginning of treatment. Drug and alcohol treatment providers need to challenge entrenched patterns of waiting for someone suffering from a sex/drug-linked problem to bring it forward. Sexual health in recovery is founded on the principle of integration of human sexuality within all levels of health care and treatment. After all, everyone is sexual.

When it comes to sexual health, I think "If you build it they will come" or "a program of attraction rather than promotion" are good slogans to summarize the approach. Many people with sex/drug-linked addiction concerns will come forward if given an opportunity to do so, especially if the process occurs during a time to talk without premature movement to change or action.

A good portion of the remainder of this book will focus on implementing and providing sexual health in recovery relapse prevention counseling. However, one more assessment issue needs to be addressed. How do you assess individual client's level of sex/drug-linked addiction? We will consider this assessment in Chapter 5.

5

Assessing Sex/Drug-Linked Relapse Risk

San Diego's Stepping Stone drug and alcohol addiction treatment program began looking at the relationship between sex/drug-linked behavior and a client's ability to succeed in recovery in 2002. To this day, it remains a new area of study. During the Stepping Stone project, we administered a client assessment survey to examine individual client's risk for sex/drug-linked relapse and to hopefully identify characteristics specific to clients reporting a high degree of linkage between sex and substance use. The client assessment survey was administered to more than 250 clients within the first 2 weeks of their admission into the program. More than 60% of those clients retook the survey after 3 months of treatment. More than one third of the original 250 completed an assessment after 6 months of treatment.

The Stepping Stone client assessment survey measured changes in risk behaviors associated with sex/drug-linked relapse in addition to client sexual attitudes and beliefs associated with risky sexual behaviors. It contained six categories:

1. drug and alcohol use
2. sex/drug-linked behavior
3. cognitive errors in coping and interpersonal style
4. sexual secrets and shame
5. sexual health attitudes and beliefs
6. risky sexual behaviors

These six categories formed the starting point for examining clients' sexual health in recovery characteristics, behaviors, affect states, motivations, and decisions to be included within the Sexual Health in Recovery Assessment described in the next chapter.

In this chapter, I will summarize the construction process of the Sexual Health in Recovery Assessment and its origins. I will discuss general outcome evaluation conclusions from each of the six categories from the original Stepping Stone study. I will describe how the Stepping Stone survey summary conclusions contributed to the building of the current 130-item Sexual Health in Recovery Assessment. I will describe how the Sexual Health in Recovery Assessment was constructed to organize and unify each specific assessment item within the core four elements of sexual health in recovery as well as the 12-skill sets for sex/drug-linked relapse prevention (these will be discussed in Chapter 10).

This chapter ends with the "Inventory Categories for Sexual Health in Recovery Assessment," which organizes all 130 scored items from the Sexual Health in Recovery Assessment (to be introduced in the next chapter).

DRUG AND ALCOHOL USE

Stepping Stone's assessment survey provided clients with a list of substances (chosen because they represented those most commonly used by men and women seeking treatment at Stepping Stone) and asked to disclose all of those they had used 3 months prior to taking the survey. The list included:

1. alcohol,
2. amyl nitrate,
3. cocaine or crack cocaine,
4. crystal methamphetamine,
5. ecstasy,
6. gamma hydroxybutyrate (GHB),
7. hallucinogens (LSD or mushrooms),
8. heroin,
9. ketamine ("Special K"),
10. marijuana,
11. sleeping pills (barbiturates), and
12. steroids.

In our evaluations, we found that six drugs were of particular interest with respect to sex/drug-linked relapse: crystal methamphetamine, cocaine or crack cocaine, ketamine, ecstasy, GHB, and amyl nitrate.

Alcohol was most frequently used 3 months prior to treatment, but it was not weighted the same as these six drugs because of the multitude of situations often associated with alcohol that are not commonly associated with sexual behavior.

If you wish to adapt the Sexual Health in Recovery Assessment for your own purposes, you should add emerging sex-linked drugs reported to be used or abused by clients within your region. You may also be interested in client use of erectile functioning medications, diuretics, inhalants, and a wide range of prescription medications. It will be important to establish a survey of drug use that addresses the sex/drug-linked behavior and use pattern of the population served by your specific treatment program.

SEX/DRUG-LINKED BEHAVIOR

This sex/drug-linked relapse risk factor combined information on Stepping Stone resident sexual activity as well as sexual activity while under the influence of drugs and/or alcohol. The higher the frequency of sexual activity, as well as the higher the frequency of sexual activity paired with substance use, the higher the score for this risk factor in the overall client assessment survey.

Sexual behavior was divided into type of sexual partnered activity in the 3 months prior to entering treatment. Clients described their sexual activity by choosing among four types of sexual partnered activity.

- *Primary partners* were defined as a significant other, spouse, domestic partner, or person with whom the client had an exclusive sexual relationship.
- *Regular partners* are men or women with whom the client reported having sex with on a regular basis.
- *Casual partners* are nonstrangers with whom the client has had one or more sexual encounters.
- *Anonymous partners* are strangers the client did not know prior to the sexual encounter. These are situations in which the sexual act is center to the sexual activity and the partner is a momentary choice not based on an interpersonal connection or even introduction.

In discussing sexual activity, the Stepping Stone client assessment survey modeled critical language skills by discussing a wide range of partnered sexual situations without using judgmental terms and shaming language. No distinction was made regarding level of emotional attachment, motivations, circumstances, or defining characteristics of the partner. No questions were asked about having affairs, paying for sex, trading sex for drugs, or other situations that might insinuate judgment. Asking a client to reveal sexual activity with a nonexclusive partner may already make the client feel significant negative evaluation (by himself or herself as well as by others). It was vital to have the assessment questions model the sex neutral dialogue that would be part of the sexual health in recovery group, counselor interactions, and other sexual discussion in treatment.

All four categories asked the gender of the partner(s) whom the client engaged with in the sexual activity. This can be another emotion-filled moment for clients. Will they acknowledge having other as well as same-sex activity? For this reason, it was essential to inform clients who would be scoring and evaluating their assessments. (I will address these procedural confidentiality concerns in Chapter 6.)

The boundaries of how and by whom your sex/drug-linked assessment is scored will be an important variable in how open clients may be around specific shame prone sex questions. Treatment programs that are conducting further research on sex/drug-linked outcome evaluations or validity of the assessment measures or constructs of this intervention will need to maintain standards established by the American Psychological Association for collecting and evaluating client assessment data (Stepping Stone rigorously adhered to these standards).

Masturbation is a significant sex/drug-linked behavior that Stepping Stone did not measure. I think this is a significant omission. In my experience with clients, solo sex activity is so frequently brought up by men and women alike that I now believe a complete sexual activity relapse risk picture can only be accomplished by including solo as well as partnered sexual activity patterns. Masturbation can be a significant focus of recovery and relapse prevention interventions, either as a relapse-linked behavior (masturbating and remembering a previous drug or sex using situation for arousal) or by practicing sexual pleasure delinked from desire, fantasy, arousal, and orgasm. Clients benefit from their counselors' ability to regulate and suspend judgmental language regarding solo sexual activity in recovery.

Sexual intercourse (including vaginal, anal, and/or oral sex), history of sexually transmitted infections (STIs) or current STIs, pregnancy, use of contraception, HIV status, and HIV partner disclosure and protection measures are also part of the assessment. The Sexual Health in Recovery Assessment prioritized frequency of these sexual health concerns as the primary relapse risk focus. Sexual activity that risks serious health consequences when engaged in at a higher frequency is often a source of shame, fear, secrecy, and increased risk for relapse.

COGNITIVE ERRORS IN COPING AND INTERPERSONAL STYLE

As we contemplated sex/drug-linked addiction patterns, we wondered if high sex/drug-linked clients would also demonstrate very low self-esteem, poor interpersonal relationship skills, and emotional reactivity, making closeness and intimacy of sexual relations profoundly difficult to navigate. Might they mitigate these interpersonal limitations through using drugs or alcohol with sex?

You will note the absence of these areas of evaluation on the Sexual Health in Recovery Assessment measure (outlined in Chapter 6). That is because in the 250 client assessment surveys, we found no significant correlation between sex/drug-linked addiction patterns and elevated levels of interpersonal symptoms or cognitive processing errors. They were definitely present among the clients, just not significantly correlated within the Stepping Stone high sex/drug-linked population. This is may be an area for further study.

Today, many drug and alcohol treatment programs integrate cognitive–behavioral therapy (CBT) approaches to improve client thinking and decisions in highly emotional situations. CBT has been demonstrated to be an essential component of overall recovery, particularly among crystal methamphetamine abusers. The curriculum and counseling approaches that I recommend for sex/drug-linked relapse prevention adopt principles of Dialectical Behavioral Therapy (DBT), a cognitive–behavioral psychotherapy for men and women with substantial and inflexible personality patterns leading to emotional, relational, and behavioral problems. Both counselor's and client's skills in suspending judgment and modeling judgmental regulation when discussing sexual health and sexual behavior require a mindful presence and self-observational ability that is defined and described quite artfully within the DBT treatment counseling manuals.

Even though this is not a measured subscale within the Sexual Health in Recovery Assessment, skills for better regulating rigid and irrational personality patterns is a significant element of effective drug and alcohol counseling. For some clients, the process of completing the sex/drug-linked assessment will challenge their rigid personality patterns and internalized judgmental thinking related to matters of sex. The assessment may trigger argumentative responses that denigrate and dismiss sexual attitudes and values that are not clearly stated as right or wrong, good or bad, and moral, immoral, or sinful. For some individuals, a clear and unyielding clarity of "correct" sexual behavior is an essential way of organizing their sexual values and attitudes. Sexual health in recovery is not an intervention to treat, change, or modify values or beliefs. The focus is primarily on identifying sex/drug-linked patterns of behavior, thinking, and/or relating that increase risk for relapse. When clients express these intense reactions (and this will happen from time to time after some women or men complete the Sexual Health in Recovery Assessment), the focus needs to remain on whether the clients exhibit high sex/drug-linked relapse risk patterns and how will this be integrated within their overall recovery plan.

I do not recommend excusing clients with anticipated high-reactivity, intense, or incredulous responses from completing the Sexual Health in Recovery Assessment, nor do I agree with those who may say that a sex/drug-linked assessment is too difficult, too invasive, and too much an invasion of privacy to measure among people in recovery. As I have discussed in earlier chapters, the act of addressing sexuality within drug treatment as well as facilitating sexual health discussions in groups or individual counseling sessions will remain highly controversial and that historic professional and personal attitudes toward sex and recovery may remain extremely negative among some clients, counselors, and administrators. As I have stated earlier, the wide spectrum of diverse responses will always be a part of sexual health discussions. Policies that omit clients with extremely negative attitudes, reactions, or levels of discomfort in response to assessing sex/drug-linked relapse risk is a significant matter of policy and treatment. Informing clients prior to entering treatment that assess for sex/drug-linked behavior is a routine part of the initial evaluation, obtaining written consent and acknowledging this notification upon admission is important. Clients should have sufficient information about sexual health in recovery treatment interventions at your program or counseling service to make an informed decision about whether or not to become a client or enter your facility.

Too often, counselors or treatment programs have little time to determine how to handle clients' high-reactivity behavior. Sex will always have the potential to raise charged emotions, thoughts, or behaviors. Both the counseling approaches in this book and the structured sexual health in recovery tools provide some specific direction on how to regulate and facilitate these client interactions.

SEXUAL SECRETS AND SHAME

The relationship between sex/drug-linked behavior, relapse risk, and shame was the most significant outcome of the Stepping Stone client assessment survey. The assessment among clients upon entering treatment demonstrated a strong correlation between high sex/drug-linked relapse risk and unusually high levels of shame. In fact, at Stepping Stone, men and women with high sex/drug linkage had doubled the levels of shame compared to individuals with low sex/drug linkage when assessed upon entering treatment. Given that many addicts already experience high amounts of shame (developed through their experiences with addiction), the group with high sex/drug linkage were considered a very high-shame group.

When we embarked on this process, we had no idea that elevated levels of shame would be the most significant correlation among men and women at Stepping Stone whose chemical dependency was intertwined with their sexuality.

This has important implications for recovery and sobriety, as intense levels of shame can complicate early recovery. These sex–shame complications are central to sexual health–based recovery. Recovery is about engaging in healthier behaviors. When attempts to change destructive addictive behavior is combined with sexual secrets and toxic sex-shame, contemplating the changes that recovery entails will likely trigger a multitude of negative emotions. Sexual health in recovery provides specific emotion regulation skills, counseling interactions, and prevention interventions to decrease sexual secret keeping and reduce sex-shame states. If this sex/drug-linked shame outcome is replicated in future evaluations and studies, addiction treatment programs and drug counselors will have compelling evidence that reducing sex/drug-linked shame is an important additional tool in which to improve treatment effectiveness and increase client retention.

As you review the sexual secret and shame items on the assessment (in Chapter 6), notice how the wording of the items invite a suspension of judgment. The items are worded to focus on internal conflict surrounding maintaining sexual secrets while simultaneously embarking on drug and alcohol recovery. The sexual secret questions defocus on the specific sexual behavior, act, or desire that is kept secret, rather, they focus on the role of the secret in risking relapse.

The shame assessment questions are adaptations from the Personal Feelings Questionnaire Revised (PFQ-2) form (Harder & Zalma, 1990). The Revised Personal Feelings Questionnaire is a relatively straightforward means for men and women to report emotions and feelings that are synonymous with shame. The assessment does not specifically distinguish between shame and guilt feelings or proneness to feeling guilt related to sexual behavior.

Shame is a fairly recognizable behavior and feeling. The shame items on the Sexual Health in Recovery Assessment rely upon recognizing shame-related behaviors and feelings without supplying a label or conclusion about the meaning of these states. Words like *embarrassment, feeling ridiculous, stupid, childish,* and *laughable* speak to the heart of shame. Shame is a moral emotion (Tangeny, Youman, & Boyle, 2009). Sexual shame is less likely to be experienced as a failure of behavior and more likely experienced as a failure of the self. Sexual shame is a public, witnessed, or seen aspect of our sexuality. Sexual guilt can be private. When sex/drug-linked shame is not given a voice, a space in which to be processed, the corrosive nature of shame and sex will increase. Sex/drug-linked shame is an internal voice of sexual judgment and punitive admonishment accompanying the client every day of treatment like an invisible tormentor. Drug and alcohol treatment professionals must create a space for men and women to air out their sex/drug-linked judgments and hold them up to evaluation outside of our own mind and perspective.

Addressing shame states in the assessment ("I worry that some aspect of my sexual behavior may cause me to have problems with my treatment program," "When sober . . . I worry my sexual behavior may not be satisfying.") disrupts shame-motivated attempts to hide sexual concerns. Escaping sexual disapproval, especially very public sexual disapproval, may feel like a reprieve. It is a false relief. As we have found among the high sex/drug-linked individuals at Stepping Stone, the internal shame, imagined judgments, feared disapproval, and moral rejection of one's sexual life are in themselves tormenting mental states that interfere with readiness to engage in treatment and early recovery.

Assessing shame poses challenges. Most people, including those in recovery, have difficulty articulating the difference between shame and guilt. A common short hand phrase is "I feel guilt for what I did" and "I feel shame for who I am." Shame related to sex can be very difficult to untangle when sex is both a behavior ("what I did") and an expression of self ("who I am"). When an addict with a high level of sex-linked shame enters recovery, his or her ability to manage the work of treatment may hinge on early sex/drug-linked interventions to decrease thoughts and beliefs that make him or her feel shame over his or her sexual self.

Identifying and informing men and women that they have a high level of sex/drug-linked addiction patterns and teaching them how to mitigate this risk factor is in itself a shame-reduction intervention. It conveys to everyone that sex/drug-linked addiction is not a hopeless situation. Addressing sex/drug-linked addiction patterns in all clients (those with low linkage through those with high linkage) will go a tremendous way toward reducing shame.

Shame is a self-focused emotion. Shame states represent a collapse onto oneself that disconnect one's ability to attend to or experience others. Shame is selfish. However, sex/drug-linked shame is not a constant state. It is not a low glow of disgust that one lives with at all times.

Addressing sex/drug-linked shame improves treatment because it initially occurs at such a disabling level that it threatens the client's ability to benefit from treatment. Think of addicts with high sex/drug linkage in recovery as some of the most shame-prone men and women in treatment. If our pilot study assessment survey outcomes at Stepping Stone are upheld in future studies, then the shame proneness of individuals with sex/drug linkage may need to be proactively assessed to provide these men and women a fair shot at recovery and treatment completion.

An important aspect of the shame measures in the Sexual Health in Recovery Assessment is to focus only on high levels of shame. The shame measure is pertinent to overall sex/drug-linked relapse risk based only on an elevated score. It has no bearing or equally opposing significance if the score is low. A low shame score does not and should not in any way be construed as a "shameless" person. This kind of either–or perspective is not applicable when it comes to measuring shame related to drugs and sex. The level of shame for sex/drug-linked men and women in treatment is relevant only in the context of the shame levels of low sex/drug-linked men and women also in treatment. It is the sex/drug-linked shame that is believed to create so many negative feelings of worthlessness, powerlessness, and humiliation compared to the rest of the shame all addicts in recovery must face that is measured in this assessment.

SEXUAL HEALTH ATTITUDES AND BELIEFS

As mentioned in previous chapters, when it comes to sexual health concerns, typical drug and alcohol treatment programs usually focus on sexually transmitted diseases (STD), unintended pregnancy, and HIV infection risks. These are all vital issues. Sexual health consequences of drug abuse and addiction include higher frequency of HIV infection, unintended pregnancies, pregnancy termination, preterm labor or early delivery, and risk of sexual assault as well as sexual exploitation.

Substance abusers vary in the scope and seriousness of sexual health problems they face. Research consistently demonstrates high numbers of women in drug and alcohol treatment with histories of sexual abuse (Covington, Burke, Keaton, & Norcott, 2008). Women are at increased risk for HIV infection not because of their own risky behavior, but for the potentially risky behaviors of their partners (Wyatt, 2007). Men in recovery tend to avoid knowing their current sexual health status, especially HIV infection. HIV infection, even among addicted men, is assumed to come about because of sexual activity with other men. The shame and fear associated with disclosing male same-sex activity is so great many men avoid this conflict by remaining uncertain of their HIV status.

When we designed the Stepping Stone sexual health in recovery program, we knew about these grim statistics. We know from sexual health and public health research that barriers to honest and informed conversations about sex are some of the most persistent obstacles in changing negative sexual health outcomes. The Sexual Health in Recovery Assessment includes various items measuring current sexual health behaviors related to HIV infection, STIs and pregnancy. However, we go beyond this basic health behavior.

Our hypothesis was that sexual health attitudes are an additional significant barrier to changing sexual behaviors that place an addict in harm's way for a sex/drug-linked relapse. Measuring these attitudes would be essential in creating a measure that reflects the overall risk for sex/drug-linked relapse. Sexual health in recovery links deficits in sexual health attitudes with sex/drug-linked patterns. (This book addresses drug and alcohol counselor attitudes and behaviors linked with poor treatment outcomes resulting from unaddressed sexual concerns among men and women in recovery. My other book, *Sexual Health in Drug and Alcohol Treatment: Group Facilitator's Manual* addresses client sexual attitudes and behaviors and their individual link with risk for relapse.)

Clients who score highly in sex-positive or even sex-neutral attitudes and beliefs have a decreased risk for relapse. Several items in the assessment ask about common sexual health habits, activities, or health care practices that are highly associated with positive sexual attitudes. These items include the following:

1. "I talk about my sexuality with my doctor as it relates to health care."
2. "I talk about my sexuality with my friends."
3. "My race/ethnicity has been a positive influence on my sexuality."
4. "I am able to keep my healthy sexual boundaries."

Items about sexual practices are fairly straightforward:

1. "I delay sex if a condom is not available."
2. "I enjoy masturbating."
3. "I can say no to a sexual partner when asked to do a sexual behavior I do not like."

Another focus of the sexual attitude subsection of the Sexual Health in Recovery Assessment is the discrepancy between a person's sexual health values, ideals, and behavioral expectations and his or her current behavior, especially discrepancies that arise when using drugs and alcohol. Sexual health is reflected in the degree of consistency and congruency between our sexual beliefs and our actual behavior. This is also central to recovery. Stephanie Covington wrote: "To me recovery mean wholeness. It means having one's inner self (thoughts, feelings, values, and beliefs) *connected and congruent* with one's outer self (behavior and relationships). Developing sexual health in recovery is essential to becoming an integrated, whole person" (Braun-Harvey, 2009, p. x).

Sexual health in recovery strives to increase congruency in each individual's personal sexual values and their behavior. It should be noted that this model of sexual health focuses on identifying and eliminating discrepancies; it is not a model of so-called healthy sexuality. Ideas about healthy sexuality tend to arise from the values, ethics, and behaviors that are generally agreed on by large institutions like religions, public health experts, government policies, or educators. Individuals are expected to conform to these ideas.

Sexual health is an individual responsibility. It lies within each person to determine his or her own vision for sexual health. This vision may or may not conform or reflect with those agreed on within the family, community, religion, or culture. Individual sexual health focuses on consistency between the evolving and changing sexual attitudes across an individual's life span. For recovering women and men, sexual health now has an added dimension of developing congruency between sexual values and attitudes that support recovery and decrease the risk for relapse. It is an added dimension of sexual health.

Everyone has a responsibility to develop and understand his or her vision for sexual health. This is not the sole realm of men and women in recovery. However, recovery may be the first opportunity for substance abusers to contemplate sexual health. Men and women with high sex/drug linkage have more on the line when it comes to sexual health. It is not just an important dimension to healthy living. It may be the essential element to entering and maintaining recovery.

Inconsistent or (to use a term from motivational interviewing) *self-discrepant* sexual behavior increases negative emotions and negative attitudes about sex and sexuality. This discrepancy is identified through assessment items that focus on the conflict between a person in recovery experiencing sexual satisfaction, having the availability of sexual partners, experiencing sexual intimacy, or taking responsible sexual action and a person remaining abstinent from using drugs or alcohol. In other words, the assessment is interested in identifying each individual's degree of unresolved conflict between the pursuit of recovery and sexual safety and pleasure. Notice as you read the items on sexual health discrepancy how they are worded to avoid judgment:

1. "I think about sexual activity that may put me at risk for relapse."
2. "I worry that sex while sober is not as satisfying as it is when I am high or drinking."
3. "The sex I have had while sober has been a disappointment."

They simply attempt to describe the conflict or the association between using and sexual behavior that is discrepant with recovery and sexual health. The assessment does not ask questions associated with common sexual values found in religion, culture, or society.

Conforming one's sexuality to systems of authority does not necessarily reduce relapse risk for sex/drug-linked addiction. It is believed the negative emotions from discrepant sexual behaviors and attitudes stem first and foremost from personal disappointment, fear, worry, and shame. Regulating negative emotions by reducing sex/drug-linked relapse provides a sense of hope in recovery. As the Alcoholics Anonymous (AA) slogan adopted from Shakespeare says, "To thine own self be true."

RISKY SEXUAL BEHAVIORS

Here we enter an area where many drug treatment programs have already made significant progress. It is rare, perhaps medically irresponsible, to not include HIV prevention, education, and intervention services within drug and alcohol treatment. In their publication of *Principles of Drug Addiction Treatment: A Research Based Guide*, the National Institute on Drug Abuse (NIDA; 2009) state emphatically that:

> Drug-abusing individuals, including injecting and non-injecting drug users, are at increased risk of HIV, HCV, and other infectious diseases. These diseases are transmitted by sharing contaminated drug injection equipment and by engaging in risky sexual behavior sometimes associated with drug use. Effective drug abuse treatment is HIV/HCV prevention because it reduces associated risk behaviors as well as drug abuse. Counseling that targets a range of HIV/HCV risk behaviors provides an added level of disease prevention. Drug

injectors who do not enter treatment are up to six times more likely to become infected with HIV than injectors who enter and remain in treatment because the latter reduce activities that can spread disease, such as sharing injection equipment and engaging in unprotected sexual activity. Participation in treatment also presents opportunities for screening, counseling, and referral to additional services, including early HIV treatment and access to HAART. In fact, HIV counseling and testing are key aspects of superior drug abuse treatment programs and should be offered to all individuals entering treatment. Greater availability of inexpensive and unobtrusive rapid HIV tests should increase access to these important aspects of HIV prevention and treatment. (section 22)

Men and women in recovery reduce their sexual-risk behaviors for HIV infection, hepatitis C infection, and STIs. When drug and alcohol treatment proactively addresses HIV prevention, testing and early intervention become part of their overall treatment program they are acting as public health allies. The standard of care in state-of-the-art drug and alcohol treatment services is to integrate HIV prevention and treatment services to ensure access to harm-reduction skills for reducing risk for HIV infection and for HIV-infected recovering men and women to have access to HIV medical treatment. Recovery decreases the risk of obtaining an STI as well as transmitting a viral or bacterial STD.

A significant sexual health relapse prevention goal is not only to reduce risk related to negative sexual health outcomes (STIs, HIV, hepatitis C virus [HCV], unwanted pregnancy) but also to reduce the risk of relapse stemming from the physical and emotional consequences of a negative sexual health outcome during or following treatment or early recovery. Sex/drug-linked relapse risk increases when the strains, secrets, shame, embarrassment, fears, denial, and self-discrepancy of acquiring an STI or experiencing an unplanned pregnancy are intertwined within the recovery process. A fundamental foundation for sexual health in recovery is to know STI, HIV, and/or hepatitis C infection status or if a woman is in the early stages of unplanned or unwanted pregnancy. It is difficult to imagine the ability to remain abstinent from drugs and alcohol or to maintain a program of recovery without maintaining sufficient sexual behavior boundaries that prevent or reduce risk for these negative sexual health outcomes.

Sexual functioning is also addressed in this portion of the assessment. We know more about the role of sexual functioning and negative effects of drug or alcohol intoxication. Men and women who chronically abuse or become addicted to drugs and alcohol experience significant deterioration in all stages of human sexual response. A recent study found a significant percentage of adolescents experiencing significant sexual dysfunction (premature ejaculation, erectile dysfunction, or low sexual desire) prior to any use of drugs stated that their first drug using experience was motivated by their sexual dysfunction. The authors recommend a possible new strategy in the primary prevention of substance abuse among adolescents. They believe their data points to a new strategy in which sexual education and early treatment of sexual disorders be considered as a prevention intervention prior to first drug use (La Pera et al., 2008). Perhaps, sex/drug-linked sexual dysfunction works in a dual direction. For some, the sexual dysfunction is an outcome of a serious drug or alcohol addiction. For others, the drug dependency or alcoholism grew out of a misguided attempt to solve a significant and untreated sexual dysfunction.

In 2002, Richard Rawson, PhD, international addiction researcher and associate director of the University of California, Los Angeles, Integrated Substance Abuse Programs, investigated the differences between men's and women's sexual thoughts, feelings, and behaviors related to their primary drug of choice (alcohol, opiates, cocaine, methamphetamine). The study participants reported correlations between specific psychoactive drugs and the effect on sexual behavior. Gender was also a significant variable among their subjects. Some drugs were more deleterious for men's sexual functioning and other drugs for women's. Rawson, Washton, Domier, and Reiber (2002) recommend the development of a valid measure that assesses not only the specific relationship between drug of choice and sexual behavior but also the strength of these relationships. Their study suggested the development of such a valid measure be implemented within drug and alcohol treatment programs and services would benefit the promotion of abstinence from drugs and alcohol as well as prevent relapse (Rawson et al.).

CONCLUSION

It is important to note that the Sexual Health in Recovery Assessment does not as of yet meet criteria as a valid measure, it is too new, and has only been implemented in one treatment setting. However, it represents an attempt to integrate acquired knowledge from the pilot program client assessment survey. The Sexual Health in Recovery Assessment is a clinical tool for drug and alcohol counselors to identify varying levels of sex/drug-linked relapse risk among men and women in treatment and to inform clients of this sex/drug-linked recovery risk. Clinicians can use the score to integrate level of sex/drug-linked relapse within initial and ongoing treatment planning.

The assessment measure also provides a significant sex-positive relational experience for clients. At Stepping Stone, the experience of engaging in dialogue with a sexual health ally was a unique and meaningful experience. Most clients reported positive feelings and affirming feedback for the counselor. Including the Sexual Health in Recovery Assessment within the general battery of intake, assessment, and evaluation instruments also establishes a useful overall acuity of drug and alcohol use patterns among clients in treatment. The assessment process will create a treatment milieu with an ever-increasing confidence and ability to engage in meaningful sexual health conversations. Clients will exhibit more open, authentic, and informative recovery integrating sexuality irrespective of level of sex/drug-linked relapse.

Although the purpose of the current Sexual Health in Recovery Assessment is limited to clinical acuity and relapse prevention planning, it is hoped that this measure may lead to research funding to develop a valid and reliable measure for identifying and researching men and women whose drug and alcohol dependency is interwoven with sexual thoughts, feelings, and behavior. Perhaps this preliminary assessment measure will change the way sex/drug-linked addiction is treated. We may one day see current approaches to sex, drugs, alcohol, and recovery as negligent, misinformed, and ill advised.

6

The Sexual Health in Recovery Assessment

The Sexual Health in Recovery Assessment is a series of 130 statements (of which 120 are included in the overall score) that assess a client's sexual behavior, drug or alcohol history, sexual behavior combined with drug or alcohol use, emotional states, and sexual safety and risk practices. The 130 items are divided into three separate assessments.

The Drug and Alcohol Use assessment (45 items; 35 are included in determining overall subscore) asks clients to describe the frequency of drug and alcohol use, links between drugs or alcohol and sexual activity, and readiness to change behaviors (see Figure 6.1).

The Sexual Health assessment (45 items) asks clients to rate their level of agreement with statements related to sexual boundaries, spirituality/religion, ability to talk about sex, out-of-control sexual behavior, body image, and sexual functioning (see Figure 6.2).

The Sex/Drug-Linked Recovery section (40 items) is divided by gender; there is one version for women and another for men. The items in this section address specific sex/drug-linked relapse risk factors that were identified within the pilot project as promisingly significant treatment interventions to reduce risk of sex/drug-linked relapse. These factors include levels of shame related to sexual behavior and addiction, the expectation of positive outcomes from treatment, sexual health practices, readiness to change, and ability to manage sexual attractions and relationships in recovery (see Figures 6.3 and 6.4).

The 120 scored items in the complete Sexual Health in Recovery Assessment are divided into 16 subscores. Each of the subscores directs the counselor to consider a specific treatment intervention for sexual health in recovery. Each subscore is linked with core concepts, curriculum lessons, recovery tool worksheets, and change outcomes within the *Sexual Health in Drug and Alcohol Treatment: Group Facilitator's Manual* (Braun-Harvey, 2009).

FIGURE 6.1 Drug and Alcohol Use Assessment

INSTRUCTIONS: Below is a list of situations, attitudes, behaviors, and concerns that people with drug and alcohol problems sometimes experience. Some items discuss drug and alcohol use combined with sex. Sex is defined as any combination of intercourse (vaginal and/or anal), oral (vaginal, penile, anal), and mutual, partnered, or solo masturbation.

Please read each item carefully and then circle the number at the right that best describes how often you have felt, thought, or behaved in this way in the past 3 months. Mark only one number for each item. Do not skip any items.
1 = Never 2 = Rarely 3 = Some of the time
4 = Frequently 5 = Almost Constantly

1. Drank any alcoholic beverages	1.	1	2	3	4	5
2. Used marijuana	2.	1	2	3	4	5
3. Used GHB	3.	1	2	3	4	5
4. Used crystal methamphetamine	4.	1	2	3	4	5
5. Used ketamine (Special "K")	5.	1	2	3	4	5
6. Used ecstasy	6.	1	2	3	4	5
7. Used heroin	7.	1	2	3	4	5
8. Used cocaine or crack cocaine	8.	1	2	3	4	5
9. Hallucinogens (LSD or mushrooms)	9.	1	2	3	4	5
10. Sexual functioning enhancement drugs	10.	1	2	3	4	5
11. Sleeping pills (barbiturates)	11.	1	2	3	4	5
12. Drank any alcoholic beverages before, during, or right after sex	12.	1	2	3	4	5
13. Used marijuana before, during, or right after sex	13.	1	2	3	4	5
14. Used GHB before, during, or right after sex	14.	1	2	3	4	5
15. Used crystal methamphetamine before, during, or right after sex	15.	1	2	3	4	5
16. Used "K" ("Special "K") before, during, or right after sex	16.	1	2	3	4	5
17. Used heroin before, during, or right after sex	17.	1	2	3	4	5
18. Used cocaine or crack cocaine before, during, or right after sex	18.	1	2	3	4	5
19. Used drugs that would make my body more attractive	19.	1	2	3	4	5

(continued)

FIGURE 6.1 Drug and Alcohol Use Assessment *Continued*

20. Ingested hallucinogens before, during, or right after sex	20.	1	2	3	4	5
21. Sexual functioning enhancement drugs before or during sex	21.	1	2	3	4	5
22. Sleeping pills (barbiturates) before, during, or right after sex	22.	1	2	3	4	5
23. Used prescription drugs for other than medical reasons	23.	1	2	3	4	5
24. Combined one or more drug/alcohol at a time	24.	1	2	3	4	5
25. Unable to stop drinking or using drugs when I wanted to	25.	1	2	3	4	5
26. Experienced blackouts or flashbacks resulting from drinking or using drugs	26.	1	2	3	4	5
27. Neglected my spouse and family because of drinking and using drugs	27.	1	2	3	4	5
28. Experienced problems at work because of drinking and using drugs	28.	1	2	3	4	5
29. Experienced problems with sexual interest, desire, or functioning because of drinking and using drugs	29.	1	2	3	4	5
30. Wondered if I have sexual problems caused by drinking or using drugs	30.	1	2	3	4	5
31. Thought I am actually going to do something about drinking and using drugs	31.	1	2	3	4	5
32. Believed that I am actively working on quitting drinking and using drugs right now	32.	1	2	3	4	5
33. Felt more free to be sexual when high on drugs and alcohol	33.	1	2	3	4	5
34. More likely to take risks during sex when high on drugs and alcohol	34.	1	2	3	4	5
35. Less likely to use a condom for sex when high on drugs and alcohol	35.	1	2	3	4	5
36. Less likely to use contraception to prevent pregnancy when I am high on drugs and alcohol	36.	1	2	3	4	5

(continued)

FIGURE 6.1 Drug and Alcohol Use Assessment *Continued*

37. People would think less of me if they knew what I did sexually after I drink or use drugs	37.	1	2	3	4	5
38. Concerned I might fail at abstaining from drugs and alcohol use	38.	1	2	3	4	5
39. Feeling uncomfortable trying to abstain from drugs and alcohol use	39.	1	2	3	4	5
40. Thinking recovery from drug addiction and alcoholism takes a lot of effort and energy	40.	1	2	3	4	5
41. I Tell myself that if I try hard enough, I can recover from my addiction	41.	1	2	3	4	5
42. Thinking I will be sexually healthier if I stop drinking or using drugs	42.	1	2	3	4	5
43. Thinking I will feel better about myself if I stop drinking or using drugs	43.	1	2	3	4	5
44. Thinking I will worry less if I stop drinking or using drugs	44.	1	2	3	4	5
45. Thinking some people will be better off if I stop drinking or using drugs	45.	1	2	3	4	5

Identification: _____ Date: _____

FIGURE 6.2 Sexual Health Assessment

INSTRUCTIONS: Below is a list of situations, attitudes, behaviors, and concerns that people with drug and alcohol problems sometimes experience. Some items discuss drug and alcohol use combined with sex. Sex is defined as any combination of intercourse (vaginal and/or anal), oral (vaginal, penile, anal), and mutual, partnered, or solo masturbation.

Please read each item carefully and then circle the number at the right that best describes how much you agree or disagree with each statement during the past 3 months. Mark only one number for each item. Do not skip any items.
1 = **Strongly Disagree** 2 = **Disagree** 3 = **Neither Agree or Disagree**
4 = **Agree** 5 = **Strongly Agree**

1. I find sex pleasurable.	1.	1	2	3	4	5
2. I avoid talking about sex.	2.	1	2	3	4	5
3. I can say no to a sexual partner when asked to do a sexual behavior I do not like.	3.	1	2	3	4	5
4. I have no interest in having sex.	4.	1	2	3	4	5
5. I can interrupt sex to use a condom.	5.	1	2	3	4	5
6. I think about sex more than I would like to.	6.	1	2	3	4	5
7. I am very certain that I know my HIV status.	7.	1	2	3	4	5
8. I attend church activities at least twice a week.	8.	1	2	3	4	5
9. I have concerns about my sexual functioning.	9.	1	2	3	4	5
10. Masturbation is a healthy way to be sexual.	10.	1	2	3	4	5
11. I talk about my sexuality with my friends.	11.	1	2	3	4	5
12. I like the look of my genitals.	12.	1	2	3	4	5
13. My sexual thoughts and behaviors are causing problems in my life.	13.	1	2	3	4	5
14. I am able to keep my healthy sexual boundaries.	14.	1	2	3	4	5
15. My sexual behaviors and sexual values are in conflict with each other.	15.	1	2	3	4	5
16. I talk about my sexuality with my doctor as it relates to health care.	16.	1	2	3	4	5
17. I easily have an orgasm receiving oral sex.	17.	1	2	3	4	5
18. It has been difficult for me to find sex partners who desire sex as much as I do.	18.	1	2	3	4	5
19. I have been avoiding an HIV test.	19.	1	2	3	4	5
20. Sex helps me express my love to my sexual partner(s).	20.	1	2	3	4	5
21. I feel condemned by God because of my sexual feelings and behaviors.	21.	1	2	3	4	5
22. I can use a condom for sexual intercourse (vaginal and/or anal) while under the influence of drugs or alcohol.	22.	1	2	3	4	5

(continued)

FIGURE 6.2 Sexual Health Assessment *Continued*

23. I think pornographic material is disgusting.	23.	1	2	3	4	5
24. My race/ethnicity has been a positive influence on my sexuality.	24.	1	2	3	4	5
25. Most of the time, I orgasm/"come" too quickly when I am with a partner.	25.	1	2	3	4	5
26. I find many sexual matters too upsetting to talk about.	26.	1	2	3	4	5
27. Recently, I have not been interested in sex.	27.	1	2	3	4	5
28. I am generally satisfied with my sexual behavior.	28.	1	2	3	4	5
29. I enjoy hearing about my sexual partner's sexual fantasies.	29.	1	2	3	4	5
30. It bothers me to talk about sex.	30.	1	2	3	4	5
31. I think I am overweight.	31.	1	2	3	4	5
32. Overall, I wish I had more of a desire to have sex.	32.	1	2	3	4	5
33. I feel that my sexual thoughts and feelings are stronger than I am.	33.	1	2	3	4	5
34. I have strong religious beliefs.	34.	1	2	3	4	5
35. I feel pressured by my sexual partner(s) to have sex (if no current partner, refer to your most recent partner).	35.	1	2	3	4	5
36. In general, I like how my body looks.	36.	1	2	3	4	5
37. I was sexually abused when growing up.	37.	1	2	3	4	5
38. I enjoy masturbating.	38.	1	2	3	4	5
39. I think I need to see a medical doctor for physical problems I am having with my penis/testicles (men) // vagina/pelvis (women).	39.	1	2	3	4	5
40. I have an interest in a specific sexual "turn-on" that concerns me.	40.	1	2	3	4	5
41. I have engaged in sexual behavior for money, alcohol, illegal drugs, or shelter.	41.	1	2	3	4	5
42. It is difficult for me to share my sexual fantasies with a sexual partner.	42.	1	2	3	4	5
43. Sex is dirty.	43.	1	2	3	4	5
44. Masturbation is a form of self-loving that is natural, normal, and morally acceptable.	44.	1	2	3	4	5
45. I have made promises to change my sexual behavior.	45.	1	2	3	4	5

Identification: _____ Date: _____

FIGURE 6.3 Sexual Health in Recovery Assessment

Sex/Drug-Linked Recovery for Women

INSTRUCTIONS: Below is a list of situations, attitudes, behaviors, and concerns that people with drug and alcohol problems sometimes experience. Some items discuss drug and alcohol use combined with sex. Sex is defined as any combination of intercourse (vaginal and/or anal), oral (vaginal, penile, anal), and mutual, partnered, or solo masturbation.

Please read each item carefully and then circle the number at the right that best describes how often you have felt, thought, or behaved in this way in the past 3 months. Mark only one number for each item. Do not skip any items.

1 = Never 2 = Rarely 3 = Some of the time
4 = Frequently 5 = Almost Constantly

1. I worry that sex while sober is not as satisfying as it is when I am high or drinking.	1.	1	2	3	4	5
2. I am pleased that I am addressing my sexual behavior as part of staying sober.	2.	1	2	3	4	5
3. I feel more comfortable talking about my sexual issues.	3.	1	2	3	4	5
4. I used drugs and alcohol to express love and affection or receive love and affection.	4.	1	2	3	4	5
5. I look for information about relationships in recovery.	5.	1	2	3	4	5
6. I talk to people in recovery who have successfully changed their sexual behavior.	6.	1	2	3	4	5
7. I used sex to get out of negative or overwhelming feeling.	7.	1	2	3	4	5
8. I talk with my partner about birth control/contraception before having sex.	8.	1	2	3	4	5
9. I am too self-conscious to enjoy sex when sober.	9.	1	2	3	4	5
10. I feel regret and remorse.	10.	1	2	3	4	5
11. I seek out immediate sex partners (anonymous sex partners, online sex, pay for sex) when I am high on drugs and alcohol.	11.	1	2	3	4	5
12. I worry I am infected with a sexually transmitted disease (i.e., herpes, gonorrhea).	12.	1	2	3	4	5
13. I used drugs and alcohol to experience a specific sex act or have kinky sex.	13.	1	2	3	4	5
14. I understand the sexual behavior guidelines for my treatment program.	14.	1	2	3	4	5

(continued)

FIGURE 6.3 Sexual Health in Recovery Assessment *Continued*

15. I feel mild guilt and worry about hurting someone or injuring someone.	15. 1	2	3	4	5
16. I become irritated, mean, critical, angry, or shaming toward people when talking about my sexual history or current behavior.	16. 1	2	3	4	5
17. I get upset thinking about giving in to using drugs and alcohol so I can have sex.	17. 1	2	3	4	5
18. I would be insulted if my sex partner put on a condom to avoid getting a sexually transmitted disease.	18. 1	2	3	4	5
19. I feel confident that my sexual behavior will not prevent me from staying sober.	19. 1	2	3	4	5
20. I have feelings of blushing, looking red in the face.	20. 1	2	3	4	5
21. I delay sex if a condom is not available.	21. 1	2	3	4	5
22. I feel freer to be sexual when I am high on drugs and alcohol.	22. 1	2	3	4	5
23. I feel ridiculous or laughable.	23. 1	2	3	4	5
24. I limit my sexual activity to one partner.	24. 1	2	3	4	5
25. I am convinced that my sexual activity is a significant concern for my recovery.	25. 1	2	3	4	5
26. I talk about my relationship history and current relationship concerns with people in my recovery support system.	26. 1	2	3	4	5
27. I talk with people in my recovery support system when I miss having sex high.	27. 1	2	3	4	5
28. I notice my habit of rationalizing and justifying my sexual behavior that is linked with drugs and alcohol.	28. 1	2	3	4	5
29. I think about sexual activity that may put me at risk for relapse.	29. 1	2	3	4	5
30. I have a sexual secret that preoccupies my thoughts that I hide from my recovery support system.	30. 1	2	3	4	5
31. I think about important recovery tools to use in my relationship (or that I would know to use if I was in a relationship).	31. 1	2	3	4	5

(continued)

FIGURE 6.3 Sexual Health in Recovery Assessment *Continued*

32. I feel humiliated, "stupid," and "childish."	32.	1	2	3	4	5
33. I feel more confident that my sexual behavior will not lead to relapse.	33.	1	2	3	4	5
34. I worry that some aspects of my sexual behavior may cause me social humiliation.	34.	1	2	3	4	5
35. Thinking that changing my sexual behavior to stay sober takes a lot of effort.	35.	1	2	3	4	5
36. I am lonely.	36.	1	2	3	4	5
37. When I feel concerned about sex and recovery I go talk to someone about it.	37.	1	2	3	4	5
38. I feel helpless and paralyzed.	38.	1	2	3	4	5
39. The sex I have had while sober has been a disappointment.	39.	1	2	3	4	5
40. I have used drugs or alcohol before or during sex in the last 30 days.	40.	1	2	3	4	5

Identification: _____ Date: _____

FIGURE 6.4 Sexual Health in Recovery Assessment

Sex/Drug-Linked Recovery for Men

INSTRUCTIONS: Below is a list of situations, attitudes, behaviors, and concerns that people with drug and alcohol problems sometimes experience. Some items discuss drug and alcohol use combined with sex. Sex is defined as any combination of intercourse (vaginal and/or anal), oral (vaginal, penile, anal), and mutual, partnered, or solo masturbation.

Please read each item carefully and then circle the number at the right that best describes how often you have felt, thought, or behaved in this way in the past 3 months. Mark only one number for each item. Do not skip any items.

1 = Never 2 = Rarely 3 = Some of the time
4 = Frequently 5 = Almost Constantly

1. I worry that sex while sober is not as satisfying as it is when I am high or drinking.	1. 1	2	3	4	5
2. I am pleased that I am addressing my sexual behavior as part of staying sober.	2. 1	2	3	4	5
3. I feel more comfortable talking about my sexual issues.	3. 1	2	3	4	5
4. I used drugs and alcohol to not "come" so quickly.	4. 1	2	3	4	5
5. I look for information about relationships in recovery.	5. 1	2	3	4	5
6. I talk to people in recovery who have successfully changed their sexual behavior.	6. 1	2	3	4	5
7. I used sex to get out of negative or tense feelings.	7. 1	2	3	4	5
8. I talk with my partner about using a condom before having sex.	8. 1	2	3	4	5
9. I am too self-conscious to enjoy sex when sober.	9. 1	2	3	4	5
10. I feel regret and remorse.	10. 1	2	3	4	5
11. I seek out immediate sex partners (anonymous sex partners, online sex, pay for sex) when I am high on drugs and alcohol.	11. 1	2	3	4	5
12. I worry I am infected with a sexually transmitted disease. (i.e., herpes, gonorrhea)	12. 1	2	3	4	5
13. I used drugs and alcohol to experience a specific sex act or have kinky sex.	13. 1	2	3	4	5

(continued)

FIGURE 6.4 Sexual Health in Recovery Assessment *Continued*

14. I understand the sexual behavior guidelines for my treatment program.	14. 1	2	3	4	5
15. I feel mild guilt and worry about hurting someone or injuring someone	15. 1	2	3	4	5
16. I become irritated, mean, critical, angry or rageful toward people when talking about my sexual history or current behavior.	16. 1	2	3	4	5
17. I get upset thinking about giving in to using drugs and alcohol so I can have sex.	17. 1	2	3	4	5
18. I would be insulted if my sex partner asked me to put on a condom to avoid getting a sexually transmitted disease.	18. 1	2	3	4	5
19. I feel confident that my sexual behavior will not prevent me from staying sober.	19. 1	2	3	4	5
20. I feel rage.	20. 1	2	3	4	5
21. I delay sex if a condom is not available.	21. 1	2	3	4	5
22. I feel freer to be sexual when I am high on drugs and alcohol.	22. 1	2	3	4	5
23. I feel ridiculous or laughable.	23. 1	2	3	4	5
24. I limit my sexual activity to one partner	24. 1	2	3	4	5
25. I am convinced that my sexual activity is a significant concern for my recovery.	25. 1	2	3	4	5
26. I talk about my relationship history and current relationship concerns with people in my recovery support system.	26. 1	2	3	4	5
27. When I miss having sex high or drunk I talk with people in recovery.	27. 1	2	3	4	5
28. I notice my habit of rationalizing and justifying my sexual behavior that is linked with drugs and alcohol.	28. 1	2	3	4	5
29. I think about sexual activity that may put me at risk for relapse.	29. 1	2	3	4	5
30. I have a sexual secret that preoccupies my thoughts that I hide from my recovery support system.	30. 1	2	3	4	5

(continued)

FIGURE 6.4 Sexual Health in Recovery Assessment *Continued*

31. I think about important recovery tools to use in my relationship (or that I would know to use if I was in a relationship).	31.	1	2	3	4	5
32. I feel humiliated, "stupid," and "childish."	32.	1	2	3	4	5
33. I feel more confident that my sexual behavior will not lead to relapse.	33.	1	2	3	4	5
34. I worry that some aspects of my sexual behavior may cause me social humiliation.	34.	1	2	3	4	5
35. Thinking about changing my sexual behavior to stay sober takes a lot of effort.	35.	1	2	3	4	5
36. I am lonely.	36.	1	2	3	4	5
37. When I feel concerned about sex and recovery I go talk to someone about it.	37.	1	2	3	4	5
38. I feel helpless and paralyzed.	38.	1	2	3	4	5
39. The sex I have had while sober has been a disappointment.	39.	1	2	3	4	5
40. I have used drugs or alcohol before or during sex in the last 30 days.	40.	1	2	3	4	5

Identification: _____ Date: _____

The remaining chapters in this book will discuss how each assessment subscore measure can be used to guide treatment planning, counseling interventions, and individualized sex/drug-linked relapse prevention.

HOW THE ASSESSMENT MEASURES THE SEX/DRUG LINK

The overall assessment score can be likened to taking someone's temperature. The higher the score, the more significantly drug and alcohol use is linked with sexuality. Higher scores reflect a strong sex/drug-linked pattern of drug and alcohol use. Lower scores reflect a low or inconsistent sex/drug-linked pattern of drug and alcohol use.

Scores may vary depending on the treatment acuity level (hospital-based detox; inpatient, residential treatment; intensive outpatient and various levels of outpatient treatment) and the primary drug of choice among the client population. Clients with high sex/drug linkage may not be seen in acute levels of care because of the wide range of medical, social, economic, and co-occurring psychiatric conditions that are typically treated within these settings. Residential and intensive outpatient programs may experience a higher frequency of high sex/drug-linked clients connected with high relapse rates and multiple treatments found within this acuity level. These are the people who may have failed at lower levels of treatment because sex/drug-linked issues were not resolved at a lower level of care.

The assessment can be administered separately from other intake evaluation measures or combined with complete intake information. It can be given at the beginning of treatment or as part of ongoing assessment and treatment planning. It can be taken at various intervals within an extended treatment over 6 months to several years to measure changes in understanding and reporting of sex/drug-linked addiction patterns as well as identifying sex/drug-linked relapse risk factors pertinent to a specific time in the recovery process.

Each of the three assessment subscales can be given separately or in any combination. Only a combined score of all three administered at the same time will determine overall level of sex/drug-linked addiction and relapse risk. The combined score is the sex/drug-linked relapse risk.

Just because a client completes this assessment (as part of a drug treatment program intake or entrance process) does not mean that the client is ready to incorporate sex/drug-linked relapse risk feedback into his or her current recovery or treatment. Rather, think of the assessment as a message to the client regarding the treatment center or counselor's readiness to attend to client sex/drug-linked addiction. The assessment also reinforces the treatment center's commitment to integrating sex/drug-linked treatment approaches within the overall program.

KEY MEASURES OF THE ASSESSMENT

The Stepping Stone's Client Assessment Survey Outcome Data identified at least one variable as statistically significantly correlated with the high sex/drug-linked group: shame. This was discussed in Chapter 5.

The combined three measures of the Sexual Health in Recovery Assessment identify client-positive outcome expectations of treatment. Preliminary outcome measures from Stepping Stone suggest a higher rate of sex/drug-linked relapse risk among clients who perceive high pessimism and negative expectations about treatment because of sex/drug-linked addiction patterns.

The "Readiness to Change" scores reflect a decrease in sex/drug-linked relapse risk associated with an increase in items that reflect more sex-positive beliefs and values, more self-efficacy, more optimism about completing treatment, more determination to address and utilize sex/drug-linked relapse prevention tools, and lesser levels of self-discrepancy between values and behavior. Higher sex/drug-linked relapse risk is reflected by client's thoughts and perceptions that frequently focus on arguments against successful sobriety and an active sexual life. The stronger a client's opinion that sexual activity and pleasure is in opposition to recovery, or that sexual life is a threat to recovery, or a focus on the negative and harmful consequences of sexual desire and activity in recovery, the less likely the individual will move toward contemplating specific sex/drug-linked recovery activities. A high score in "Sex/Drug-Linked Use Patterns" in tandem with a high score on "Precontemplative Readiness" elevates risk for treatment failure related to sex and drugs.

Sex/drug-linked relapse risk is decreased when the motivational stage of readiness to change items reflects increasing frequency of positive, favorable, optimistic, self-efficacy, and confidence to utilize sex/drug-linked relapse prevention tools in recovery. Prochaska, Norcross, and DiClemente (1994) describe two principles of progress that can be predictive of the degree of self-change. One principle ascribes progression from precontemplation to action as when significant focus is given to the benefits of making a healthy behavior change. The second principle contrasts the same process beginning from not considering a change (precontemplative) to taking actions directly designed for changing. This principle states that a much smaller decrease in the arguments against considering change is necessary for movement toward action stage changes. In other words, a high Sexual Health in Recovery Assessment motivation subscore reflects increasing client perceptions and beliefs in the benefits and optimism for reducing sex/drug-linked relapse. It is not necessary for the same level of an equivalent change in frequency and client perceptions related to the opposing precontemplative defenses that obstruct addressing sex/drug-linked relapse prevention.

ADMINISTERING THE SEXUAL HEALTH IN RECOVERY ASSESSMENT

The Sexual Health in Recovery Assessment is a tool for assessing level of sex/drug-linked relapse risk. Relapse linked to sexual behavior or desires can be of concern at any time in the process of recovery. The assessment is designed so that it can be given to people at any time in their treatment or recovery. Therefore, who administers the assessment will vary over time.

The first time a person completes the Sexual Health in Recovery Assessment measure may be with his or her original drug and alcohol treatment program. Clients may be very unfamiliar with disclosure of their relationship with drugs and alcohol. They may be even less experienced with contemplating and reporting their sexual behavior and attitudes. Treatment programs that include this measure as part of their comprehensive initial assessment should have a team of trained staff to administer this measure. These staff members will need preparation and practice to clearly articulate the purpose of the Sexual Health in Recovery Assessment and how the outcome information will be used in their treatment.

Clearly stating boundaries around privacy will be important. Will all staff at the center have access to the answer sheet for the assessment? Will the raw data sheet be included in the patient record? Will only the scores and subscores be in the patient chart? Each treatment program will need to anticipate these privacy concerns and be clear with clients before giving them the measure. If the outcome measures in the original pilot study at Stepping Stone are supported by further study, then *shame reduction procedures* in the process of administering this measure will be essential for a more accurate and useful determination of sex/drug-linked relapse risk. Good, clear boundaries that are consistently maintained will be central to this shame-reduction approach when administering the assessment.

I suggest that the first time this assessment is given to a client, they be given the option of completing the assessment with a staff member available (or in the room) with the client to answer questions and address reactions. Written instructions are printed on each assessment. Have the client read aloud the directions to ensure clear understanding of the directions. Provide time for clarifying any questions prior to taking the assessment. Observing a client's response to completing this measure can be valuable nuanced information in ascertaining a more comprehensive picture of the client's initial level of shame and defenses in addressing sex/drug-linked patterns. The staff assisting the client in completion of the assessment should document any specific reactions, concerns, or behaviors of the client to prepare the treatment staff.

Upon entry into the program, clients should be informed that sex/drug-linked issues are part of the overall treatment program. Having some brief but specific statement about the program's commitment to reducing relapse and improving treatment by addressing the sex-drug link is an important boundary of informed consent. Informing clients that sex/drug-linked addiction patterns are part of the overall discussion that will occur in the treatment program sets the stage for a more open response to the assessment.

I suggest that each employee, volunteer, and ancillary staff member at the treatment program take the assessment. Have each new employee complete the assessment. It is important to demystify the content. Anxieties around sexual health conversations can be lessoned by a transparent, open, and personal encounter with the exact measure clients will complete. My experience of working in a wide variety of hospital, residential, and outpatient treatment settings is that you never know what staff member clients will look to for support and trust. When each staff member has taken the assessment, then the entire team is able to be a resource for client's reactions, opinions, and feelings in response to completing the questionnaire.

Do you remember your first sex education class (if you had one)? Do you remember wanting to talk more after the class than during? Do you remember how important it was to know what your peers thought or how they reacted to the class? Did you seek out one-on-one interactions or small group discussions after the class? This will become part of the culture of your treatment setting once the Sexual Health in Recovery Assessment is conducted with each patient. As soon as clients complete this assessment, many of them will seek out a trusted confidant—a roommate, a group member, a family member, their spouse or partner, and/or a counselor—at the treatment center, to talk about the experience. Sexual health conversations often trigger thoughts of "is that normal?" The most consistent way people find normality in their sexuality is to find others with whom to compare their experience. As part of the assessment procedure, clients should be given permission and be encouraged to discuss any part of their experience in completing the assessment with as many people as they want. Encourage openness. When it comes to matters of sexual health, we all need clear messages from leaders and authority figures that we welcome discussions of sexuality. Clients will not assume it is acceptable to discuss their experience of completing the assessment unless a clear statement is given and then backed up by welcoming responses from staff when sexual health conversations are observed or initiated by clients.

PRIVACY ISSUES

As mentioned earlier in this chapter, firm boundaries of privacy among staff will be essential to the success of this intervention. If you have not yet done so, take a moment and read the assessment items. Notice how you feel as you read them and imagine how clients may experience answering these questions and not knowing who will review their answers. All you need is for a resident to overhear a few staff talking about someone's answers to the questionnaire; this will be spread among the residents and patients like wildfire, not only within the treatment program but also within the 12-step programs that most patients attend as part of their treatment.

I have found that treatment programs with excellent boundaries about clients' private medical record can fail to stem lurid sex talk about clients among staff, primarily because boundaries about the sexual lives or histories of clients is a less common focus of most drug and alcohol treatment. It will be important to conduct in-service training and review written policies about procedures and confidentiality to ensure clear boundaries of how and where the assessment measure is retained after completion as well as developing a treatment staff that has a reputation for handling these sources of shame with respect and empathy.

Have an envelope that is sealed by the staff in front of the client when she turns in the assessment. This will limit client thinking that the staff can't wait to look at their answers. Again, having procedures that are open and consistent will go far in establishing trust and in reducing fears about future shame and humiliation in treatment for how the client answers the items on the assessment.

Create a confidential identification system in your program so clients use the identification number rather than their name on the form. This will ensure that the person scoring the measure does not know the identity of the person who completed the assessment. The client's sexual health in recovery ratings will be placed on the Sexual Health in Recovery Assessment Raw Data Answer Sheet. There is a place for overall total score and a subtotal score for each of the 16 subscales. The raw data scores are transferred to the Client Sexual Health in Recovery Assessment Outcome Form. This is the form that is to be placed in the client record and used by the treatment staff for treatment planning. The overall score combined with staff's or counselor's evaluation is the client's sex/drug-linked relapse score. It is vital to explain these procedures to the client as part of preparation for taking the assessment. Boundaries are essential to sexual health. Modeling boundaries in the administering of this assessment is all part and partial to building confidence among your clients or residents that your treatment program is determined to provide a useful and respectful sexual health relapse prevention service.

After the client has completed the assessment, let him or her know when the assessment results will be discussed and with whom the results will be discussed. Clarify again that the raw data answer sheets are not part of the client file, only the summary sheet. We found it very helpful to include a few moments for the client to debrief with the assessment proctor. Taking a sexual health–based information questionnaire is a rare experience for most people. Normalizing the uniqueness of this experience is yet another shame reduction opportunity.

SCORING THE SEXUAL HEALTH IN RECOVERY ASSESSMENT

To score the assessment, use the raw data sheet provided in Figure 6.5.

There are 16 subsets to score. Each item on all three measures directly links with one of these subsets. Each subset has a letter as an identifier linking the question to the subset. They are the following:

- Drug and Alcohol Use
    - Sex/Drug-Linked Behavior—BE
    - Sex/Drug-Linked Motivations—M
    - Readiness to Change—C

FIGURE 6.5 Sexual Health in Recovery Assessment Raw Data Answer Sheet

DIRECTIONS: Each item number answer of 1–5 must be transferred from the original assessment to this raw data scoring sheet. This form has a numbered item that corresponds with the listed acronym letter(s) next to each item on the client assessment. For example: A number 1–5 from the answer to item #3 from the "Drug and Alcohol Use" section goes in the line under BE [Sex/Drug-Linked Behavior] in the blank numbered "3. Used GHB." To reduce human error in recording the data on this scoring collection sheet, the number on the raw data sheet corresponds with the numbered item on the original answer form. Notice no name or identifying information is included on this sheet. This is a scoring tool, not part of the client's record.

Each of the 120 items to be included in the scoring must be recorded in the same way, by placing the answer in the corresponding coded section. At the end of this process you will have 16 separate sections with each line filled in with a number 1, 2, 3, 4, or 5. Simply add each column of numbers for each separate subsection and write the total in the Subtotal line. Do this for each of the 16 sections [Readiness to Change **{C}** is a combination of two subtotals from Drug and Alcohol Use and Sex/Drug-Linked Recovery Assessments]. Do the same for all 16 sections. Record all 16 subscores on the "Client Sexual Health in Recovery Assessment Outcome Form."

The Assessment Level of Client Sex/Drug Link is obtained by adding all 16 subscale scores and dividing by 120 (see Figure 6.6).

Inventory Categories for Scoring Sexual Health in Recovery Assessment

Drug and Alcohol Use

[Seven items reversed scored marked **(R)**]

BE Sex/Drug-Linked Behavior

_____ 3. Used GHB
_____ 4. Used crystal methamphetamine
_____ 5. Used ketamine ("Special K")
_____ 6. Used ecstasy
_____ 8. Used cocaine or crack cocaine
_____ 12. Drank any alcoholic beverages before, during, or right after sex
_____ 13. Used marijuana before, during, or right after sex
_____ 14. Used GHB before, during, or right after sex
_____ 15. Used crystal methamphetamine before, during, or right after sex
_____ 16. Used ketamine ("Special K") before, during, or right after sex
_____ 17. Used heroin before, during, or right after sex
_____ 18. Used cocaine or crack cocaine before, during, or right after sex
_____ 19. Used drugs that would make my body more attractive

(continued)

FIGURE 6.5 Sexual Health in Recovery Assessment Raw Data Answer Sheet
Continued

_____ 20. Ingested hallucinogens (LSD or mushrooms) before, during, or right after sex

_____ 22. Sleeping pills (barbiturates) before, during, or right after sex

_____ Subtotal

M Sex/Drug-Linked Motivations

_____ 10. Sexual functioning enhancement drugs

_____ 21. Sexual functioning enhancement drugs before or during sex

_____ 29. Experienced problems with sexual interest, desire, or functioning because of drinking or using drugs

_____ 30. Wondered if I have sexual problems caused by drinking or using drugs

_____ 33. Felt more free to be sexual when high on drugs and alcohol

_____ 34. More likely to take risks during sex when high on drugs and alcohol

_____ 35. Less likely to use a condom for sex when high on drugs and too much alcohol

_____ 36. Less likely to use contraception to prevent pregnancy when I am high on drugs and alcohol

_____ 37. People would think less of me if they knew what I did sexually after I drink or use drugs

_____ 42. (R) Thinking I will be sexually healthier if I stop drinking or using drugs

_____ Subtotal

C Readiness to Change

_____ 27. Neglected my spouse and family because of drinking and using drugs (C)

_____ 31. (R) Thought I am actually going to do something about drinking and using drugs (C)

_____ 32. (R) Believed that I am actively working on quitting drinking and using drugs right now (A)

_____ 38. Concerned I might fail at abstaining from drugs and alcohol use (C)

_____ 39. Feeling uncomfortable trying to abstain from drugs and alcohol use (P)

_____ 40. Recovery from drug addiction and alcoholism takes a lot of effort and energy (P)

(continued)

FIGURE 6.5 Sexual Health in Recovery Assessment Raw Data Answer Sheet
Continued

_____ 41. **(R)** I tell myself that if I try hard enough I can recover from my addiction (A)

_____ 43. **(R)** Thinking I will feel better about myself if I stop drinking or using drugs (P)

_____ 44. **(R)** Thinking I will worry less if I stop drinking or using drugs (P)

_____ 45. **(R)** Thinking some people will be better off if I stop drinking or using drugs (P)

_____ Subtotal

Items Omitted From Drug and Alcohol Use Score

1. Drank any alcoholic beverages
2. Used marijuana
7. Used heroin
9. Hallucinogens (LSD or Mushrooms)
11. Sleeping pills (Barbiturates)
23. Used prescription drugs for other than medical reasons
24. Combined one or more drugs/alcohol at a time
25. Unable to stop drinking or using drugs when I wanted to
26. Experienced blackouts or flashbacks resulting from drinking or using drugs
28. Experienced problems at work because of drinking and using drugs

Sexual Health
[18 items reversed scored marked **(R)**]

SP Sex-Positive Attitudes

_____ 1. **(R)** I find sex pleasurable.

_____ 10. **(R)** Masturbation is a healthy way to be sexual.

_____ 20. **(R)** Sex helps me express my love to my sexual partner(s).

_____ 23. I think pornographic material is disgusting.

_____ 24. **(R)** My race/ethnicity has been a positive influence on my sexuality.

_____ 28. **(R)** I am generally satisfied with my sexual behavior.

_____ 29. **(R)** I enjoy hearing about my sexual partner's sexual fantasies.

_____ 38. **(R)** I enjoy masturbating.

(continued)

FIGURE 6.5 Sexual Health in Recovery Assessment Raw Data Answer Sheet *Continued*

_____ 42. It is difficult for me to share my sexual fantasies with a sexual partner.

_____ 43. Sex is dirty.

_____ Subtotal

BU Boundaries

_____ 3. **(R)** I can say no to a sexual partner when asked to do a sexual behavior I do not like.

_____ 5. **(R)** I can interrupt sex to use a condom.

_____ 7. **(R)** I am very certain that I know my HIV status.

_____ 14. **(R)** I am able to keep my healthy sexual boundaries.

_____ 19. I have been avoiding an HIV test.

_____ 22. **(R)** I can use a condom for sexual intercourse (vaginal and/or anal) while under the influence of drugs or alcohol.

_____ 35. I feel pressured by my sexual partner(s) to have sex (if no current partner, refer to your most recent partner)

_____ 37. I was sexually abused when growing up.

_____ 41. I have engaged in sexual behavior for money, alcohol, illegal drugs, or shelter.

_____ 45. I have made promises to change my sexual behavior.

_____ Subtotal

SR Spirituality or Religion

_____ 8. I attend church activities at least twice a week.

_____ 15. My sexual behaviors and sexual values are in conflict with each other.

_____ 21. I feel condemned by God because of my sexual feelings and behaviors.

_____ 34. I have strong religious beliefs.

_____ 44. **(R)** Masturbation is a form of self-loving that is natural, normal, and morally acceptable.

_____ Subtotal

T Talking About Sex

_____ 2. I avoid talking about sex.

_____ 11. **(R)** I talk about my sexuality with my friends.

(continued)

FIGURE 6.5 Sexual Health in Recovery Assessment Raw Data Answer Sheet
Continued

_____ 16. **(R)** I talk about my sexuality with my doctor as it relates to health care.

_____ 26. I find many sexual matters too upsetting to talk about.

_____ 30. It bothers me to talk about sex.

_____ Subtotal

OC Out-of-Control Sexual Behavior

_____ 6. I think about sex more than I would like to.

_____ 13. My sexual thoughts and behaviors are causing problems in my life.

_____ 18. It has been difficult for me to find sex partners who desire sex as much as I do.

_____ 33. I feel that my sexual thoughts and feelings are stronger than I am.

_____ 40. I have an interest in a specific sexual "turn-on" that concerns me.

_____ Subtotal

SF Sexual Functioning

_____ 4. I have no interest in having sex.

_____ 9. I have concerns about my sexual functioning.

_____ 25. Most of the time, I orgasm/"come" too quickly when I am with my partner.

_____ 27. Recently, I have not been interested in sex.

_____ 32. Overall, I wish I had more of a desire to have sex.

_____ Subtotal

B Body Image

_____ 12. **(R)** I like the look of my genitals.

_____ 17. **(R)** I easily have an orgasm receiving oral sex.

_____ 31. I think I am overweight.

_____ 36. **(R)** In general, I like how my body looks.

_____ 39. I think I need to see a medical doctor for physical problems I am having with my penis/testicles (men) // vagina/pelvis (women).

_____ Subtotal

(continued)

FIGURE 6.5 Sexual Health in Recovery Assessment Raw Data Answer Sheet *Continued*

Sex/Drug-Linked Recovery
[Eighteen items reversed scored marked **(R)**]

PE Positive Outcomes Expectancy

_____ 2. **(R)** I am pleased that I am addressing my sexual behavior as part of staying sober

_____ 3. **(R)** I feel more comfortable talking about my sexual issues

_____ 19. **(R)** I feel confident that my sexual behavior will not prevent me from staying sober

_____ 25. **(R)** I am convinced that my sexual activity is a significant concern for my recovery

_____ 33. **(R)** I feel more confident that my sexual behavior will not lead to relapse

_____ Subtotal

R Relationship/Dating Sex/Drug-Link

_____ 4. I used drugs and alcohol to express love and affection or receive love and affection (W)

_____ 4. I used drugs and alcohol to not "come" so quickly (M)

_____ 5. **(R)** I look for information about relationships in recovery

_____ 26. **(R)** I talk about my relationship history and current relationship concerns with people in my recovery support system

_____ 31. **(R)** I think about important recovery tools to use in my relationship [or that I would know to use if I was in a relationship]

_____ 39. The sex I have had while sober has been a disappointment

_____ Subtotal

D Sexual Decisions in Recovery

_____ 7. I used sex to get out of a negative or overwhelming feeling (W)

_____ 7. I used sex to get out of negative or tense feelings (M)

_____ 16. I become irritated, mean, critical, angry or shaming toward people when talking about my sexual history or current behavior (W)

_____ 16. I become irritated, mean, critical, angry or rageful toward people when talking about my sexual history or current behavior (M)

(continued)

FIGURE 6.5 Sexual Health in Recovery Assessment Raw Data Answer Sheet
Continued

_____ 29. **(R)** I think about sexual activity that may put me at risk for relapse

_____ 37. **(R)** When I feel concerned about sex and recovery I go talk to someone about it

_____ 40. I have used drugs or alcohol before or during sex in the last 30 days

_____ Subtotal

L Sex/Drug-Linked Addiction Patterns

_____ 1. I worry that sex while sober is not as satisfying as it is when I am high or drinking

_____ 11. I seek out immediate sex partners (anonymous sex partners, online sex, pay for sex) when I am high on drugs and alcohol

_____ 13. I used drugs and alcohol to experience a specific sex act or have kinky sex

_____ 22. I feel more free to be sexual when I am high on drugs and alcohol

_____ 24. **(R)** I limit my sexual activity to one partner

_____ Subtotal

S Shame

_____ 9. I am too self-conscious to enjoy sex when sober

_____ 10. I feel regret, remorse

_____ 15. I feel mild guilt, worry about hurting someone or injuring someone

_____ 20. I have feelings of blushing, looking red in the face (W)

_____ 20. I feel rage (M)

_____ 23. I feel ridiculous or laughable

_____ 30. I have a sexual secret that preoccupies my thoughts that I hide from my recovery support system

_____ 32. I feel humiliated, "stupid", "childish"

_____ 34. I worry that some aspects of my sexual behavior may cause me social humiliation

_____ 36. I am lonely

_____ 38. I feel helpless, paralyzed

_____ Subtotal

(continued)

FIGURE 6.5 Sexual Health in Recovery Assessment Raw Data Answer Sheet *Continued*

SH HIV/STI/Pregnancy

_____ 8. **(R)** I talk with my partner about birth control/contraception before having sex (W)

_____ 8. **(R)** I talk with my partner about using a condom before having sex (M)

_____ 11. I take responsibility to protect my sex partner from getting HIV infected

_____ 12. I worry I am infected with a sexually transmitted disease (ie. herpes, gonorrhea)

_____ 18. I would be insulted if my sex partner put on a condom to avoid getting a sexually transmitted disease (W)

_____ 18. I would be insulted if my sex partner asked me to put on a condom to avoid getting a sexually transmitted disease (M)

_____ 21. **(R)** I delay sex if a condom is not available

_____ Subtotal

C* Readiness to Change

Precontemplation

_____ 6. **(R)** I talk to people in recovery who have successfully changed their sexual behavior

Contemplation

_____ 17. **(R)** I get upset thinking about giving in to using drugs and alcohol so I can have sex

Preparation

_____ 14. **(R)** I understand the sexual behavior guidelines for my treatment program

_____ 27. **(R)** I talk with people in my recovery support system when I miss having sex high

_____ 35. Thinking that changing my sexual behavior to stay sober takes a lot of effort

_____ Subtotal* Add this subtotal with **C** scores from first section for total subscore

_____ + Subtotal from first section for total subscore

_____ Subtotal for **C**

- Sexual Health
  - Sex-Positive Attitudes—SP
  - Boundaries—BU
  - Spirituality or Religion—SR
  - Talking About Sex—T
  - Out-of-Control Sexual Behavior—OC
  - Sexual Functioning—SF
  - Body Image—B
- Sexual Health in Recovery
  - Positive Outcomes Expectancy—PE
  - Relationship/Dating Sex/Drug Link—R
  - Sexual Decisions in Recovery—D
  - Sex/Drug-Linked Addiction Patterns—L
  - Shame—S
  - HIV/STI/Pregnancy—SH
  - Readiness to Change—C*

Here is the tedious part. Follow the direction on the Sexual Health in Recovery Assessment Raw Data Scoring Sheet to transfer each item answer of 1–5 from the original assessment form to the Inventory Categories for Scoring Sexual Health in Recovery Assessment (Figure 6.5). The Inventory Categories for Scoring Sexual Health section has each numbered item from the original assessment organized within each sexual health sub-category listed by acronym and name. For example BE Sex/Drug-Linked Behavior lists all 15 items by number and sentence from original assessment measure. A number 1–5 from the answer to item #3 from the Drug and Alcohol Use section goes in the line under **BE** in the blank numbered _____ "3. Used GHB." The number on the sheet corresponds with the numbered item on the original assessment answer form. This will help to reduce human error in recording the data on this anonymous sheet. Notice that no name or identifying information is included on this sheet. This is a scoring tool, not part of the client's record.

Most items are a direct transfer (direct score) of the client number rating on the assessment to the raw data answering sheet. There are 43 items on the assessment that are *reversed scored*. Some items on the Sexual Health in Recovery Assessment are worded such that a given response (e.g., "Almost Continually" or "Strongly Agree") represents a low sex/drug-linked relapse risk response for one item, but a high sex/drug-linked relapse risk response for another. When

---

*Note that the readiness to change subscale is a 10-item combination score from the Drug and Alcohol Use assessment and 5-item from Sex/Drug-Linked Recovery assessment.

reverse scoring an item marked "**(R)**" on the raw data sheet, the highest and lowest numerical values are substituted for each other, the next highest and next lowest values are substituted for each other, and so on.

For each item that is reversed scored, a #5 becomes a #1 for tabulation. A #4 rating becomes a #2. A #3 remains a #3, no reverse necessary. A #2 rating becomes a #4, and a #1 becomes a #5. For example, item #10 **SP** on the "Sexual Health" section of the assessment "Masturbation is a healthy way to be sexual" is reversed scored because this attitude about masturbation is a desirable response in terms of sex/drug-linked relapse. High scores are the less desirable behaviors. So this item needs to be reversed scored. A #1 answer by the client is scored as #5 on the Inventory Categories for Scoring form. This is essential to understand and implement to accurately complete the scoring.

Each of the 120 items must be recorded in the same way, by placing the answer in the corresponding coded section. Experience will make this process go faster. Transfer each subscale total (ranging from low of 5 to high of 75 depending on the category) to the Client Sexual Health in Recovery Assessment Outcome Form (see Figure 6.6). Add all 16 subtotals. Divide this number by 120 for overall score. Score will range from a low of 1 to a maximum score of 5. Place this score on the gradient line score. Leave the other gradient score lines blank for now.

Interpreting the Results

The results of the assessment measure are linked with the sexual health in recovery group and individual relapse prevention interventions. The overall assessed level of sex/drug-linked addiction is first and foremost a means of feedback for everyone involved in the clients treatment to understand the degree to which each client's initial treatment plan needs to include sex relapse concerns in understanding the clinical issues that may emerge as staff get to know the client.

- A low score (1–2) most likely means that sex linked with drug use will not likely emerge as a significant issue for recovery in the immediate future.
- Midrange scores (2–3.0) may indicate a need to look more closely at specific subtotals to identify clustering of sex/drug-linked recovery concerns. For example, consider a client whose elevated subtotals from the drug and alcohol use scale and the sexual health scale comprise most of the high scores, whereas the sex/drug-

FIGURE 6.6 Client Sexual Health in Recovery Assessment Outcome Form

---

Identification _____

Date assessment completed _____

Assessment scored by _____

BE _____ Subtotal

M _____ Subtotal

SP _____ Subtotal

BU _____ Subtotal

SR _____ Subtotal

T _____ Subtotal

OC _____ Subtotal

SF _____ Subtotal

B _____ Subtotal

PE _____ Subtotal

R _____ Subtotal

D _____ Subtotal

L _____ Subtotal

S _____ Subtotal

SH _____ Subtotal

C _____ Subtotal

Total _____ ÷ **120** = _____

Assessment Level of Client Sex/Drug Link

0	120	240	360	480	600
0	1	2	3	4	5

very low   very high

Professional Staff Perceived Level of Client Sex/Drug Link

0	1	2	3	4	5

very low   very high

Client Perceived Level of Client Sex/Drug Link After Assessment Feedback

0	1	2	3	4	5

very low   very high

_____

linked recovery scale may be much lower. This may indicate a history of situational drug use with sex as well as elevated sexual concerns that are not tied specifically to drug or alcohol use. These distinctions will be explored in case examples within the remaining chapters. For now, it is important to interpret midrange scores as requiring a more individualized approach. The degree to which specific sexual health concerns are linked with their addiction will be the work of the treatment staff, counselor, and/or physician.

- Scores more than 3.0 most likely indicate a high degree of sex/drug-linked addiction. These clients need the sexual health in recovery tools, counseling, and staff guidance to learn and implement sex/drug-linked relapse prevention tools. They will require an early and effective intervention (matched with their stage of readiness for change) that begins to link treatment completion and relapse prevention with abstinence from drugs and alcohol *and* sexual health education. Scores in this range indicate a client who may need to focus most, if not all, 16 areas of sexual health in recovery as well as sex/drug-linked relapse prevention.

Each subtotal score is a guide for establishing a recovery plan, not a conclusion. An elevated score on shame may need to be closely watched. Sex-positive interactions that are not focused on judgment or evaluation but rather relapse prevention and open, safe group discussions may reduce the levels of shame in a short time. A client may be given one of the three separate measures at closer intervals after initial assessment as an objective clue for how the client is changing or reducing relapse risk.

Subscales may also guide the client or treatment staff to do more in-depth education, counseling, or referral to target a specific relapse risk that may risk treatment completion. For example, a client may report high levels of risk for HIV infection, may have little confidence in maintaining boundaries to prevent HIV infection, and has avoided knowing HIV status. A high score may target knowing HIV status as first sexual health goal in recovery.

Conveying a sense of optimism and hope to each client regardless of level of sex/drug link will be an important skill for interpreting the results. Congratulate clients on taking the measure and for their considering sexual health information as an important component of their recovery. Normalize that this is a new process for everyone and how discussing the results contributes to comfort with future sexual health conversation.

Discussing Assessment Results With the Treatment Team and Other Providers

Drug and alcohol treatment is essentially a tag team mental health care process. It takes a village for an addict to recover. The process of recovery is not one of isolation, autonomy, or "going solo." Treatment professionals work together to create a path of recovery. Discussing the Sexual Health in Recovery Assessment results among the team of treatment professionals is important for integration of sexual health principles within the entire treatment program.

Make sure the assessment outcome form is included in the client record. A delegated staff person (typically the staff member who completed the assessment feedback session) should facilitate whatever discussion forum the program uses for establishing and reviewing the client's sex/drug-linked treatment. Key issue for the treatment team is to isolate the primary factors that will be addressed cross-discipline. The team may identify a specific sexual relapse risk factor within the treatment program that everyone will address in client interactions and interventions. For example, the team may agree that a client's oversexualized behavior creates distance and mistrust among their recovery support system. The team may identify clients whose precontemplative stage of readiness to change contributes to their disregarding sexual boundaries of safety and respect within the treatment program. Clients may have very high levels of shame and be quite anxious or paranoid about sexual issues being brought up in a manner that will potentially be humiliating. It is important for the treatment team to discuss shame reduction approaches to increase these clients' ability to talk about their sexual patterns of behavior to reduce relapse risk in treatment. For high-shame clients, the staff may focus on the clients' attendance and participation in the sexual health in recovery group rather than specific relapse risk prevention actions. Some clients may need to test out the counselors and observe them addressing sex/drug-linked issues with other clients before placing their own concerns within a particular group or recovery situation.

The more experience the staff has with discussing sex/drug-linked relapse, the more confident and useful these clinical planning discussions will be. In my role as consultant at Stepping Stone, once a month, I observed the staff meet with two clients for about 20 minutes each. Each client was a very high risk for sex/drug-linked relapse and had concerns about dropping out of treatment because of these risks. The meeting was a proactive prevention to collaborate with the client and staff and address this risk prior to a relapse or possible treatment termination.

My role was to observe the staff talking with the client and, after the client left the room, to give feedback to the staff on sexual health language, sex-positive attitudes and perspectives, sex/drug-linked clinical discussion, and collaborative sex/drug-linked relapse prevention strategic planning. All levels of staff expressed increasing confidence and optimism about addressing sex/drug-linked recovery and treatment planning not only in these observed client encounters but also in their day-to-day work in group sessions, individual counseling, and treatment program management.

The most significant aspect of interdisciplinary exchange of sex/drug-linked relapse prevention interventions was the decrease in client sexual behavioral disruptions in the treatment program. As staff began to speak and discuss sexuality related to client sex/drug-linked recovery, common sexual behavior management concerns plummeted. Staff was spending far less time managing sexual boundaries of clients. Instead, they were increasingly sought out by clients for thoughtful contemplation of sexual issues relevant to treatment success.

I believe when adults are given safe, respectful, and informed opportunities to address matters of sexual health, most will take advantage of the situation for constructive dialogue. It is as if everyone knows how rare these sexual health safe zones are in our culture. The hunger is real. When the meal is provided, nourishment ensues.

PROFESSIONAL STAFF INPUT ON CLIENT SEX/DRUG LINK

The client's overall Sexual Health in Recovery Assessment process is more than the numeric assessment level rating from the Sexual Health in Recovery Assessment. The overall clinical picture includes summarizing professional staff assessment and perceptions of each individual client's level of sex/drug-linked addiction patterns (this will be discussed in next chapter). As I have referenced in earlier chapters, we cannot reliably predict what staff or counselor(s) individual clients will be most open and willing to discuss their sexuality. The Professional Staff Perceived Level of Client Sex/Drug Link Evaluation (Figure 6.7) is a form that can be completed by any staff member or counselor that has client sexuality information from either clinical observation or client discussion.

After all staff have completed this form, average this overall rating and place the score on Client Sexual Health in Recovery Assessment Outcome Form in the space provided.

Each staff choosing to give input about a client's sex/drug-linked addiction pattern or history will complete this two-page form prior to the

Chapter 6 The Sexual Health in Recovery Assessment   **153**

FIGURE 6.7 Professional Staff Perceived Level of Client Sex/Drug Link Evaluation

---

Client name _____
Admission date _____
Name of staff completing this evaluation _____
Number of sexual health in recovery psychoeducational group lessons _____
Number of individual counseling sessions _____
Unplanned pregnancy or impregnated sex partner since admission? YES NO
   If yes, was the pregnancy linked with drug use or drinking? YES NO
Please explain circumstance. _____
_____
_____

Client contracted a sexually transmitted infection (STI) since admission? YES NO
   If yes, check which STI
      _____ syphilis
      _____ gonorrhea
      _____ chlamydia
      _____ herpes
      _____ HPV (genital warts)
      _____ other (describe) _____
Client HIV status: HIV negative _____ HIV Positive _____
   Unknown _____
Has client been tested for HIV since admission? YES NO unknown
Has client tested HIV positive since admission? YES NO unknown
In your opinion, how important is sex/drug-linked addiction and relapse prevention skill acquisition to the client's recovery?

|―――――|―――――|―――――|―――――|―――――|
0   1   2   3   4   5
not at all important   extremely important

In your opinion, what is your current perceived level of client relapse risk due to sexual behavior?

|―――――|―――――|―――――|―――――|―――――|
0   1   2   3   4   5
not at risk   extremely at risk

Add any additional information important to understanding this client's current sex/drug-linked relapse risk. _____
_____
_____
_____

Look over all the information on this sheet and rate your overall perceived level of this client's sex/drug link pattern of addiction.

Professional Staff Perceived Level of Client Sex/Drug Link

|―――――|―――――|―――――|―――――|―――――|
0   1   2   3   4   5
not at risk   extremely at risk

assessment feedback session (this session will be discussed in the next chapter). It may be interesting to note that specific staff may have certain information on the form and another staff member may round out client information different from other staff completing this form. Individual rating sheets may be kept in the client's file. The important feedback to include is the overall average score (1–5) of the total ratings given by each staff member to the last item on the form Professional Staff Perceived Level of Client Sex/Drug Link Evaluation. This number is totaled and averaged with every other individual staff rating to determine the overall "Professional Staff Perceived Level of Client Sex/Drug Link" on the Client Sexual Health in Recovery Assessment Outcome Form (Figure 6.6).

Staff perceptions of the level of client sex/drug link provide an additional clinical perspective to balance overdependence on the assessment measure data. Clinical observations, sexual health tests and information, client interactions, treatment session discussions, group therapy sessions, family contact, and adjunct professional exchanges can all be part of the summarizing of counseling staff observations and perceptions. This rating provides an important opportunity for potential discrepancy or agreement between client and staff perceptions pertaining to client sex/drug link.

LIMITATIONS AND DRAWBACKS TO THE SEXUAL HEALTH IN RECOVERY ASSESSMENT

I cannot end this chapter without acknowledging the current limitations and caveats for the sex/drug-linked relapse prevention approaches outlined in this book. First and foremost is that this is only the first of what I hope are many additional perspectives on sex/drug-linked addiction treatment. I see this work as a catalyst to further a much-needed sexual health conversation. Professional criticism and evaluation of these concepts, approaches, and interventions will be an essential component of this process. I hope this book stimulates curious and expansive thinking about the potential role of sexual health principles within drug and alcohol treatment.

This intervention is primarily designed to accomplish two goals: to increase client retention in all levels of drug and alcohol treatment and to prevent relapse. As such, it is not focused on wider issues of sexuality that are common among men and women in treatment. It is not a program to address recovery for men and women with a history of sexual violence, abuse, and/or trauma. It is not an HIV-prevention intervention. It is not a sex education class to review basic components of reproduction, anatomy, and transmission routes for sexually transmitted infections or contraception. It is not an intervention to treat sexual disorders and dysfunction. It is not designed to treat various concerns about sex that occur throughout the maturation and aging process.

Sexual health information and education is so hard to come by for adults that one narrowly defined sexual health intervention can be a setup for disappointment because of the many additional needs men and women may bring to the situation that are not within the parameters of the specific sexual health service. I observed this when I supervised an HIV prevention team who provided HIV testing and early intervention at San Diego County addiction treatment programs. Drug and alcohol treatment clients were often pressed into talking about their sexual concerns in recovery during the brief 15 minutes of pretest counseling time. It was as if this HIV testing appointment was the one chance they had to talk openly and confidentially about sexual concerns in recovery. The drug treatment program provided no space for this. The counselors conducting the pretest interview were constantly trying to refocus the clients to information about preparing to take an HIV test.

This is a limitation of the *Sexual Health in Recovery* group and individual counseling program. It does not and cannot attempt to be a comprehensive sexual health education and prevention program. It is limited to the role of an adjunct clinical focus for addressing relapse concerns linked with sexual behavior in treatment and recovery. Sexual health in recovery is to improve drug and alcohol treatment outcomes. It is not an intervention to change overall sexual health attitudes or beliefs.

The most significant drawback to sex/drug-linked relapse is the frequent perception among drug and alcohol treatment professionals as a sex addiction treatment intervention for women and men entering addiction treatment. It is by far the most common misunderstanding among a wide range of mental health care providers. It seems when the sexuality of drug addicts or alcoholics is mentioned, the notion that their sexuality could only be of clinical pertinence if it is a co-occurring sexual addiction is so automatic that it is unconsciously assumed. It is only when I slowly describe the purpose and function of sexual health relapse prevention that people turn away from their automatic sex-addict framework and open their minds to a health-based framework for discussing sex in recovery. A vision for sexual health as a relapse prevention skill is yet to become a common sentence or thought within drug and alcohol treatment. It will not become a common notion without many other drug and alcohol treatment specialists, sexologists, therapists, researchers, grantees, and government funding onboard. We will all need to work together to improve the lives of the men and women currently entering treatment with high sex/drug-linked addiction patterns.

7

The Sexual Health in Recovery Assessment Feedback Session

I have a very fortunate marriage. My husband, Al Killen-Harvey, is a licensed clinical social worker clinically supervising a team of trauma counselors at the Chadwick Center for Children and Families. The Chadwick Center is a program of Rady Children's Hospital in San Diego. In 2005, the Chadwick Center created an intervention model, *Assessment-Based Treatment for Traumatized Children: A Trauma Assessment Pathway* (TAP) with support from the Substance Abuse and Mental Health Services Administration (SAMHSA), as part of the National Child Traumatic Stress Network (NCTSN).

I became aware of the TAP model through Al. He trains therapists and trauma treatment providers throughout the United States in the TAP model. As I listened to Al describe the model, I began to see the similarities with my own model for sex/drug-linked relapse prevention counseling. The TAP model is an elegantly developed process for using multifaceted assessment measures and procedures to provide psychotherapy and guide the course of trauma treatment. Unwittingly, the same process emerged from the Stepping Stone sexual health intervention in a much more rudimentary fashion. Assessing client sex/drug-linked risk factor lead to various treatment and measures of progress to reduce sex/drug-linked relapse risk. Like the TAP model, sexual health–based relapse prevention would approach each client's sex/drug-linked situation as a unique clinical picture requiring individualized approaches to more effectively treat drug and alcohol addiction.

The TAP model provided a language framework for sexual health relapse prevention as a "pathway" model. The pathway is not only a screening and assessment for sex and drug use but also a clinical counseling process for integrating assessment information into all phases of recovery. The pathway is also a process for drug and alcohol treatment professionals to develop a more comprehensive understanding of each client sex/drug-linked relapse risks, select specific relapse prevention skills, and monitor and reevaluate sex/drug-linked relapse at all stages of recovery.

This chapter adapts the TAP as a sequence of counseling decisions based on current sexual health and drug and alcohol recovery research and relapse prevention modalities. I will guide readers in completing the Sexual Health in Recovery Assessment client feedback session. Clinical case examples will illustrate specific approaches for this session.

SEXUAL HEALTH IN RECOVERY PATHWAY (SHRP)

The SHRP is a three-stage pathway from Assessment to Triage and finally Treatment. Each stage has a sequence of steps leading to the next stage with the focus on creating an individualized sex/drug-linked relapse prevention plan for men and women in recovery. The pathway is outlined in Figure 7.1 (Sexual Health in Recovery Pathway).

It may be repetitive at this point, but it is important to reiterate the centrality of sex/drug-linked relapse prevention as the central goal of this pathway. The entire process is an enhancement to the individual drug and alcohol treatment plan and recovery process. Because of the cutting-edge nature of this work, counselor readiness is the first step in the pathway. Chapter 4 combined counselor's self-assessment and suggestions for an initial sex/drug link client screening (see Figures 4.1 and 4.2). In Chapters 5 and 6, we discussed a process for integrating the assessment measure outcomes with professional staff perceptions to create a unique picture of client relapse risk factors combined with their readiness to change. The Sexual Health in Recovery Assessment guides the counselor to focus on relapse prevention interventions within any of the three subcategories: drug and alcohol use, sexual health, and sex/drug-linked recovery.

Subscores within each of these three categories contribute to the overall counseling pathways selected by the counselor. The pathway model is a collaborative model between counselor and client to decide specific sexual health in drug and alcohol treatment lessons and skills sets for initial treatment planning including client attending the Sexual Health in Recovery Psychoeducational Group (see Braun-Harvey, 2009).

ADDITIONAL SEXUAL HEALTH SERVICES

The Sexual Health in Recovery Pathway outlines seven specific additional issues that are basic to integrating sexual health within drug and alcohol treatment. Determination of client level of sex/drug-linked relapse risk includes identifying any one of seven additional sexual

FIGURE 7.1 Sexual Health in Recovery Pathway

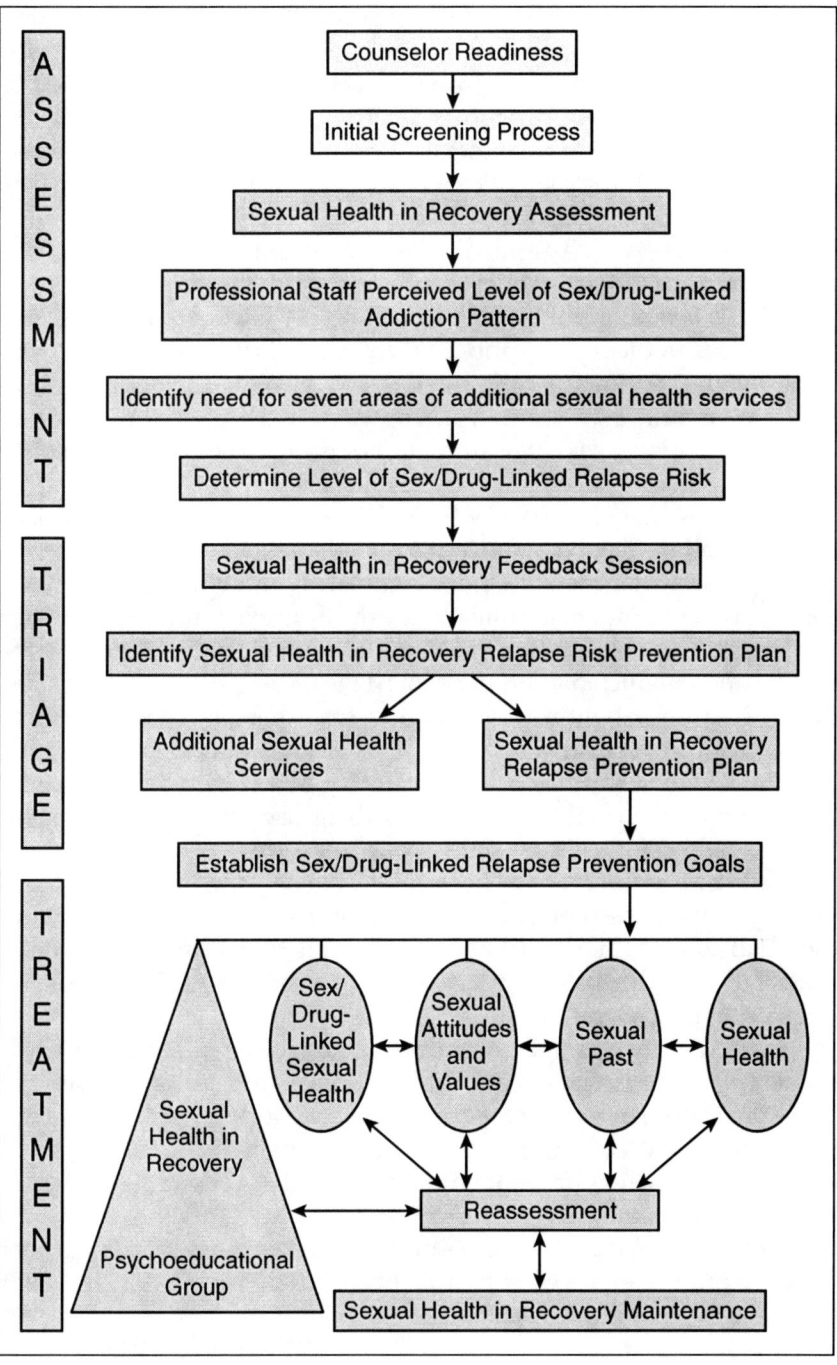

health services that may be pertinent to each client's drug and alcohol treatment. Additional specialized sexual health services are indicated when client, counselor, and assessment point to specific sexual health issues that, if left unattended, are a risk factor for recovery regardless of the specific level of sex/drug-linked pattern of substance abuse. If any or all of these seven additional sexual health services are left unresolved or set aside it will create significant barriers to treatment completion (see Figure 7.2).

Remember Sabrina from Chapter 1. Her untreated social anxiety combined with a high level of sex/drug-linked addiction contributed to multiple sexually transmitted infections (STIs) and two miscarried pregnancies in the 5 years prior to recovery. Sabrina had not been to a gynecological appointment in more than 2 years (since her first pregnancy spontaneously aborted after 2 months). Assessing Sabrina's need for additional sexual health services is important for establishing an initial recovery baseline of physical health.

The assessment identified which of the seven sexual health services to access and the feedback session included a sexual health relapse prevention plan recommendation for completing these health care tasks. Sabrina was referred to a women's health clinic in the first weeks of her treatment. The examination evaluated the health of her reproductive system and conducted a full panel of STI tests as well an HIV test. Her doctor inquired about any side effects from her psychiatric medications, including sexual side effects. This clinic works closely with the treatment center and has begun including brief questions about history of nonconsensual sex during her drug use. In this appointment, Sabrina talked for the first time about her second pregnancy, which resulted from a gang rape at her dealer's house. Men had sex with her while she was passed out. She had no memory of the sex or how many men had violated her. The spontaneous end to the pregnancy was a relief but a source of enormous shame. It was the beginning of her decision to get sober.

Sabrina's story is not uncommon among women entering treatment. For this reason, sexual health services are recommended for those beginning in recovery—even those that do not demonstrate high sex/drug-linked addiction patterns. These specialized sexual health services can address immediate concerns that are relevant to relapse-risk prevention and early treatment success. Often these sexual health services are provided by community clinics or medical centers that have a working referral and treatment coordination relationship with a drug and alcohol treatment center.

Chapter 7 The Sexual Health in Recovery Assessment Feedback Session

FIGURE 7.2 Seven Additional Sexual Health Services

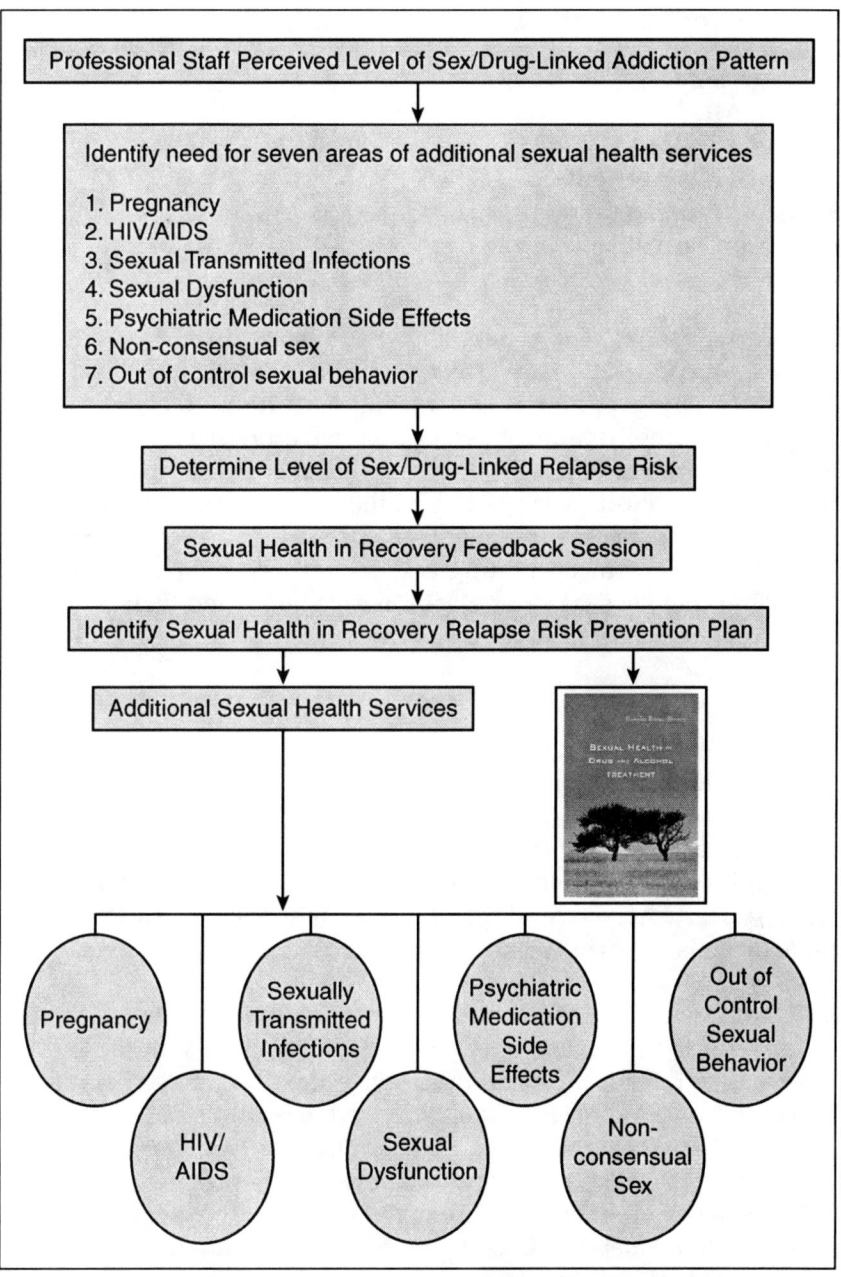

There are seven areas of additional sexual health services for both men and women entering treatment:

1. pregnancy
2. HIV/AIDS status
3. STIs
4. sexual dysfunction
5. psychiatric medication sexual side effects
6. nonconsensual sex
7. out-of-control sexual behavior

Some drug and alcohol treatment centers bring an HIV counseling and testing specialist to their treatment center. A hospital-based inpatient treatment program or a very high-end freestanding for-profit drug and alcohol treatment center may have physicians and sexual health practitioners on staff. Access to sexual health–based medical care and evaluation varies greatly in the United States. Sexual health based drug and alcohol treatment includes this pathway as a preliminary step toward incorporating sex/drug-linked relapse prevention programming. Let's take a brief look at each factor and their relevance to the Sexual Health in Recovery Pathway.

Pregnancy

Women addicted to drugs and alcohol tend to continue their use throughout pregnancy (Loebstein & Koren, 1997). She may be initially concerned about the effects of her drug use on the developing fetus, but this is not to be an indication of readiness to become abstinent or enter recovery. An active addicted woman will not necessarily discontinue drug use or drinking upon learning that she is pregnant.

- "I have been addicted to heroin for almost 2 years. Yesterday I found out I am 9 weeks pregnant. My menstrual cycle was messed up because of the dope. I am worried I have already damaged my baby."
- "For the last 8 years I have been addicted to painkillers. My husband wants to have another child. Have I ruined by body? Will the fetus still be affected even if I stopped before getting pregnant?"
- "Is there any number to call anonymously to get information on how hydrocodone may be affecting my pregnancy? I am too ashamed to talk to ask my doctor. She doesn't know I am pregnant."
- "My boyfriend was using crystal meth, pot, and alcohol when I got pregnant. Can a father using drugs cause birth defects?"

Women entering drug and alcohol treatment during the prenatal period increase their likelihood of successful recovery from alcohol and drug abuse. Comprehensive prenatal–obstetrical care for pregnant substance-abusing women is basic to drug and alcohol treatment. Drug and alcohol treatment professionals often understand the dangers to the fetus when exposed to maternal substance abuse. Premature birth, low birth weight, retarded growth, brain and central nervous system damage, as well as physical congenital malformations are caused by alcohol or other drug abuse by the pregnant woman (Wilson & Thorp, 2008). Recovery interventions following the birth must address many complex social needs related to poverty, violence, isolation, single motherhood, domestic/family violence, or sexual abuse. Pregnant and new mothers in recovery need gender-specific drug and alcohol treatment. The recovery needs of pregnant women are not exclusively relevant to level of sex/drug-linked relapse risk. This triage step requires substance abuse counselors to use data outcomes of the Sexual Health in Recovery Assessment in concert with established treatment approaches with pregnant women. Discerning what specific sex/drug-linked addiction patterns are best addressed in early recovery will need to be balanced with the significant focus on pregnancy, delivery, and newborn care.

HIV/AIDS Status

Since the onset of the HIV epidemic, injection drug use has been linked with HIV infection. Over time, alcohol and drug use linked with HIV infection is associated with poor decision making, which can lead to high-risk sexual practices. Early in the epidemic, research demonstrated a significant reduction in unsafe sex practices and injection drug use during and following addiction treatment. Because of this, drug and alcohol treatment became a primary means of HIV education, testing, counseling, intervention, and case management. Drug treatment programs became experts in HIV education and prevention as well as significant sources for HIV related referrals. Most treatment programs across the United States now provide HIV education or contract with HIV education and testing services. Contemporary studies have identified biological and immune-suppressing effects of drug addiction that make some abusers more susceptible to HIV infection, worsen the progression and consequences of disease progression, as well as identify specific drugs (such as methamphetamine) as particularly harmful to the brain and cognitive functioning among HIV-infected individuals (NIDA, 2010).

HIV infection and the prevention of HIV infection among men and women in drug and alcohol treatment are not specific to sex/drug-linked behavior. Infection risks are not always directly linked to the sexual behavior of the person who becomes infected. The behavior of partners, the inability to assert safe sex boundaries with a committed partner, and lack of knowledge about partners or one's own HIV status (positive or negative) all contribute to risk for infection well beyond the scope of sex/drug-linked relapse risk.

Every person in recovery, whether he or she is 1-day sober or has years of sobriety, must be certain of his or her relationship with HIV to begin and sustain a life in recovery. This is basic to sexual health in drug and alcohol treatment.

Sexually Transmitted Infections

"Research has documented the association between substance use and STDs" (Centers for Disease Control and Prevention, 2010). STI screening for all patients at a drug treatment program may not be necessary. However, the Sexual Health in Recovery Assessment identifies client's in need of further follow-up for "HIV, STI, Pregnancy" sexual health services. The Sexual Health in Recovery Assessment is an additional screening tool for identifying clients that do not fit the typical STI risk profile of a young adult, injection drug user (IDU), or sex worker in drug and alcohol treatment.

Sexual Dysfunction

"Sexual functioning problems are health issues of significant concern" (Carpenter, Janssen, Graham, Vorst, & Wicherts, 2008, p. 36). Many men and women believe alcohol and most other drugs will arouse or intensify their sexual desire or functioning. In reality, smoking, drinking, and psychoactive drugs tend to damage all aspects of sexual function (Bang-Ping, 2008).

This contradiction is important for sexual health in recovery. A drug treatment professional assessing for sexual dysfunction needs to focus on the client's self-report of his or her individual experiences with alcohol and/or drugs on sexual functioning. A referral to a specialist is indicated when clients report lifelong sexual dysfunction and/or a high motivation for using substances to self-medicate sexual dysfunction. Recovery may be a formidable choice for a client who has a history of polysubstance use to engage in or enjoy sexual interactions.

This correlation between drug use and sexual interactions may be even more prevalent among recovering women with a history of sexual assault and sexual dysfunction. A recent study found that a history of sexual inhibition and sexual assault each predicted the use of alcohol or other drugs to increase sexual desire (Sanjuan, Langenbucher, & Labouvie, 2009). The researchers suggested that women who self-medicate their sexual dysfunction may be on a path to relapse.

Sexual functioning is an interaction between the body and our emotions, relations, social conditions, psychology, culture, gender, religion, sexual expectations, and inhibitions. All of these factors can increase or decrease sexual arousal (even when completely drug and alcohol free). Lack of knowledge about the effects of drugs and alcohol on sexual functioning is extremely common among men and women in recovery. A useful sexual health step is to offer clients additional information about sexual functioning. This can be as basic as directing them to reputable online education resources. Treatment programs may collaborate with community sexual health services who provide assessment and treatment for sexual dysfunctions. Counseling clients to understand sexual functioning as essential for sexual health in recovery is a key relapse prevention intervention for everyone in recovery.

Psychiatric Medication Sexual Side Effects

Dealing with alcoholism and drug addiction is not easy. When a mental health diagnosis accompanies drug and alcohol treatment, recovery becomes exponentially more complicated. Many men and women in recovery or just entering treatment have co-occurring psychiatric conditions. According to the National Alliance for the Mentally Ill, more than 50% of drug abusers and more than one third of alcohol abusers have at least one serious mental illness (National Alliance on Mental Illness, 2003).

Psychopharmaceutical drug treatment is a basic treatment intervention for most psychiatric conditions. Combining talk therapy with medications significantly improves mental health treatment outcomes (Consumer Reports, 2004).

Sexual dysfunction resulting from psychotherapeutic drugs is an important sexual health concern for men and women in recovery. They may have been using alcohol or drugs to self-medicate sexual inhibitions or issues. Removing the self-medicating effects of alcohol and drugs and then introducing sexual side effects as a result of psychiatric medications can cause exasperation and frustration for men and women in recovery.

Counselors should provide significant empathy, interest, reinforcement, and validation for the client's medication related sexual functioning concern. Time and again I hear stories of clients discontinuing their psychiatric medications, in part, because the psychiatrist, physician, therapist, or drug counselor dismissed, minimized, or failed to empathize with the clients concern over diminished sexual functioning. Men and women may be motivated and ready for recovery and for treating their mental illness. However, they do not want sexual dysfunction as the trade-off. This concern should not be seen as a sign of decreased motivation for sobriety and mental health. The medication induced sexual side effects may lead clients to have very low confidence that they can succeed at recovery and their mental health treatment when their medication decimates sexual desire, arousal, and or functioning. Clients can tolerate sexual side effects for a much greater period if their recovery and mental health care team empathizes with the problem and is committed to [over time] finding a solution.

Counselors should encourage clients to advocate for their sexual health as part of recovery. Finding a psychiatrist who is a specialist in addictionology may be an important first step. A board-certified addictionologist will be familiar with the intricacies of co-occuring disorders and medication sexual side effects. He or she will be familiar with strategies for managing sexual side effects and candidly discussing possible subsiding of sexual side effects as the client adjustments, stabilizes, and reaches therapeutic levels for medication dosage. Specific treatment planning may include switching medication or adding an erectile dysfunction medication (for men). A sex-positive counseling approach that provides options for long-range recovery and sexual health is an essential triage skill.

Nonconsensual Sex

Experts now recognize childhood sexual abuse as a risk factor in all forms of drug dependence (Rosellini, 2002). Swan reports as many as two-thirds of patients in drug abuse treatment centers report physical or sexual abuse before the age of 18 (Swan, 1998). Women who experience any type of sexual abuse or nonconsensual sex in childhood may be three times more likely than unabused girls to report drug dependence as adults (Kendler et al., 2000). Researchers from the Harvard Medical School and McLean Hospital found that repeated sexual abuse during childhood causes physical changes in the brain that can explain why abused children often develop substance abuse problems (Anderson, Teicher, Polcari, & Renshaw, 2002).

Nonconsensual sexual relations are a violation of bodily integrity and sexual self-rule and control. This leads to harmful distress and psychological injury. Some sexual abuse survivors may themselves commit forced sexual violence or rape or may use drugs to manipulate another adult or child into sex. Sobriety may lead to an increase in thinking about or remembering sexual abuse or committing sexual violence.

More often than not, the very places society deems safest for children are the most common places for child sexual abuse to occur. "Most abusers are family members or others close to the family" (Saisan, Smith, & Segal, 2009). Men and women in recovery reflect these trends through stories of sexual abuse in their homes, schools, places of worship, and health care facilities. This is important for drug and alcohol counselors to understand. Clients seeking drug treatment will not assume they are safe just because they are in a professional health care setting. In fact, for some clients, it will trigger the fears that were experienced when a trusted person nonconsensually violated or exploited them for their own sexual gratification. A sexually abused adult understands that a person cannot be trusted just because they occupy a position of trust. They know that position of authority could be the very weapon used against them. When counselors understand that this is a common perception among addicts, they will be in a better position to provide the essential triage skill for work with sex/drug-linked relapse (Best, 2005).

Nonconsensual sex is often a highly charged topic within drug and alcohol treatment. Concealing childhood sexual assault or abuse is very common among people in recovery. Perpetrators of abuse, too, will commonly conceal their actions. The sexual health in recovery counseling skill is to assume that every client has most likely experienced nonconsensual sex prior to entering treatment. I believe that making this assumption spares client and counselor alike from prematurely discussing sexual abuse or perpetration. A gradual, guided disclosure of nonconsensual sex with professionals, sponsors, therapists, and other mental health care providers is the sexual heath step. Secondly, it is the responsibility of drug and alcohol treatment providers to acknowledge and treat their *own* history of sexual abuse or perpetration. Counselors who have not addressed their personal history of nonconsensual sex (in either role) will be ill equipped to effectively facilitate the sexual health concerns surrounding sexual abuse among men and women in recovery.

A common concern among many drug and alcohol counselors is their ambivalence over discussing sexual abuse:

- "What if she wants to talk about her history of abuse? I am not trained in that."
- "If he raped someone, I just don't think I could ever work with him or have him in the treatment program."
- "I don't feel good about listening to a man talk about being sexually abused, I just don't see how it is the same thing as what happens to a woman."

Implementing a triage step of assuming the topic is relevant without an inquiry, or disclosure will allow for a more client-centered unfolding of this material in the context of recovery.

Out-of-Control Sexual Behavior

The last sexual health in recovery triage consideration is addressing symptoms of what is commonly called *sex addiction, compulsive sexual behavior, love addiction,* or *sex compulsion*. A high risk or immediate concern for some people entering a rehabilitation program is inability to manage sexual attractions, sexual behaviors, or sexual responses to other people. These clients are likely candidates for disciplinary actions, safety concerns, and significant behavior management focus from staff. Frequent management of sexual behavioral concerns prohibits clients from fully engaging in their treatment and recovery process.

The sexual health skill is to effectively address sexual boundaries, which threaten the client's ability to remain in treatment. Relapse and recovery issues related to sexual boundaries, as well as co-occurring symptoms of out-of-control sexual behavior, must be addressed in a methodical and contemplative manner. Counselors risk misdirecting treatment by prematurely assuming clients require an assessment for out-of-control sexual behavior, sex addiction, or compulsive sexual behavior. Setting limits on staff language and client assumptions of "he's a sex addict" are crucial and necessary for a suspended judgment zone to observe and discuss sexual boundary concerns with the client.

Some clients may enter treatment with a co-occurring diagnosis of out-of-control sexual behavior. Most treatment programs in the United States are ill equipped to attend to this dual condition. This leaves many programs to rely on perhaps a specific counselor with experience in sexual recovery. The essential sexual health service consideration is to have a plan for addressing sexual safety issues and to be able to address sex/drug-linked addiction and relapse risk concurrently with compulsive sexual behavior.

After evaluation of the seven additional sexual health concerns, it is time to review the Sexual Health in Recovery Assessment recommendations with the client. The pathway from this point forward is directly focused on establishing goals for relapse prevention focused on sex/drug-linked recovery skills. The first step is the assessment feedback session.

SEXUAL HEALTH IN RECOVERY FEEDBACK SESSION

The Sexual Health in Recovery Assessment feedback session has several purposes. One is to provide a verbal client exchange with a drug and alcohol treatment professional that integrates sexuality and sexual health issues within the larger context of recovery. Secondly, it empowers clients to discuss sexuality and sex/drug-linked addiction patterns within treatment, their recovery community, therapists, doctors, psychiatrists, and other significant members of their support community. Lastly, the assessment allows counselor and client to proactively plan to prevent sex/drug-linked relapse risk factors. The Sexual Health in Recovery feedback session is an essential discussion to increase the client's potential for treatment completion and sustained abstinence within sexual situations or relationships.

This face-to-face meeting will be one of many sex-positive interactions in the treatment program. However, the assessment feedback session will set the tone and expectations for how the treatment program and staff members discuss sex/drug-linked issues. It is one thing to provide a written assessment and policy of positively and proactively addressing sexuality as a factor in treatment success. But no matter how well thought out the policies and procedures, when it comes to establishing a credible relationship between client and treatment center, the individual counselor and client sessions are where the real trust will be built and maintained.

Clients will be at their most vigilant in evaluating the treatment center's ability to address sex/drug-linked concerns in this feedback session. The choice of staff member who provides the feedback is an important one. Sex is a vulnerable and personal experience for clients to discuss. Staff members who have invested in their own personal growth and professional knowledge regarding human sexuality should be strongly considered for this work. A counselor's ability to suspend judgmental thinking (as discussed in Chapter 2) is put to the test when he or she individually reviews the Sexual Health in Recovery Assessment feedback with a client. A common defense used by addicts is to complain about the counselors' behavior or language as a means of avoiding examining their own issues. Having adequately prepared staff, specifically staff who provide individual counseling related to sex/drug-linked relapse risk or prevention, is essential to the successful implementation of the overall intervention.

Starting the Session

I suggest the counselor start by asking clients their feelings and thoughts about the appointment. Are there some concerns they have been worried about? Is there a specific feedback, which they are concerned, that may be brought up? Acknowledge the likelihood of the clients having some trepidation about the "sex talk." Remember, this may be the first time clients have ever discussed their sexuality with another adult in a safe, respectful, and informed manner. Thus, it might be helpful to acknowledge the unusual nature of this appointment. Give clients credit for doing something that is uncommon for most adults, not just men and women in recovery. Remind them that the reason for this appointment is to discuss the assessment and to address their level of relapse risk related to sex/drug-linked patterns of addiction. Some clients may need the counselor to reiterate that she is not here to judge or criticize their sexual behavior. It is important to emphasize that the primary purpose for this assessment interview is to increase clients' likelihood of completing the treatment program and sustaining abstinence by preparing in advance for a recovery process that includes clients' sexual health as a central element of sobriety.

Provide Subscore Feedback

Start by organizing the feedback in three areas: drug and alcohol use, sexual health, and sex/drug-linked recovery. Give the client his or her subscore of each of the three areas. Then briefly discuss what each subscore means. The "Client Sexual Health in Recovery Assessment Outcome Form" (Figure 7. 3) provides a numeric rating for the three subscores.

The Drug and Alcohol Use subtotal (from 35–175) is a reflection of how closely associated the client's drug and alcohol abuse patterns coincide with some aspect of his sexual behavior. In other words, this section addresses how the client's sex life alters when he

Chapter 7   The Sexual Health in Recovery Assessment Feedback Session

FIGURE 7.3   Client Sexual Health in Recovery Assessment Outcome Form

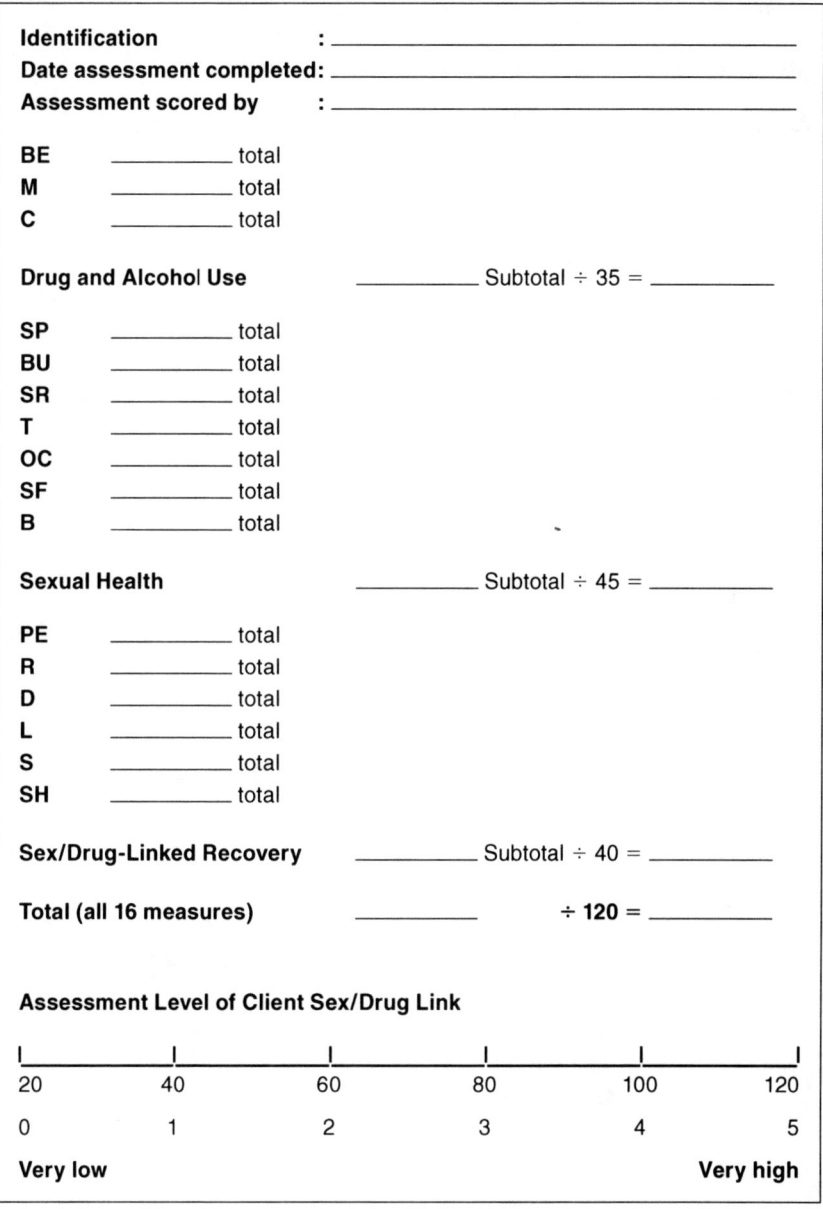

(continued)

FIGURE 7.3 Client Sexual Health in Recovery Assessment Outcome Form *Continued*

Professional Staff Perceived Level of Client Sex/Drug Link

|⎯⎯⎯⎯⎯|⎯⎯⎯⎯⎯|⎯⎯⎯⎯⎯|⎯⎯⎯⎯⎯|⎯⎯⎯⎯⎯|
0　　　　1　　　　2　　　　3　　　　4　　　　5
Very low　　　　　　　　　　　　　　　　Very high

Client Perceived Level of Client Sex/Drug Link After Assessment Feedback

|⎯⎯⎯⎯⎯|⎯⎯⎯⎯⎯|⎯⎯⎯⎯⎯|⎯⎯⎯⎯⎯|⎯⎯⎯⎯⎯|
0　　　　1　　　　2　　　　3　　　　4　　　　5
Very low　　　　　　　　　　　　　　　　Very high

Summary of assessment interview _____

_____

_____

_____

_____

_____

_____

_____

or she is high or drunk. It reflects how certain substances are more closely associated with sex, sexual behavior, or sexual situations for the client. This section looks at how much the client's motivations for using drugs may be linked with the sexual outcomes. These outcomes could be negative or positive. The higher the number the more closely associated sex and drug use is with motivations and behavior. Drug and Alcohol Use subtotal is a clinical treatment planning tool and to identify treatment areas for specific client attention as part of overall sex/drug-linked relapse prevention. For example, a client may have scored highest on readiness to change and in the middle range on sex/drug-linked motivations and sex/drug-linked behavior. A client may benefit from hearing feedback about high readiness to change as an affirming source of optimism to counterbalance specific worries of their sex/drug-linked behavior.

The Sexual Health subtotal describes sexual attitudes, behaviors, influences, and functioning that are significant for clients in recovery. It is not a comprehensive sexual health assessment; rather, it is a guide to general overall sexual health as it relates to sobriety and recovery. The subtotal ranges from 45–225. The higher the total score the more important it will be for the counselor and client to discuss how sexual health factors may impede or support recovery or relapse. There are seven sexual health scales within the subtotal. Clinical treatment planning and client awareness of the highest total areas and lowest total areas (sexual health strengths) may be important to focus upon. If a client has elevated subtotals on both Sexual Health and the Drugs and Alcohol Use section, there may be an increased risk for relapse due to the emotional conflicts and stressors of experiencing a higher degree of sexual health concerns. It is the emotions and avoidance of these sexual health concerns that must be addressed in early recovery.

The most important goal is to familiarize the client with the range of treatment areas related to sexual health that require extra attention and focus at this time in his or her recovery. Remind the client that these recommendations are based on the last 3 months of his or her life; the scores may change over time. Taking the assessment again in 3 months to see changes in sexual health can be a rewarding and encouraging experience for someone new to recovery or who has been through a series of sex/drug-related relapses.

The Sex/Drug-Linked Recovery scale focuses on predictive variables for sex and relapse. Scores range from 40–200 among a cluster of six sex/drug-linked relapse factors. This section also addresses shame. By now the reader knows the significance of sex/drug-linked shame upon entering treatment. Only the shame subscale contributes up to

50 points to this score. This is a reflection of the hypothesized significant correlation between client high sex/drug link and shame. It will be important for counselors to address the shame score contribution to the overall level of sex/drug-linked recovery. For example the shame score could be 40 points out of a total score of 110. This would alert treatment planning to focus the client on early relapse prevention by reducing sex/drug-linked shame. The psychoeducational curriculum class is a vital tool for addressing this shame reduction in the very first stages of treatment.

Elevation on this subscale should direct the counselor and client to address future behaviors that may be common (perhaps unavoidable) in recovery, and prepare to avoid relapse if and when they occur. This is the equivalent of the Boy Scout motto "Be Prepared." This subsection focuses on the changes necessary for a recovery that integrates sexual health and sexual relationships.

Let's consider a case example: "John," a client who subtotals 155 (out of 175) is 4.4 on the Drug and Alcohol Use scale (155 total score ÷ 35 total number of items in subscale), 110 (out of 225) is 2.4 on the Sexual Health scale (110 total score ÷ 45 total number of items in subscale) and a 95 (out of 200) is 2.3 (95 total score ÷ 40 total number of items in scale) on Sex/Drug-Linked Recovery. His total score of 360 translates to a 3 (360 total score ÷ 120 total number of items in scale) on the Assessment Level of Client Sex/Drug Link scale (see Figure 7.3). John's sexual behavior concerns are linked to the development of his alcoholism but are not as likely an immediate and urgent early treatment relapse risk. Perhaps his sexual behavior is more commonly a problem when he drinks. He may have a fairly solid sense of his boundaries when he is sober. John may benefit from a focus on how he will discuss his sexual history as an active alcoholic. He also may have a higher shame level because of his drinking sex history. Notice how the measures are used to guide treatment recommendations and early sex in recovery treatment focus.

The last step is to show the client where his overall sex/drug-linked score falls on the continuum. This rating is a translation for the overall score (120–600 points) when placed on the Assessment Level of Client Sex/Drug Link continuum on the second page of the Client Sexual Health in Recovery Assessment Outcome Form (Figure 7.3). Translating the larger number to a 0–5 number provides a more readily understood scale of sex/drug-linked relapse risk level for a wide range of clients. The number 1-2-3-4-5 or increments between give both a quantified and a visual representation of where he is in reference to fellow addicts in recovery regarding overall sex/drug-linked addiction.

Chapter 7 The Sexual Health in Recovery Assessment Feedback Session   **175**

Also show clients the professional staff perceived level of client sex/drug link score (discussed in Chapter 6). The cumulative staff perception is also a score of 0–5. Thus both scores can easily reflect discrepancy or concordance between client self report and staff perceptions and opinions about the client's level of sex/drug link. The discussion will vary depending on the level of congruency between these two measures. The first score reflects the information they provided on the assessment scale. The second measure is an accumulation of subjective impressions by a number of the staff. Over time, staff will become more experienced at identifying sex/drug-linked trends and patterns; this may explain the wide discrepancy between client self report and staff perceptions related to level of sex/drug link.

Discuss Sexuality and Sex/Drug-Linked Addiction Patterns

Now the focus of the interview shifts from assessment feedback to client response and discussion. Encourage the client to discuss aspects of sexuality that are important at this time in his or her treatment. The counselor may signal the transition by saying something like, "I know this is a lot of information, and we are not going to address all of this today. But I am interested in what aspects of the assessment we discussed that seem to be on your mind right now, today, or in the last few days."

If the counselor has some experience with typical concerns at this stage of treatment (just entering, recent relapse, mid treatment assessment) as well as the treatment setting (outpatient, inpatient, residential, short-term treatment, self-help group) he or she may discuss typical concerns of previous clients with similar scores or circumstances. For instance, "I know that your husband has taken the two children to their grandmothers while you are in treatment. When you go home on passes, it will be just you and your husband. Have the two of you talked at all about what is expected or wanted sexually during these home visits? Based on the feedback today, are you having any different ideas on how to approach this with your husband?"

As another example, a single 27-year-old male client with a history of combining sex and drugs may need some coaching to discuss masturbation in recovery. It may be important to reinforce attitudes about masturbation and how his solo sex activity may be an important area for relapse prevention. Laying the groundwork for such discussions can be important for establishing frank discussion of this often-silent relapse trigger.

This portion of the session should establish early client confidence in talking about sexual concerns related to recovery. The role of the counselor is to listen, provide nonjudgmental responses, and reinforce and support the client's attempts to discuss sexual matters relevant to recovery and relapse prevention. This is not the time to focus on problem solving or specific in-depth concerns. Facilitating good boundaries in this portion of the assessment will be discussed further in Chapter 8.

DISCUSS CLIENT PERCEIVED LEVEL OF SEX/DRUG-LINKED RELAPSE RISK

At this point, the counselor asks the client to rate his or her perceived level of sex/drug-linked relapse risk. There is no correct answer to this. Simply give the client the Client Sexual Health in Recovery Assessment Outcome Form (discussed in Chapter 6) and ask him or her to mark the "Client Perceived Level of Client Sex/Drug Link After Assessment Feedback" section at the bottom of the form (Figure 7.1).

This rating is valuable in establishing the client's stage of readiness for change to address sex/drug-linked risk. Less ambivalent clients may demonstrate a more candid and thoughtful response to this request. Others may respond with minimization, denial, rationalization, excuses, blame, or self-blame that sounds like contempt, criticism, or hopelessness. These defenses are common in clients who are in the precontemplation stage. The counselor will benefit from experience and knowledge of effective interactions with precontemplators. Counselors who resort to confrontation will contaminate the effectiveness of the assessment and will likely inhibit a constructive focus on targeting specific relapse prevention recommendations.

The self-rating scale is the tool to meet the client at their current stage of readiness for linking recovery with sexual health. Consider this case example: A 43-year-old recently divorced man, has rated his perceived level of sex/drug link around 1.5, which is fairly low. The assessment level total for all three subtotals is 350 which translates to just under 3 (350 total score ÷ 120 total number of items), which is midrange risk and the staff perceived level of risk is close to four, which is high. (This level of discrepancy is a more common scenario with precontemplators.) The counselor should inquire what thoughts or considerations did they include in this rating based on the assessment feedback. In other words, the counselor is interested in the client's ability to listen and consider new sexual health information with openness and curiosity. These characteristics are important to consider in planning for initial sex/drug-linked relapse risk factors.

Discuss Additional Sexual Health Services

The seven high-risk sexual concerns, discussed earlier in the chapter, will also need to be reviewed. The counselor should review each of the seven and outline which are relevant or not. The focus of the assessment is to review the client's plan for addressing these factors in conjunction with the sexual health–relapse prevention goals.

ESTABLISHING SEX/DRUG-LINKED RELAPSE PREVENTION GOALS

The last step in the assessment feedback interview is to establish the client's initial goals for addressing level of sex/drug-linked relapse. The focus here is to summarize level of sex/drug-linked relapse as low, midrange, or high risk and end the interview with an immediate plan. The Sexual Health in Recovery Relapse Prevention Plan (see Figure 7.4) is organized around the Core Four Concepts of sexual health in drug and alcohol treatment curriculum. Each of the twelve lessons of the curriculum correlate with measured levels of sexual health from the assessment. The pathway is a visual description of how the key relapse prevention skills are connected with four primary treatment core issues for sexual health in recovery.

Low-Risk Sex/Drug-Linked Relapse Risk

Depending on the treatment setting, client population, and other demographics, the percentage of men and women with low risk for sex/drug-linked relapse will vary from a small to a very large percentage of the clients completing the assessment. Counselor's feedback for clients scoring in the low range (1–2) has several important goals. The counselor will need to emphasize that sex/drug-linked relapse is but one of a wide range of relapse risk factors for early recovery. Even though sex/drug-linked addiction is not an urgent

FIGURE 7.4 Sex/Drug-Linked Recovery

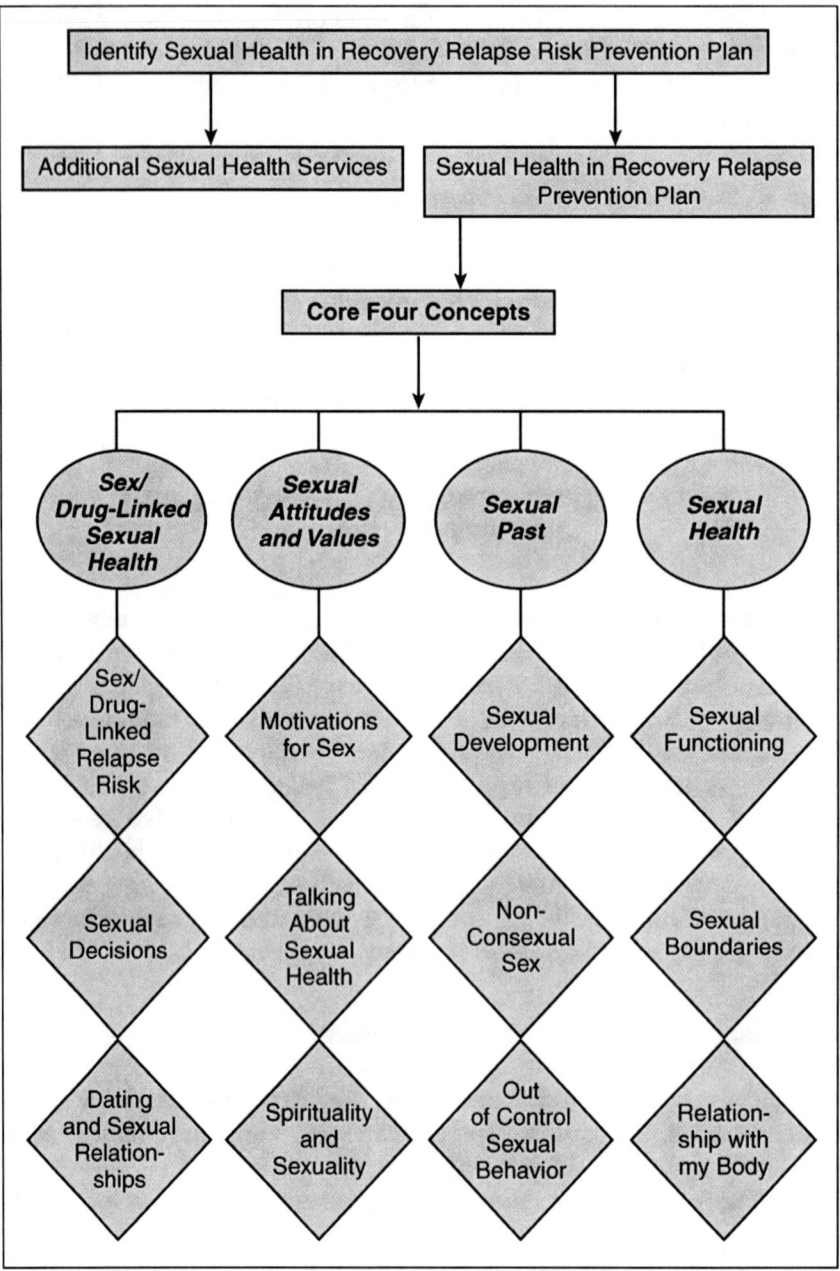

Chapter 7 The Sexual Health in Recovery Assessment Feedback Session   179

issue for this particular client, sexual health in recovery is important for everyone in recovery. The counselor may focus on sexual health strengths that the client may want to maintain as important sources of self-esteem and confidence.

> *Allisa is a 37-year-old woman in a family residential sober living program where she lives with her two preteen children. Her assessment reveals strong religious beliefs surrounding sexuality; Allisa has and maintained these values despite her alcoholism. She has been a single mother for 9 years and has focused her life primarily on raising her children. She was a weekend binge drinker, especially when her children were away for summer vacations. Her assessment showed concerns about talking about sex and some sex-negative attitudes; however, they are not linked with her drinking. Thus, Allisa shows a low level of sex/drug-linked relapse risk. Alyssa's recovery home requires all residents to participate in the sexual health in drug and alcohol curriculum. Alyssa's counselor focused on useful ways for Alyssa to use the class sessions. Alyssa revealed that she hopes to find a new partner as part of recovery. Her counselor suggests that she focus on the lessons on dating and relationships in recovery and motivations for sex in recovery. These lessons may help Alyssa talk more openly about her vision for sexual health in recovery.*

If your treatment center requires participation in the psychoeducational group sexual health curriculum, it is important that the counselor explain to clients with low sex/drug linkage how the group lessons and participation can be important to them. At Stepping Stone for example, we found that the curriculum offered clients with lower risk an alternative perspective on sexuality delinked from substance abuse. Clients with low risk need to see sexuality as an essential issue in recovery, despite their presenting of a relatively low immediate risk for relapse or not completing treatment. The counselor may also encourage the client to take the assessment again before leaving the treatment center to see if any sexual concerns have emerged during the course of treatment.

Midrange Sex/Drug-Linked Relapse Risk

Men and women with midrange scores (2–3.0) provide counselors with an interesting challenge. A midrange score is an indication that sex/drug-linked addiction patterns are an important component of overall relapse prevention and recovery. This group of men and women may benefit from the psychoeducational group curriculum not only to learn the skill sets but to clarify which sex/drug-linked risk factors they identify as a significant addiction pattern.

A common feedback from the participants at Stepping Stone was how the psychoeducational class clarified its vague sense of specific relapse risk patterns. Here are a few case examples that demonstrate this clarifying effect:

> Alex, was a 25-year-old gay male whose boyish appearance conveyed a sense of sexual immaturity. His sex/drug-linked pattern, however, was pretty well established. When he used crystal, he had sex. When he had sex, he used crystal. He was also a daily drinker and pot smoker, although he rarely combined sex with either of these substances. He had lost his job, had two DUIs in the past 3 years and was living at friends' houses to avoid homelessness.
>
> Alex scored a 2.6 on the Sexual Health in Recovery Assessment. The professional staff and Alex's perceived level of sex/drug-linked addiction was also midrange. This congruency between the assessment, staff, and client perceptions makes relapse prevention planning easier.
>
> His elevated scores centered on sex/drug-linked motivations, boundaries, sexual decisions, shame, and sex/drug-linked addiction patterns. He had a strong motivation for recovery, reported little body image, sexual functioning, out-of-control sexual behavior symptoms, and was consistent in presenting sex-positive attitudes as well as comfort in talking about sex.
>
> Alex's counselor focused on the importance of the sexual health in recovery psychoeducational group. His counselor identifies the specific lessons that will be important for Alex, so Alex can maximize his relapse prevention skill development. The counselor suggested Alex follow-up with individual counseling sessions if any classes brought up difficult or painful experiences that he did not feel comfortable discussing with his recovery network or that were not appropriate levels of discussion for the psychoeducational group.

Or consider the case of Shawna:

> Shawna is 41, married with two preteen daughters and a husband who is also in recovery (he for 15 years, Shawna for 17, until her unexpected and humiliating relapse). Shawna began taking prescription pills to cope with pain during sex. She and her husband had tried various solutions: different positions, lubrication, different times of the day, and taking a bath to relax before sex. Unfortunately, nothing worked.
>
> Then one day, Shawna turned her ankle. She decided to take some old pain medication she had left over from some dental work. When Shawna and her husband had sex that night, the pain was gone. Instead Shawna felt an usually pleasant sense of well-being. It was a feeling she had associated

with sex earlier in her marriage. She delighted in this feeling of pleasure and closeness. Her husband was happy and relieved. Shawna did not tell him about taking the pain medication. But she decided to keep the supply on hand for the next time. Gradually her addiction grew.

Shawna scored in the midrange on the sex/drug-linked assessment. She had elevated scores in sex/drug-linked motivations, sex-positive attitudes, boundaries, talking about sex, sexual functioning, body image, shame, and sex/drug-linked addiction patterns. Her relapse was precipitated by motivation to address pain during sex, an often-misunderstood sexual problem. This would be a difficult story to bring to the rooms of recovery. Shawna's sex/drug-linked relapse risk factors centered on her talking openly and honestly first within her treatment groups, then her home meeting, and sponsor. Shawna and her husband agreed that she should discuss her relapse circumstances at meetings. Disclosing her addiction to pain medication without the linked sexual motivation and circumstances would undermine the central value of living a life of "rigorous honesty." Given that her husband was part of the recovery community, this negotiation and decision between the couple was vital for reestablishing recovery. They also mutually agreed what to reveal to their children and what was to remain private about the sex/drug link.

The assessment counselor, who was experienced with facilitating couples in recovery, was able to help Shawna and her husband reveal, negotiate, and discuss all of these issues as part of Shawna's recovery.

High-Level Sex/Drug-Linked Relapse Risk

Scores in the high range (3.0–5.0) indicate a strong need for sex/drug-linked relapse prevention skill building. Without such skill building the client will likely remain at a high level of relapse risk as well as not completing treatment. These clients also have greater risk for STIs, undiagnosed HIV infection, unintended pregnancy, termination of pregnancy, and/or unprepared parenthood. In addition, these clients may feel greater levels of shame, regret, demoralization, hopelessness, and isolation when relapse is once again paired with sexual behavior and desires. For some, sex/drug-linked relapse includes boundary violations involving sexual coercion, nonconsent, illegal activity, and risk of remaining free from incarceration.

For clients with high sex/drug linkage, the assessment results may be elevated in many of the subtotal areas, as opposed to the midlevel clients, who typically have the option of focusing on specific high-scoring areas. Elevated subtotals for men and women with high sex/drug linkage will commonly be evenly distributed throughout the entire assessment. A frequent emotional experience for clients with high sex-drug linkage during the assessment is likely relief combined with shame. The client's response may be, "I know this is true, but it is really embarrassing to see the truth." To help the client, a counselor can focus on here-and-now questions:

- "What feedback were you expecting to get after you completed the assessment?"
- "Are there questions you have about the assessment process?"

Let the client talk, and let your focus be on suspending any further opinions and recommendations until later in the meeting. Review the material on suspending judgment in Chapter 2. Avoid these common defensive and judgmental responses:

- Interrupt to give opinion or advice.
- Make disgusted sounds or disgusted facial expressions because you think what the client said is immoral.
- Make confrontational, aggressive, and harsh comments.
- Look for evidence of delusions, impaired judgment, or denial and try to catch the client in self-deception.
- Assume the client is untrustworthy or cannot be responsible in their sexual behavior.
- Laugh, snicker, or express shock.
- Say sexually titillating or flirtatious comments.
- Point out what is healthy and what is unhealthy sex.
- Expect client to agree with assessment or counselor about what is healthy or unhealthy sex.
- Assume the client is a sex addict in denial.

The key experience for men and women with high sex/drug linkage at this point is to understand that their ability to talk about and honestly reflect upon their sexual lives will be central to their recovery and relapse prevention. Linking recovery with understanding sexual behavior, feelings, fantasies, interests, and history is the most important counseling message to impart during this meeting.

You may focus on selected subcategories from the assessment. The first preliminary area to highlight in the assessment for early sex/drug-linked relapse prevention is the "Readiness to Change" subtotal in the Drug and Alcohol Use section. High sex/drug-linked clients may express hesitancy in their readiness to change as a result of many previous attempts at sobriety failing due to sexual issues. They may be chronic relapsers who have been to several drug treatment programs

Chapter 7 The Sexual Health in Recovery Assessment Feedback Session

before entering a program with sex/drug-linked relapse prevention services. Their belief that they can do this, their self-efficacy, may be quite low compared to clients with less sex/drug-linked addiction patterns.

In the Sexual Health in Recovery Assessment scale, the talking about sex measure may be an important focus. The client may need to develop a strategy for with whom and under what circumstances to discuss sex/drug-linked addiction. The counselor may focus on offering the client sex/drug-linked resources within the program. Remind the client that these treatment contacts can be useful for everyone. The difference for high sex/drug-linked clients is the stakes are higher.

The Sex/Drug-Linked Recovery assessment section has several subscores that are important for men and women with high sex/drug linkage. The Positive Outcomes Expectancy subtotal reflects client confidence in linking sexuality with a better treatment outcome and hopeful attitudes about recovery. Client optimism is an important ally during the emotion-filled journey of sex and recovery.

The Sexual Decisions in Recovery subtotal provides the counselor some insight into the kinds of defenses, behavior, and attitudes that a client may exhibit when he or she is having difficulty addressing sex/drug-linked recovery issues. A counselor may help the client by offering some alternative choices rather than the typical disruptive, distancing, defensive behavior.

I used many clips from the HBO documentary "Rehab" to demonstrate how counselor feedback to clients with high sex/drug linkage is central to treatment completion. Consider this segment, which I have discussed in previous chapters:

> *Tiffany, 21-year-old resident of the Santa Cruz California Drug and Alcohol Treatment Center where the documentary was filmed, exemplifies a typical experience of clients with high sex/drug linkage. Tiffany became a heroin user at age 16. She describes having an orgasm the first time she used heroin.*
>
> *Later, as she is sitting on a curb with another resident (no treatment professionals are nearby), she disclosed a gang rape at her dealer's house that resulted in a terminated pregnancy. Still later, she is seen sobbing on the shoulder of a female resident after learning that her mother knows she has traded sex for money to buy heroin. Again, no treatment professionals are present as she makes this disclosure. That night Tiffany left the treatment program, drank, spent the night on the street, and returned the next morning.*

Had Tiffany been provided a Sexual Health in Recovery Assessment upon entering treatment, I believe there is a strong possibility she would be assessed within the high sex/drug-linked range. At the time of assessment feedback, the counselor would talk with her about how comfortable she feels talking about sexual issues, how linked she sees her sexual life with using drugs, and to what degree she is concerned that her sexual history with drugs effecting her confidence in staying sober and in recovery. Counselors can use the assessment feedback to prepare a client for the important sexual health conversations that Tiffany and others like her need to have throughout treatment to reduce their sexuality-based relapse risks.

Tiffany's story also illustrates clients' needs for people, places, and groups where they can talk openly about sex/drug-linked behavior. Coaching clients about group, family, psychoeducational, couples, individual, and medical therapy sessions for proactively addressing sexuality in recovery is an important task during the initial assessment feedback session.

The Sexual Decisions in Recovery subtotal is also useful during the initial assessment. This addresses common defenses, coping patterns, and thinking related to sex/drug-linked addiction. The counselor may suggest learning about the defenses that interfere with knowing how sexual life impacts recovery. In Tiffany's case, the counselor may select one defense that is common for Tiffany and ask her if she knows the meaning of this defense, what it behaviorally looks like, and if she can relate a time since she has been in the treatment center when she may have used this defense. This provides a practice opportunity for Tiffany to demonstrate an ability to self observe her defenses. The ability for a person in early recovery to understand different defenses is critical not only for overall recovery but also for processing sexual decisions in recovery to reduce relapse risk. The counselor could focus exclusively on building on this specific sex/drug-linked relapse prevention skill rather than risk overwhelming Tiffany with too many sex/drug relapse issues at once. Counseling approaches for high sex/drug-linked clients in the first few days and weeks of treatment are best accomplished by a more finite focus on early recovery tools that will build toward a more detailed and comprehensive sex/drug-linked relapse prevention plan over time.

CONCLUDING THE SEXUAL HEALTH IN RECOVERY FEEDBACK SESSION

Summarizing the assessment and providing the next step for sexual health relapse prevention provides much-needed closure for both client and counselor. For clients in the mid-to-high range, a structured review of the content and of what the client heard is central to the summary. Allow the client to find his or her own language for what was reviewed. Using the terms from the assessment, practicing sexual health relapse prevention talk, and experiencing the feelings associated with forming one's own statements about sex/drug-linked relapse is an ongoing sexual health recovery skill. There is no time like now to begin building this skill set.

Counselors may transition to the closure by relaying how much time remains and having clients discuss key points they are leaving with as well as what recommendations they are particularly interested in following up with.

Shawna emphasized her need to clarify boundaries with her husband about discussing her sex-motivated relapse with prescription drugs. Shawna was relieved to have a starting point for addressing what has seemed a daunting problem to even think about. She expressed appreciation for the straightforward manner her sexual life was discussed in the assessment feedback. She was looking forward to attending the psychoeducational classes for more learning about sexuality and to improve her comfort with talking about sex with people in recovery. Shawna asked about a couples session with her husband to discuss the feedback. The counselor said she would discuss this with the family therapist and have him discuss this with Shawna. Medical referrals for follow-up on her sexual pain were also provided.

The counselor emphasized Shawna's strengths in discussing her sexual history in the appointment as well as her agreeing to follow up with a key recommendation for establishing sexual health relapse prevention in her life.

To end the session, ask clients what is one sex/drug-linked concern regarding relapse risk or maintaining recovery that they think will be important for them at this stage of recovery. Do not look for a correct answer. Look for the attitude, thoughtfulness, and consideration of the question and how much their answer integrates the recent information from the assessment feedback. Welcome clients' consideration and tell them that their opinion is important.

Before ending, review the boundaries of how this information will be recorded and what will be in the client record. Discuss what was done with the original answer sheet and data collection sheet. Review any feedback the client has about the assessment process. Write summary comments in space provided on the Client Sexual Health in Recovery Assessment Outcome Form.

III

Sexual Health in Recovery Counseling Skills

8
Sex-Positive Drug and Alcohol Counseling

Counselors arriving at this place in the sexual health in recovery pathway have completed quite a process. At this phase, counseling moves to the center of the process. This stage may include combining the Sexual Health in Drug and Alcohol Treatment psychoeducational group program (Braun-Harvey, 2009) with individual counseling. The Sexual Health in Drug and Alcohol Treatment psychoeducational group is still only available in a handful of treatment centers across the country. I hope this changes over time. However, for now, the vast majority of men and women in treatment and recovery have not been provided sexual health relapse prevention skills.

The good news is many men and women in recovery participate in individual, couples, or group psychotherapy. Men and women in recovery who have co-occurring mental illness and substance abuse benefit from integrating mental health services with substance abuse treatment (McGovern, Matzkin, & Giard, 2007). When mental health professionals and drug and alcoholism counselors encourage drug- and alcohol-addicted clients to talk about sex, clients will develop skills to identify feelings and emotions associated with sex/drug-linked addiction patterns. Counselors equipped with the sexual health topic skill sets can introduce clients to coping skills that develop important relapse prevention and maintenance for sexual health in recovery. Sexual health in recovery counseling focuses primarily on increasing specific sexual health coping skills combined with increasing client coherence of the link between sexuality and their addiction to drugs and alcohol.

The remaining chapters of this book offer some basic sexual health counseling skills that can be used repeatedly with clients. Remember that these will need to be reinforced in many counseling sessions with the same client. They are not onetime clinical experiences. This chapter will demonstrate how to implement the five sex-positive counseling skills introduced in Chapter 2 that guide the structure of the counselor assessment feedback session discussed in Chapter 7. Case examples will return to characters previously introduced in earlier chapters to demonstrate sex-positive skills in action. I also include worksheets that can help counselors and clients better understand the issues under discussion.

SEX-POSITIVE COUNSELING SKILLS

Establishing sex/drug-linked prevention within individual or couples counseling will require drug and alcohol treatment professionals to develop basic skill areas. Chapter 2 introduced five sex-positive counseling skills within the framework of eight key concepts for sexual health in recovery:

1. suspending judgment
2. affirming sexual pleasure
3. understanding that sexuality is a central and basic need
4. understanding how a client's behavior might indicate an attempt to address a sexual worry or concern
5. focus on client motivation

As discussed in the previous chapter, the sexual health in recovery assessment outcome is the framework through which counselors can implement sex-positive counseling skills and establish sexual health–based relapse prevention goals. The purpose for integrating the five sex-positive counseling skills is to reduce sex/drug-linked slips or relapses, provide efficient client learning of sexual health principles for recovery, and facilitate client movement toward integrating sexuality within the lifelong process of recovery.

What goes through the mind of counselors doing sexual health relapse prevention work? What kind of judgments must be suspended? What does a counseling session look like when sexuality is being affirmed as central to being human? The case examples in this chapter will describe the counseling relationship as well as the counselor's thinking and decisions during key sexual health counseling skill moments with a client.

TRISH: SUSPENDING JUDGMENT

When we met Trish in Chapter 1, she was sending sexual pictures and provocative text messages to her addiction counselor. For Trish, playing the "slut" was familiar. After three treatment programs in 6 years, she was now in counseling with Jackie, a therapist trained in sex/drug-linked relapse prevention. Trish was enthused to complete the sexual health in recovery assessment. "I am good at sex, . . . this will be my first A since grade school." Trish was not surprised to learn of her high level of sex/drug-linked behavior when Jackie reviewed her results. Her total assessment score of 92, combined with Jackie's [Client] perceived level of risk at 3.5 and Trish's [Professional Staff] perceived level of risk at 4.5, made for a sound conclusion that addressing sexuality early and proactively with relapse prevention skills was a well-targeted treatment plan.

In creating Trish's sexual health relapse risk prevention plan, Jackie identified several additional sexual health services that would need immediate attention. Trish had not been tested for sexually transmitted infections (STIs) or HIV since her first course in addiction treatment more than 6 years ago. Several terminated pregnancies since then make it clear that Trish has been at risk for a STI. Trish's voice quieted as she recalled her continued drug and alcohol use during these pregnancies. "I hate myself for that. Can you believe that even knowing I had a baby growing inside me didn't stop me?"

Jackie is a mother of two preteens and a recovering alcoholic for 12 years. She is glad her children never saw their mother drunk, and she is proud that she did not drink while she was pregnant. However, she harbors judgments about women who continue to use when pregnant. Her training in sex/drug-linked relapse prevention counseling has been helpful; Jackie now focuses on suspending her judgmental thinking rather than expecting herself to eliminate the judgment.

As Trish speaks about using while pregnant, Jackie implements a brief exercise. She notices how long it takes for her body to react to the client disclosure. When she feels the predictable stomach clench and facial muscle tension as she listens without interrupting, she says to herself, "I, too, am a person in recovery and a woman in recovery." She is not sure why, but as soon as she implements this thought, she calms, becomes more present, and moves past the wave of judgment.

Jackie, like many counselors, had to move out of the unrealistic expectation of being "without judgment" and to try to learn how to suspend judgment. She first identified behaviors that she noticed she did have when women discussed pregnancy and their addictions. The most common behavior was interrupting or giving an opinion. She also had judgmental thoughts ranging from "That is so selfish," "That is so disgusting," even "Why am I in this profession?" to "I do not want to hear this again."

She was determined to improve her ability to listen to women discuss pregnancy while active in their addiction. At first, she practiced breathing. She would slowly place her hand on her stomach area, breath through her nose and out her mouth and just relax. She found she could do this as an alternative to interrupting the client or moving to her mind and focusing on her opinion. Many times, the client did not notice this small action. If they did notice, Jackie would be honest about just taking a few deep breaths.

Jackie was able to suspend her judgmental behavior over time by reminding herself that the client's honesty was a positive sign for the client's recovery. She understood many of the women were deeply conflicted about their history of continued use during pregnancy. For these women, this level of honesty was a sign of hope. If she could keep her judgment suspended by focusing on hope, she could live with her more pernicious judgmental thoughts, just as long as she suspended her behavior.

Upon hearing Trish's history of pregnancy and STIs, Jackie recommended additional services to address high-risk sexual concerns (one of the seven additional sexual health services discussed in Chapter 7). Jackie introduced the seven areas and briefly reviewed why they are important for high sex/drug-linked recovery. Trish noticed Jackie's calm, nonjudgmental tone as they discussed her history of terminating pregnancies, missed periods, and sexual activity without condoms. They discussed the importance of HIV and STI testing as preliminary steps in sexual health in recovery.

Trish was not prepared for the next few questions that Jackie had been trained to discuss:

Jackie: I appreciate you letting me know about your history of pregnancies in the last few years. It sounds like using a condom or other forms of birth control was not part of your sexual health in the past. What are your thoughts about preventing sexually transmitted infections or HIV infection now?

Trish: I feel so lucky, I can't believe I haven't gotten it.

Jackie: Gotten what?

Trish: AIDS, I thought for sure I would have it by now. That's why whenever I found out I was pregnant, I had an abortion every time. I didn't want my baby to get sick from me.

Jackie: So you ended your pregnancies partly because you did not want your baby to get HIV?

Trish: Yes, of course, wouldn't you?

Jackie: Have you ever told anyone this before?

Trish: No, it's just when I took the assessment and all those questions about sex and condoms made me feel like I could talk with you about this.

Jackie: I am glad you did. What do you think about getting tested for HIV and for STIs now?

Trish: I am so scared. I think my luck has run out, I think I may have it.

Jackie: Have what?

Trish: Have AIDS. I just don't think I could be that lucky. I have been such a slut.

Jackie: Do you think you are ready to know your HIV status rather than guess?

Trish: I am not sure, I just don't know if I can handle that.

Jackie: That is why, it is so important to be talking with me. Just talking with me so honestly is a good step toward recovery.

Notice that Jackie summarized how Trish's pregnancy termination behavior (despite her reactions to a woman using when pregnant) was an attempt to address another worry or concern, giving a baby HIV. This provides Jackie with another sex-positive counseling tool. She emphasized how one behavior that is easily judged (terminating a pregnancy), when put into a larger perspective, can be understood as an attempt to address a more essential client concern. In this case, for Trish, passing on HIV to a baby was a very high self-discrepant motivation. She values being a mother who does not harm her baby with HIV infection. This is a value that even in the depths of addiction was important and intrinsically motivating for Trish. Jackie is learning something about Trish today. When Trish clearly understands central cherished values, she is able to take action to implement them. Jackie used sex-positive counseling skills when pointing out this strength to Trish.

Jackie: So Trish, it appears that when you are very certain of something that is very important to you, like not passing on HIV to a baby, you were able to make clear decisive action, even in the throes of your addiction. I think this is a positive skill you can use in your recovery. When you are certain about your values, you take action. What do you think about the value of knowing for certain if you are infected or not with an STI or HIV?

Trish: Well, I. Ummm . . . I guess I get what you are saying, I am just so scared.

Jackie: I understand you are scared. I am wondering if you understand how strong and certain you can be, even when it is scary, like going to terminate a pregnancy, when you really know what is the most important to you? It just seems you can be a pretty strong woman when you are clear about what is important to you.

Trish: I hadn't thought about it that way. Well, I am still scared. Can I think about it?

Jackie: Yes, let's get back to this next session.

Jackie's work with Trish is setting the standard for sexual health in recovery by emphasizing the necessity of maintaining a baseline level of physical, sexual, and mental health as a foundation for establishing specific sex/drug-linked recovery skills based on the assessment.

Trish did test for HIV and returned to the testing site for her results. She was negative. With great relief, she went to her next session with Jackie to talk about her very good news. Jackie shared in Trish's relief. However, she was also prepared in case Trish returned with a positive result. Within a few minutes of letting the news of her negative test settle in to the counseling session, Trish began to cry. She talked about the missed opportunities for motherhood, how her addiction controlled everything and her shame for terminating pregnancies without having information about preventing mother child transmission of HIV. Jackie sat quietly with Trish, listened to her grief and deep regret. She knew Trish would have many opportunities in recovery to visit this loss. Trish's tears were an outcome of her own awareness of another dimension of living with an untreated addiction. Today was another moment of living in the process of recovery.

Later in the session, Jackie discussed other high-risk sexual concerns. What was Trish's thinking regarding preventing future unplanned pregnancies in recovery? What about other STIs? Trish agreed to make a follow-up appointment at her local community health clinic to discuss these concerns. Jackie recommended a specific doctor who had experience with women in early recovery and could recommend contraception methods compatible with early recovery.

Jackie now moved to relapse prevention planning. The assessment data prioritized the treatment plan to immediately establish sex/drug-linked relapse prevention goals. Jackie used several sex-positive counseling approaches. First, she affirmed sexual pleasure as part of recovery. Trish was a person whose sexuality is central to her life. Trish's idea of early recovery was not nonsexual. Trish and Jackie talked about establishing her sexual health in recovery relapse prevention plan. Jackie talked with Trish about the boundary crossing of "sexting" a picture to a male staff member. Trish agreed it was a "stupid thing to do." Jackie said she was less interested in her judgment about her behavior but was more interested in Trish learning about sexual boundaries as a necessary skill while in drug and alcohol treatment. Jackie shared with Trish a worksheet on Sexual Boundaries in Recovery (see Figure 8.1)

Chapter 8 Sex-Positive Drug and Alcohol Counseling

FIGURE 8.1 The Sexual Boundaries in Recovery Inventory

Take a few minutes to reflect on your day. Did you experience any sexual boundary issues today? The checklist offers a few examples of sexual boundary challenges, sexual boundary crossings, and sexual boundary violations. If you experienced a boundary challenge, crossing, or violation, check your level of concern in response to this boundary issue.

Remember the sequence for resolving any sexual boundary issue is:

1. The sexual boundary issue is identified and described clearly.
2. Talk about the boundary issue with the person who was involved in the boundary challenge or crossing. Talk with a trusted helper after a boundary violation.
3. The boundary challenger, or crosser, listens and negotiates a resolution. The helper asks if your are safe, if you are hurt, and how you are feeling.

Sexual Boundary Challenges	Very Concerned	Somewhat Concerned	No Concern
Sharing the bathroom			
Interrupts when you are talking			
Talks about himself or herself without asking how your are doing			
Makes sexual jokes in response to sex/drug-linked relapse concerns			
_____			
_____			

Sexual Boundary Crossings	Very Concerned	Somewhat Concerned	No Concern
Offensive sexual comments			
Being constantly sexualized			
Sexual stories or exploits			
Intrusive sexual questions			
Gossiping about client's sex life			
_____			
_____			

(continued)

FIGURE 8.1 The Sexual Boundaries in Recovery Inventory *Continued*

Sexual Boundary Violations	Very Concerned	Somewhat Concerned	No Concern
Sex with another client			
Sex with a newcomer to AA/NA			
Sponsor wanting to have sex			
Counselor asked me for a date			
Masturbated with someone in the treatment program			
Sex that could lead to contracting HIV or another STI			
_____			
_____			

Definitions

Sexual boundary challenges: One person is very clear about his or her boundary and clearly communicates the boundary or request. The other person is given the challenge. The person listening to the request has the challenge of choosing to cooperate, respect, and honor the request. This is sexual boundary challenge.

Sexual boundary crossings: Your own sexual limits, boundaries, or personal sexual space are crossed by another person. He or she is physically closer, emotionally closer, or mentally closer than you want him or her to be. The previously established sexual boundary has been altered. When a sexual boundary has been altered without our consent, we usually have feelings and reactions.

Sexual boundary violations: These are the most severe sexual violations, and they always result in harm. Harm and pain results from the loss of control of one's boundaries. Violations of sexual intrusion can happen by breaching a physical or emotional boundary. A physical boundary is defined by our skin, body, and self. I decide how I am touched, who touches me, and where I am touched. An emotional boundary is defined by our age, role, relationship with those around us, our personal requirements for safety, and how we want to be treated.

Remember: "Boundaries bring order to our lives. As we learn to strengthen our boundaries, we gain a clearer sense of ourselves and our relationship to others. Boundaries empower us to determine how we'll be treated by others. With good boundaries, we can have the wonderful assurance that comes from knowing we can and will protect ourselves from the ignorance, meanness, and thoughtlessness of others." (Katherine, 1993, p. 17) and suggested Trish spend the next few days discussing the sexual boundary sheet with other clients, staff, counselors, or people at recovery meetings. Jackie said she would tell staff members that Trish might approach them to discuss boundaries.

FRANK: AFFIRMING SEXUAL PLEASURE

Frank, introduced in Chapter 1, decided to keep his enjoyable solo sex life to himself after scolding judgmental comments about online masturbation from his sponsor and rehab counselor. He is now in outpatient individual therapy with John after successfully completing a drug and alcohol treatment program. Frank left the program disappointed that his sexual history with drugs had barely been talked about with the treatment professionals in his program. He talked with his roommate more about sex and drugs than anyone who worked at the center. John, 45, has been married for 18 years. He has been sober since he was a patient in the Navy drug and alcohol treatment program. It was there he first experienced the lack of sex/drug-linked discussions in treatment.

He twice contracted gonorrhea as well as herpes before getting sober. He was disciplined several times for his conduct while drunk. His last drinking binge was during his deployment in South Korea. He was arrested after threatening to kill a bar owner in response to a "price dispute" over a prostitute's fee for sex. He had always been cautious about telling the sexual circumstances of his "bottoming out." He had a distaste for the judgments and looks he would get.

As a counselor, John had both personal and professional experience to support his supposition that not talking about sex with clients was a significant relapse risk. John began the session by asking Frank about his personal assessment of his sex/drug-linked behaviors. Frank talked about how he knew his sexual life was a significant issue for his recovery. Frank's history of drinking and crystal meth combined with a high frequency of sexual activity resulted in a demoralizing decline into poverty and estrangement from family and friends. Frank always had sex with someone when he used crystal. Sometimes he had sex with men; mostly with women. He was not sure what this all meant. Frank was curious about working with a counselor who could help him talk more about this part of his life without judgments and shame. He has already has plenty of his own shame and judgmental self-talk in his own mind.

Now in a sober living home, he is eager to discuss his difficulty with sobriety and sex. He told John of his treatment plan for sex/drug-linked relapse prevention: masturbation.

To Frank's relief, John did not offer predictable warnings of "too much jerking off" and the "dangers of porn."

On the assessment, Frank scored 78 overall, just on the cusp between middle and high range. Several attitudinal factors prevented his score from being higher: Frank's generally sex-positive attitudes, his willingness and comfort with talking about sex, and his readiness to discuss his sex/drug-linked relapse risk patterns. John explained to Frank that his relapse risk level was lowered because of his attitudes and confidence in wanting to discuss sex in recovery.

John: So let's talk about what all this means. It looks like the most important relapse risk areas to address have more to do with your sexual decisions, motivations, and choice to remain single without engaging in partnered sex. Your decision to not date or enter a relationship seems like one you feel good about. You talk openly about your plan for maintaining an active masturbation sexual life using online imagery as part of preventing relapse, is that right?

Frank: Absolutely. I do not want my life going down the drain anymore with sex and drugs. But I like having sex; I just have it with myself right now.

John: There are a few areas in a sexual health recovery relapse prevention plan that I thought we could go over. The reason for talking about this is to give you a plan for learning how to maintain recovery and enjoy a sexual life.

Frank: Well, everyone keeps telling me I am a sex addict because I watch porn. I just stopped talking about it with anyone. I was tired of having to take their crap.

John: What do you think people mean when they say watching porn makes you a sex addict?

Frank: That sex is like a drug to me and I am just substituting one drug for another.

John: Well that is a concern for some people in recovery, but certainly not for everyone. I find people use that term "sex addict" because most people really aren't that comfortable talking about sex, masturbation, and looking at sexual images online. So, sometimes people just quickly call it a sex addiction to make sex talk be more comfortable. People in recovery are more comfortable talking about addiction; it is what they are learning a lot about. So, it is an easy leap to make any sexual activity that may be disapproved of or not what the person thinks is okay, to be a possible sex addiction.

Frank: Mmmm, that's interesting. I hadn't thought that some people might just say that because they are uncomfortable.

John: Well, you seem like a person who is more comfortable talking about sex and recovery than wanting to avoid it. Your assessment supports that impression. But just because you are comfortable talking about sex doesn't mean everyone else is.

Frank: Yeah, that makes sense. What may be missing is a way for you to determine when you may want to consider pursuing dating or sex with partners in recovery.

At this point, John summarizes that Frank's commitment to maintaining a solo sex life in early recovery represents his attempt to address his relapse concerns centered on his history of combining drugs with partnered sex. (This models the sex-positive counseling skill of addressing how a person's current behavior is indicative of an attempt to address a sexual worry or concern.) John also emphasized that Frank's recovery seemed very important to him. Frank was trying to honor two important values: his recovery and his sexual pleasure while in recovery. John emphasized that it is important for Frank to not assume that sexuality is a contradiction to his central motivation to be in recovery. He would work with Frank to identify what aspects of sex/drug-linked relapse prevention are important for him to learn to accomplish both goals.

John: There is one area of your assessment I wanted to discuss as a starting point in sex/drug-linked relapse prevention. It has to do with practicing a recovery tool of stopping and thinking about how sexual activity may or may not be linked with previous motivations for sex that involved getting high. Masturbation can have some motivations that may be sex/drug-linked that may not be so obvious to you. If you do not see this, or learn to think about this, even though you are staying within your plan to not have sex with another person, it will not guarantee you will not trigger a sex/drug-linked relapse risk.

Frank: So, what are you telling me, that if I masturbate, I could still be putting my sobriety at risk?

John: No, not that, it is not masturbating that puts your sobriety at risk. It is not thinking about your motivations for choosing to masturbate. There were probably times when you had sex and got high for reasons that were not about because you were horny and wanted to have sex. It may have been to escape from how your life was falling apart, or because you had a terrible day, or you just couldn't take it anymore.

Frank: Yeah, I remember one time I went on a real binge, I hung out at a strip club, spent hundreds on lap dances, later that night picked up a woman at a bar and we did crystal for I don't know how long, we ended up going online to Craigslist and finding some guys who had more crystal to join us. That was right after my wife said she was leaving me. I had moved out to live in some grungy studio apartment and just didn't give a shit about anything.

John: Exactly, just like in your addiction, in recovery you will also be faced with some intense feeling or situations. It will be important that you be aware of yourself enough to know when you might be fleeing into online solo sex to avoid or escape feelings rather than face them. That pattern is a big sex/drug-linked relapse risk. I think it will be very important for you to practice understanding this pattern and how to interrupt it as a way to make your sole sex life not an easy way to repeat this pattern in recovery.

Frank: So what does that mean I have to do?

John: Well, first of all, you don't have to do anything. This is your choice to learn sex/drug-linked relapse prevention. It is very important that it be your choice to do this. No one is forcing you here.

Frank: Yeah, I know, it's just that I am not used to someone talking to me like this. It doesn't feel quite real. So many others in my treatment program and at meetings just tell me what to do, "Stop doing that online sex thing." I'm not really used to thinking that this is something I am choosing to do.

John: I understand, it will take getting used to not just being given some quick sex advice and be expected to do it.

Frank: Okay, so now what did you want to talk with me about.

Frank introduced John to his belief that men and women in recovery need to connect a current sexual situation with their level of risk for relapse. Frank emphasized that this is an essential sexual health in recovery tool for people who have a high to very high levels of sex/drug-linked addiction. They discussed the importance of taking time to think and rate the level of relapse risk before entering into sexual circumstances that may be commonly linked with drinking and drugs. John taught Frank how to use the Stopping and Thinking About Sex/Drug Situations in Recovery Worksheet (see Figure 8.2). Frank agreed to fill out the form before masturbation at least one time between now and his next session. John explained that there was no right or wrong answer for what Frank chose to do after filling out

FIGURE 8.2 Stopping and Thinking About Sex/Drug Situations in Recovery Worksheet

---

What sexual situation or behavior do I need to stop and think about?

_____
_____

Put a check mark next to each sex/drug-linked motivation in this specific sexual situation.

_____ Increase ability to sexually function. Using drugs or alcohol to sexually function.
_____ Change level of sexual interest, desire, or arousal. Using drugs or alcohol to feel interested in sex.
_____ Experience a specific sexual turn-on. Using drugs or alcohol to perform a specific sex act or an unusual or kinky sex act.
_____ Escape from negative or overwhelming feelings. Using sex to get out of a negative or overwhelming feeling and to experience sexual pleasure or excitement instead.
_____ Express feelings of love, affection, and commitment. Using drugs and alcohol to express love to a partner or to receive expressions of love from a partner.

Stop and think for a moment and then rate how often this sexual situation or behavior was linked with using drugs or drinking before recovery:

  0   1   2   3   4   5   6   7   8   9   10
Never   Always

Stop and think for a moment and then rate how likely this sexual situation or behavior will increase your risk for relapse:

  0   1   2   3   4   5   6   7   8   9   10
Not at all likely   Very likely

Stop and think for a moment and then rate how likely this sexual situation or behavior will increase your likelihood of staying sober:

  0   1   2   3   4   5   6   7   8   9   10
Not at all likely   Very likely

Read the specific sex/drug-linked situation again. Review the motivations you checked. Review the three ratings. Pause and think for a moment. Now write an answer to the question: Why am I still motivated to pursue this sexual activity?

_____
_____
_____

the form. Recovery is about thinking before acting. Sometimes, the thoughts will lead to changing your mind. Other times it will not.

John planned to use a more detailed assessment for out-of-control sexual behavior if Frank began to describe low confidence in his ability to control his urges and thoughts associated with seeking sex despite his strong interest in maintaining recovery. John looked at Frank's answers to each of the five "out-of-control sexual behavior" items from his Sexual Health in Recovery Assessment. The only statement John scored more than a three was #13 [My sexual thoughts and behaviors are causing problems in my life]. This was consistent with his self-report and his masturbation only in early recovery sex life. Frank said he gave this item a "strongly agree" in part because he was dealing with high levels of sex negativity about masturbation at treatment programs and with his early sponsorship relationships. A more accurate picture of sex/drug-linked relapse concerns in early recovery is the primary focus at first.

When a counselor provides sexual health–based relapse prevention tools, it is important to not overwhelm the client with multiple skills to learn simultaneously. Pacing one skill at a time as a component of overall recovery is essential. Sexual health in recovery is a part of overall recovery. The focus on sex/drug-linked relapse prevention needs to be proportional to assessed level of sex/drug-linked addiction pattern.

MARCUS: SEX-POSITIVE SUPERVISION

Developing confidence and comfort with sex-positive counseling will take time. Beyond practice, it will take ongoing supervisory support (group or individual) that will provide counselors opportunities to examine, question, and challenge anxiety surrounding sexuality and recovery. Supervision provides opportunities for counselor acquisition of additional sexual knowledge and has been correlated with increasing counselor comfort and willingness to initiate sexual discussions with clients (Harris & Hays, 2008). Counselors, therapists, and treatment program professionals participating in supervisory encounters to process emotions, worries, anxieties, and hesitancies with implementing sex-positive counseling skills as well as individual successes and accomplishments will lead to real change throughout the entire treatment program.

Marcus, 37-year-old African American gay man, is now 6 years in recovery and working at an inpatient drug and alcohol treatment program. When we met him in Chapter 1, he was "freaking out" because his last sex and crystal meth partner was now checking himself into the treatment program where Marcus is a counselor. Silent for 5 days and restlessly anxious, frightened, and ashamed, he knew what he had to do. He walked down the hall to his supervisor, Angela, and knocked on her door.

Angela knew she should not be alive. A 44-year-old single mother, she spent her early adult life drinking almost every day from age 15–32. She gave birth to a daughter while continuing her addiction. Her daughter lived with her grandmother on and off for most of their first 10 years. After a day that Angela calls "my suicide day," she has been clean and sober almost every day since.

Angela's stepfather was an angry violent drunk. She spent her early adolescent years watching her mother live in terror of his drunken rages. She could not remember exactly how it started, but her then 17-year-old stepbrother started coming into her room. He had pot, he had booze, and wanted to have sex. Angela was 15.

The next 17 years Angela rarely spent a day without drinking or getting high. She managed to "cut down" on her drinking during her pregnancy but started again after the birth of her daughter. Her mother was now single and free from domestic violence and alcoholism in her home, and eventually, Angela left her daughter with her.

At 32, Angela was arrested after brandishing a gun at her connection's house. She briefly thought about suicide. Instead, Angela took full advantage of the drug court program rather than extended time in prison. She wanted to reunite with her daughter and stop the madness. Now a respected drug and alcohol treatment professional, she supervises drug and alcohol counselors at a large drug treatment center not more than 30 miles from her childhood home.

What is sex-positive supervision? It is the ability to translate the same elements of sex-positive counseling within the supervisory relationship. Supervisors need to develop skills for suspending judgment, affirming the sexuality of their supervisees, as well as including supervisees' sexual life within the overall clinical and treatment oversight. Supervisors need to listen to counselors' case presentations and clinical questions with an additional perspective. Is it possible the counselor is describing an honorable attempt to address an as-of-yet unidentified sexual worry or concern for the client, the counselor, or both?

Marcus: (As the door is closing.) I have something I need to talk about, but I don't know if it is going to stay here.

Angela: What are you saying?

Marcus: Well, I want to talk about something with you that is about a client in our program, but I just don't know how private what I want to talk about is. Do you have to tell everything to Victoria (the program director) what we talk about?

Angela: It depends. I can't give you a yes or no answer to that. Is there a way you can talk with me about this and we will see if there is a problem as we go along? You look really distressed.

Marcus began to cry. Angela sat quietly until he was ready to talk. Then he told her the entire story.

Angela: Have you told anyone else this story before?

Marcus: Just my sponsor and a friend in NA.

Angela: So you have never discussed this part of your history with coworkers or in your work with clients.

Marcus: No, I couldn't imagine ever talking about how I got HIV with hardly anyone. I only put it in my fourth step because my sponsor made me do it.

Angela: The first thing we need to establish is boundaries for you and what you will disclose to anyone else at the treatment center. I am so glad you came to me.

Angela knew that the boundaries around Marcus's dual relationship with this new resident would be important to have clear. Angela had not been faced with this circumstance as a supervisor before. She told Marcus that she would have to seek out guidance from Victoria. They talked about what facts Marcus discussed that he is concerned about Victoria knowing. Then they discussed the situation some more.

Angela: What has your interaction with the patient been?

Marcus: Well, I decided to wait and see if he remembered me. So I didn't say anything about our history.

Angela: That was an excellent choice.

Marcus: Well, he seems to have no recollection of ever knowing me. I made sure I was not his primary counselor. But I have only been able to do this for a few shifts. I am not sure what to do about this.

Angela: This is why I am so glad you came to me. I can help you with that. What else has come up?

Marcus: Well, I have been having really bad dreams and almost called in sick today. Having him here has just brought up so many things. It is hard to be here.

Angela: I am glad you came to work and decided to talk with me. That was another good choice. Being alone with this would not be good for you, the client, or our program.

The remainder of the session focused on establishing boundaries on with whom and under what circumstances Marcus would discuss this. They talked about how he could discuss anything with his therapist and with Angela. He could not disclose the identity of the patient to any member of the 12-step community, including his sponsor. He would not discuss the previous history with this client with anyone at the treatment center unless this was part of a bigger plan yet to be determined.

Lastly, Angela praised Marcus for coming forward, caring about himself, his work, the patient, and the treatment program.

As soon as Marcus left the office, Angela took time to take some very long, deep breaths. She told herself that she had just gotten through a very difficult situation. She took some notes so as to not forget some key thoughts. Then, much to her surprise, she began to think about her stepbrother. She was glad her own therapy appointment was just a few days away.

She decided to call Victoria.

Supervision and the Sexual Lives of Supervisees

Surprisingly complicated sexual themes may present themselves in drug and alcohol treatment. If you are a supervisor, a key sexual health question is, "Where are the staff and professionals talking about the sexual concerns that emerge in their work? If not with me, then *with* whom? If not with me, then *why* not me?"

Marcus came to Angela because Angela had a history of demonstrating good boundaries in other, less frightening supervision disclosures. I remind therapists and counselors that working on small, everyday boundary concerns is one way to become good at maintaining boundaries when they really count. The focus of supervision is to support, guide, and contain a counseling relationship that facilitates the counselor's work in treatment for the client.

Angela balanced Marcus's immediate supportive needs with a focus on establishing boundaries that addressed both administrative and clinical agendas. By not expecting an answer to all three of these supervisory areas, Angela exhibited a self-regulation and self-discipline to create a tutorial experience that would be a model for Marcus to use in his own management of boundaries with his colleagues and his patients. Angela's evaluative focus was on what Marcus did well (assuming he has enough of his own critical self-evaluation) and used her own experience with bringing difficult issues to Victoria.

The lack of training for supervisors and administrators in understanding sex/drug-linked addiction patterns is beyond the scope of this book. Such training would combine the skills discussed in this book with the added dimension of training in sexual health supervision. It would eventually cause a cultural transition from entrenched sex-avoidant and sex-negative treatment policies and procedures to a more sex-positive perspective that supports ongoing recovery, prevents sex/drug-linked relapse, and minimizes the shame that is so common in our culture in response to sexual health conversations.

CULTURAL COMPETENCY AND SEX-POSITIVE DRUG AND ALCOHOL COUNSELING

One early criticism of my sexual health in recovery curriculum was its perceived limitations in scope and sexual health concerns; as one reviewer said, "It looks like a gay-male HIV prevention program." I was humbled by this assessment of my limitations in gender, sexual orientation, and sexual health perspectives. I started over.

I was determined to create an experience that was more than gender neutral. If sexual health in recovery was to be relevant, it must understand and reflect the differences between how men and women experience sexuality in the context of recovery. I was determined to fundamentally define sexual health in recovery to carefully and intentionally express the realities of men and women's different sexual lives both in addiction and recovery. As a sexual health–based intervention, it must also honor and respect diverse and differing strengths and priorities.

The key at Stepping Stone to move beyond programming that is primarily male based and reflects male cultural norms for drug and alcohol treatment was to first be open to thinking of sexual health relapse prevention as an intervention that in and of itself challenges male gender dominant treatment approaches for recovery. A basic gender difference among men and women is how they perceive safety in any given situation. To include sexuality in drug treatment means opening the door to evaluating a multitude of sexual safety concerns that go unaddressed in many treatment settings.

This is why sexual health in recovery includes fundamental sexual safety issues that tend to be experienced very differently by men and women. These fundamental principles help both men and women in recovery to understand their basic sexual ethics and values within the context of living in recovery.

Treatment programs can begin to address gender differences by forming program and counseling interventions that address consent/nonconsent in sexual relations; nonexploitation; protection from STIs, HIV, and unplanned pregnancy; honesty; and mutual pleasure.

To further understand gender responsiveness, imagine putting 10 women in one room and 10 men in a separate room and have them each discuss nonconsensual sex for 1 hour. The conversations, the content, the group dynamic, and the tone of the group would most likely be entirely different. This is not a judgment on either process. The observation of the difference is an important lesson in how men and women experience sexuality and sexual expression differently.

The authors of "Evaluation of a Trauma-Informed and Gender Responsive Intervention for Women in Drug Treatment" in the November 2008 Journal of Psychoactive Drugs (Covington, Burke, Keaton, & Norcott, 2008) developed a women's integrated treatment model using gender responsive and trauma informed curricula. Study participants reported improved treatment outcomes (less substance abuse– and less trauma-related symptoms). I recommend this work as essential reading for counselors who wish to understand gender informed drug and alcohol treatment for women.

HIV prevention can also benefit from gender-specific approaches. Gender-specific HIV risk reduction substance abuse treatment manuals have been developed by the National Drug Abuse Treatment Clinical Trials Network (see *Real Men Are Safe* [Calsyn, Berns, Hatch-Maillette, & Tross, 2009] and *Safer Sex Skills Building: A Manual for HIV/STD Safer Sex Skills Groups for Women in Outpatient Substance Abuse Treatment* [Tross et al., 2009]). Both of these evidence-based manuals use gender-specific group therapy to increase rates of less risky sexual behavior than standard therapy (see Song et al., 2009). The REMAS intervention was recently shown to significantly reduce rates of sex under the influence of drugs or alcohol compared with men completing standard HIV prevention programs (Calsyn et al., 2010).

The Centers for Disease Control and Prevention has designated *Safer Sex Skills Building* a "Promising Evidence Intervention" (Centers for Disease Control and Prevention, 2009). These gender-informed

HIV prevention interventions demonstrate how substance abuse treatment outcomes improve when gender-specific sexuality in recovery skill proactively sets target-specific behaviors, skills, problem-solving, and critical thinking techniques.

Sex-positive drug and alcohol counseling is strengthened when gender, racial, ethnic, religious, sexual orientation, and cultural concerns are integrated with the sex/drug-linked learning and implementation of relapse prevention tools. Most drug and alcohol counselors will experience cultural differences with their clients. As in all cross-cultural communication, it is important to first respect that a difference exists. No one benefits if we dismiss the many cultural and personal differences that sexual health integration within drug treatment will generate. I, first and foremost, discuss this intervention as a means to improve treatment and decrease risk of sex/drug-linked relapse. It is not a means of dismissing or disrespecting values and differences among treatment professionals regarding how sex should or should not be addressed in the delivery of drug and alcohol treatment. The differences in how sexuality is addressed among the wide array of drug and alcohol treatment providers replicates the panoply of sexual attitudes, values, and opinions within our larger culture.

9

Improving Counselor Confidence in Talking About Sex

Sex-positive counseling skills are fundamental for sexual health in recovery programming. However, like all skills, the "devil is in the details." That detail is confidence. Sexual health counseling requires counselor confidence in talking about sex. The counselor's language, words, tone, attitude, and ease will all help the client recognize and experience the counselor's comfort with sexual discussions.

Sex/drug-linked relapse prevention may be integrated into recovery in several ways: group therapy, family sessions, and adjunctive therapies as well as individual counseling, psychiatry, medicine, nursing, social work, case management, administration, supervision, and clinical program leadership. Sexuality may emerge as a topic in any one or more of these situations. Much like drug and alcohol treatment had to evolve to integrate HIV prevention, testing, and treatment, sexual health is an emerging skill set that will one day be seen as fundamental to standards of care in addiction treatment.

BASIC SKILLS FOR SEX-CONFIDENT COUNSELORS

I propose a basic skill set for sex-confident counselors (psychotherapists, physicians, nurses, and a wide array of additional drug and alcohol treatment professionals may also benefit). These skills will help counselors increase their sexual knowledge and comfort with sexual matters.

A recent survey of 175 clinical members of the American Association for Marriage and Family Therapists suggests that therapists' perceived sexual knowledge is a better predictor of the counselor's likelihood to engage in sexuality discussions than the professional's actual sexual knowledge (Harris & Hays, 2008). Drug and alcohol treatment professionals who perceive themselves as sexually literate and informed (or are perceived by other staff members as the "sex experts") are most likely the counselors who are overly relied on to carry the responsibility of addressing sexual issues.

I have noticed a common denominator among these professionals. They are often lone wolves who do not know other sexual health colleagues in drug and alcohol treatment. They have a gift for nonverbal intimacy and relationship attunement skills. They tend to have wonderful engaging eye contact. They express attentive gestures automatically. Some use voice tones and speech patterns that belie not an ounce of tension, fret, or hesitancy when they use sex-specific language. They have an ability to discuss sexual questions with the same ease as any other client-recovery issues. These are wonderful personal gifts that are nonetheless insufficient to fully address sex/drug-linked concerns in addiction treatment.

Sexual Knowledge

A counselor's perceived sexual knowledge versus his or her actual sexual knowledge is not always equivalent. In my trainings, I discuss how most mental health professionals are expected to be an excellent source for sexual information. Members of the public commonly assume that health care professionals should know more about sex than the general population. Unfortunately, most health care providers are from the same sexually silent or sexually negative culture as the client. The reality is that comfort with talking about sexuality is a fairly uncommon experience. It is rare to have a combination of health care provider and their client simultaneously ready, willing, and able to effectively engage in sexual health conversation.

Counselor Comfort

"Without proper training, a therapist may be perceived (by the public) as being an 'expert,' and yet know less and be more confused and secretive about sex than the client" (Harris & Hays, 2008). Knowledge alone is not enough to be competent in sexual health. Other factors such as the counselor's comfort level with sexual material, both their own and clients', will greatly influence the likelihood of counselor initiating or avoiding sexual conversations. A structured guide for basic sex counseling skills that improves counselor comfort and increasing sexual health knowledge is especially useful for improving drug and alcohol treatment. With a set of sexual health counseling skills that can be practiced with current clients and under the guidance of a competent supervisor,

I believe many drug and alcohol counselors can become increasingly comfortable and willing to effectively address sex/drug-linked relapse risk. This on-the-job training was the approach at Stepping Stone. A specialist in facilitating the psychoeducational curriculum received weekly supervision and additional training on sexuality at conferences, reading sex research, consultation, and discussion. Staff received numerous in-services, case consultation, language acquisition development, and feedback from supervisors and trainers. The entire drug and alcohol treatment facility was committed to becoming a space of comfort for addressing sexuality. To accomplish this, we needed to develop a staff that became less and less anxious in the presence of clients' ambivalence, shame, and tension surrounding their life of combining drugs, alcohol, and sexual behavior. Just "staying sober one day at a time" is not sufficient recovery skills for the subset of clients whose sex and substance use mutually triggers risk for relapse.

Overcoming Counselor Anxiety

Harris and Hays (2008) propose that counselors avoid sexual discussions to relieve their anxiety about addressing client sexuality. This avoidance can be either conscious or unconscious and can be linked with patterns similar to a phobic reaction. The counselor may feel uneasy, a sense of dread, and an onset of anxiety. In a more intense situation, the counselor may experience body reactions like stomachache, perspiration, sweaty palms, or perhaps a sudden tearfulness or anger. Unfortunately, drug and alcohol treatment providers have few places to acknowledge or address these confusing and embarrassing reactions. Just as addicts in recovery may not be aware of their sex/drug connection, the sex-phobic drug and alcohol counselor may avoid sex talk as a personal, as well as professional relief from the tension and panic induced by client sexual health discussions.

Chapter 3 addressed the precontemplative and contemplative counselor. The remainder of this book is for counselors at the preparation and action stage of change. I will propose a fundamental set of sexual health counseling skills to substitute for automatic undesired responses. These substitute behaviors are the essential aspect of the action stage of change. Prochaska, Norcross, and DiClemente (1994) describe countering as a powerful process to work against returning to old avoidant patterns among active changers. I believe detailed counseling skills that circumvent counselor avoidance of sexual health concerns in recovery is essential and fundamental for sexual health recovery counseling.

COUNSELOR READINESS

Recent articles advocating for sexual health in drug and alcohol counseling have drawn attention to the absence of sex education and training, in particular, the "counselor competencies required for helping clients understand the sex/drug connection. When counselors are not routinely trained to address sexual issues in addictions treatment, counselors may avoid sexual discussions altogether" (Haynes, Calsyn, & Tross, 2008, p. 9). The authors propose counselors obtain the necessary skills in discussing sex through training and clinical supervision. "Counselors will benefit from learning interventions that are skill-based, gender specific and ongoing" (Haynes et al., 2008, p. 9).

Sexual health counselor training and skill development must be stage dependent. The counselor's stage of readiness to integrate sex/drug-linked relapse prevention must be well coordinated with both the content and process. I have intentionally delayed describing specific sexual health counseling relapse prevention techniques until now to avoid premature movement to action. Counselors need to respect the process of ambivalence, making space for contemplation.

The sexual health in recovery pathway model places counselor's readiness as the first step in sexual health in recovery. Counselor's readiness increases levels of counselor's confidence in sexual health behaviors, attitudes, and feelings. Confidence develops from counselor's comfort with sex and sexual discussions. Without increasing levels of comfort, sexual health counselors will not expand and develop within drug and alcohol treatment.

In *The Handbook of Clinical Sexuality for Mental Health Professionals*, Stephen Levine, observes:

> For most of the 20th century, sexuality was seen as a vital component of personality development, mental health, and mental distress. During the last 25 years, the extent of sexual problems has been even better defined, and their negative consequences have been better appreciated. Mental health professionals' interest in these matters has been thwarted by new biological paradigms for understanding the course and treatments of mental conditions, the emphasis on short-term psychotherapy, the constriction of insurance support for non-pharmacological interventions, the political conservatism of government funding sources, and the policy to consider sexual problems inconsequential. As a result of these five forces, the average well-trained mental health professional has had

limited educational exposure to clinical sexuality. The professional is neither comfortable dealing with sexual problems, skillful in asking relevant questions, nor able to efficiently provide a relevant focused treatment. (Levine, Risen, & Althof, 2003, pp. xiv–xv)

Because of the high percentage of counselors who are in recovery from their own addiction, it is equally important to consider counselor attitudes and approaches to addressing sexual issues in their recovery. It is highly likely that most recovering counselors are involved in some form of their own counseling, therapy, and/or recovery fellowship. Counselors will also need to assess and prepare their current recovery and therapy support system as they begin to employ sexual positive counseling approaches in their work. It is likely that many of the professional and self-help men and women in your support circle may have equally avoidant drug or alcohol counselors, therapists, sponsors, or psychiatrists. Counselors who take responsibility for including sex/drug-linked materials in their work and who respect this process of professional and personal change will be ready to learn and implement basic sexual health in recovery counseling skills.

COUNSELING SKILLS FOR BEGINNING SEXUAL HEALTH IN RECOVERY

Here, I will discuss two counseling practice skills that can be learned on the job. The first is to disrupt the avoidant patterns in discussing sexuality. The second is to practice simple anxiety management skills *while in session with the client* to reduce counselor anxiety and model nonanxious clinical responses in the presence of clients. This combination of stopping avoidance and managing anxiety will increase counselors' affect regulation and will improve listening, focusing, and staying clinically attentive with the client.

DISRUPTING AVOIDANT PATTERNS

Counselors and therapists working with men and women in recovery will often avoid the topic of sex through six sex avoidant verbal or nonverbal behaviors: silence, silliness, shame, shyness, suppression, and superstition.

Silence

- "I saw him wink at her in group, it looked like a come-on. I decided not to say anything."
- "She opened her satchel and I just happened to see a condom inside. I didn't want her to know what I saw, so I just didn't say anything."
- "I knew that the upcoming pass over the weekend would be the first time he would be most likely being seeing his boyfriend alone for over 3 weeks. I wanted to bring up any concerns he had about being sexual, especially being sexual without being high, I waited for him to bring it up, he was focused on other things, so we just never got to it. I hope he does okay."
- "She told me she met this most amazing guy at her home meeting last week, she can't stop thinking about him. I didn't want to come across judgmental, but I didn't feel confident of what to say, so I just let her do the talking."

Counselor silence can take many forms. The common denominator is the counselor resolving lack of confidence, worry, and uncertainty about addressing a sex/drug-linked relapse risk by choosing (often in the immediate moment) to remain silent. This retreat from interaction is often seen as preferable to risking an intervention that will lead to defensiveness, awkwardness, or conflict with the client. The silence is not often noted by the counselor as a significant issue in the clinical work because of the typical professional culture of limiting sexual conversations to specific topics within their training. The counselor may feel embarrassed or strange in speaking about the sexual matter. Silence may be a means of emotion regulation for the counselor.

It is for clients as well. Augusten Burroughs (2004), in *Dry: A Memoir*, writes about his 90-day sobriety share at an Alcoholics Anonymous (AA) meeting:

> I'm amazed by how nervous I am, how dry my throat suddenly is. Even though I make a living talking in front of people, presenting advertising campaigns to CEOs, I'm terrified and speechless. My hands are almost dripping with sweat. I can't think of how to begin, what to say. My mind is filled with two-ply facial tissues. Yet, my mouth somehow switches to autopilot and words come out of me, like involuntary farts. I talk about how it was when I was drunk. I begin with the Faberge egg exhibit, then being forced into rehab by my boss. I talk about rehab, and then coming back into my life, sober. *And I'm obsessed with a handsome, hairy-armed crack addict from my group therapy*, I don't say. (p. 160)

Burroughs (2004) effectively distills his discomfort and complications when addressing sexual conflicts and concerns within his recovery. He chose silence at the meeting. This is the common self-editing of a sex/drug-linked recovery share. The ongoing conflict in discussing sex in recovery is an amalgamation of competing priorities between personal honesty, privacy, secrecy, and sexual disclosure decorum and talking about sex/drug-linked addiction patterns.

Silliness

Humor, jokes, innuendo, smirks, smiles, and laughter are all counselor responses to sexual issues among clients or fellow professionals. Humor is a wonderful coping mechanism for tension, including sexual tension. In drug and alcohol counseling, sexual humor may be the release valve for the unspoken sexual issues in recovery. Take the time for a week to tune in to the sexual humor that passes between clients and staff at your treatment program. They are all around. Take notice.

At Stepping Stone, everyone became invested in decreasing the use of sexual humor as an avoidance of more straightforward sex talk. Counselors and staff began to understand how the clients mirrored the sex humor defenses so common among the staff. A significant contribution to developing a more sex-positive treatment environment was to reduce sexual humor. This relieved sexual anxiety, tension, discomfort, and shame among clients and staff. Managing anxiety with sexual humor interferes with sex/drug-linked relapse prevention discussions because it models silliness as the primary entrée into sex/drug-linked relapse prevention discussions.

Shame

Counselors may find it difficult to admit engaging in shaming behavior with clients. A counselor's facial expression, action, or inaction can communicate shame. An interesting contradiction may exist among drug and alcohol counseling when it comes to shame and sex. In their response to certain client sexual behaviors or attitudes counselors may present a disgusted face or may experience internal feelings of disgust and think that it may be an important reaction to have the client experience. This may be because the counselor believes that the client needs to sense disapproval about a particular sexual issue to discourage him (through shaming) from engaging in a dangerous sex/drug-linked relapse pattern.

Counselors unprepared for an unexpected sexual discussion may suddenly feel disgust, anger, contempt, or rage. Some may have an impulse to say or do something immediately to display their disgust; others may attempt to suppress their feelings (I will get to this response when I discuss suppression).

When a counselor internally feels disgust stemming from a sexual image or story relayed by the client, the counselor will need to have a place to express or discuss this reaction. Without a suitable outlet, the counselor may not be able to rid himself of this uncomfortable feeling. This accumulation of unexpressed antipathy and averse feelings can contribute to a growing experience of sex negativity within the individual and the treatment center. When counselors have a space to process, acknowledge, and understand their responses, they increase their empathy for not only their own sex negative feelings but also for their clients own disgust for their most shameful sex/drug-linked addiction experiences.

Research has identified positive consequences for subjects who express their disgust. Subjects who processed their disgust both verbally and emotionally found themselves less bothered by a similar situation the next time. When subjects were prevented from expressing disgust they reported frequent disgusting thoughts and feelings that found their way into alternative situations. The researchers believe the suppression of the facial muscles engaged in disgust is a more significant contributor to this leakage than a cognitive constraint of verbalization of disgust (Grob, 2009).

The unprepared counselor is much more likely to have an unexpected moment of revulsion or disgust, surrounding a specific sexual disclosure by a client. The client may, in turn, feel shamed by the counselor over this particular sexual behavior. This is why it is so vital for counselors to have supervision, training, and education to experience these feelings away from clients. The good news is when these feelings have been processed in a useful manner, counselors will likely no longer be bothered by the sexual situation or image that previously triggered this most unpleasant and intrusive of feelings.

Shyness

Counselors who feel insecure, self-conscious, or nervous may present as shy in sexual conversations. The counselor may blush, shake, begin to have more shallow breathing, and feel speechless. The counselor may hesitate to say or do anything in response to the client's sexual conversation. Drug and alcohol counselors are more likely to feel shy when they're not sure how to act and when they're uncertain about what may happen, how the client will react to the counselor response, or how the client may perceive the counselor's response.

When counselor's shyness is visible to the client, the clinical focus may move from the client's sexual concern and shift to counselor's feelings. "Oh, that's okay, I didn't mean to embarrass you." The client may just change the subject or get a small satisfaction out of seeing the counselor fidget. This shift, deflection, or refocusing of attention on the counselor's feelings could discourage the client from continuing to explore matters of sex and recovery.

Suppression

Most drug and alcohol treatment programs suppress sex/drug-linked addiction discussions within group, self-help, or individual counseling sessions. Sexual talk, sexual thinking, sexual memories, sexual behavior, or sexual desires are typically excluded from treatment. This pattern of intentionally and consciously avoiding sex is a suppression approach to counselor anxiety. This suppression is often founded on the notion that moving attention toward sex and sexuality, especially in early recovery, will direct important resources away from successful treatment and abstinence. A secondary gain is to get rid of the intolerable anxiety sex talk can produce in some counselors.

Suppression of client sex/drug-linked concerns is not exclusively motivated by counselor anxiety. There may be times when the counselor unwittingly colludes with the client's own motivations for suppression. Clients may worry about rejecting responses by the counselor; this can lead to a high-anxiety state for many clients. They may manage high anxiety through suppression defenses. When the client manages her anxiety through suppression, it will in turn reinforce the *counselor's* suppression of sex talk motivated by her lack of confidence and self-efficacy in sexual conversations.

In everyday life, individuals may use inhibitory processing strategies (suppression) to regulate awareness of sexual thoughts and memories that cause negative emotions. Unfortunately, for some drug and alcohol treatment centers, suppression of sex is the staple for sex/drug-linked relapse approaches. Clients are directed to just not think about anxiety-producing sexual concerns and instead, get on with the process of recovery. When clients do not exhibit enough self-regulation skills to suppress sexual thought, impulses, or discussions, they may become extremely worried about negative or rejecting responses from their counselor.

Augusten Burroughs (2004) describes this client bind in another of his stories of recovery from *Dry: A Memoir*. Augusten is talking with his close friend in recovery, Hayden, about his crush on Foster, the hairy-armed hunk in his group therapy.

> "It's Foster, I say. Oh, God. You didn't sleep with him?" I exhale, blow smoke into the room. "No, but it was close." ". . . I think I love him." "Maybe you do." "But I'm not sure if I love him, or if I'm obsessed with him." "Have you talked to Wendy [group therapist] about this?" I look at him. "What? Are you kidding? I'd get thrown out of Group if they knew." "I think you should talk to her. I think you should be honest with her. You'll feel better." I feel so frustrated and angry. Angry with Hayden for suggesting I talk to Wendy. Angry at myself for being in this position in the first place. (p. 174)

Within a few days, Augusten has cancelled his group therapy, blown off AA meetings (with the usual rationalization of just not doing it for me anymore). He soon finds out the man he has had a crush on has been using crack and not telling anyone. He eventually has sex with him, returns to therapy and begins to lean on his group therapist for advice on his situation. Augusten asks Wendy,

> "As a general principle, should recovering alcoholics be with other recovering alcoholics? Or should we find teetotalers?" She of course says there are no hard and fast rules. And this annoys me because I want her to tell me what to do . . . Wendy crosses her legs. One of the qualities I have seen in my experience as a therapist, one of the 'traits' if you will, is that people I associate with long-term sobriety all have a sense of perspective in common. As if they can step back from their life, step back from play, and watch the performance and make judgment calls. You seem to have this quality. (pp. 242–243)

What Augusten did not have during this entire process was a specific location, group, treatment intervention, or resource designed to counteract suppression of sex talk. His story is a common outcome of the suppression of sexual issues among men and women with high sex/drug-linked relapse risk factors: A crisis leads to open discussion of sex. Too often, the solution to the counselor and client suppression of sex talk is to *create* a sexual crisis. The advantage is that in an extreme crisis, the risk of counselor rejection and judgment may be less because of the urgency of the matter. Drug and alcohol counselors may be surprised to find a deep well of empathy and concern when their client is in a sexual crisis, especially when the crisis involves sobriety. I continue to be moved by the generosity of drug and alcohol treatment professionals to overcome their automatic defenses when it is clear that they are working with a person in recovery who may be at a high risk for relapse and to address this risk the counselor may need to move beyond the usual approaches to sex in recovery.

Superstition

Most of our understanding of human sexuality has been developed in the last 40 years. In contrast, AA was founded 75 years ago at a time when sexual knowledge and information was primitive and extremely difficult to find. Sexual superstitions reign when data and facts are not available. These superstitions contribute to precontemplative resistance among drug and alcohol counselors and program leaders. They may rely upon simple either–or or yes–no categories of sex/drug-linked behaviors. "A major challenge to American thinking about sexuality requires that we stop viewing sexuality in simplistic terms of male or female, black or white, gay or straight, marital or nonmarital, or normal or abnormal" (Barthalow & Weis, 1998, pp. 297–298). Counselors should instead think about how much we *do not* know about sex/drug-linked addiction. Counselor by counselor, program by program will need to go through a process of deconstructing superstitions that have been the clinical foundations for working with sexuality in early recovery.

The primary superstition is that there exists an essential and specific way in which to function sexually in recovery. I have discussed in previous chapters the simplistic guidance of limiting relationships and/or dating, especially within the first year. Relationships are assumed to be the access to sex, so too often, the guidance surrounding sex is merged within concepts such as relationship, falling in love, and dating. Masturbation is rarely discussed and proactively endorsed as an important part of getting to know yourself sexually.

Sexual health in recovery proposes a process for individuals to evaluate their own readiness for sexuality within their recovery process, with the primary evaluation criterion being based on risk for relapse. When counselors are provided with a set of tools to offer clients that can be used for individual evaluation for readiness, then it puts areas of widespread fear of future relapse founded on premature dating or falling in love in a sphere beyond a collective (but very important) advice based on personal stories of thousands of women and men in recovery.

William White (n.d.), in his interview with AA historian "Merton," discussed the roots of the idea that romantic relationships pose a serious danger on success in the first year of recovery. Merton reports "eastern branch alcoholic" Hank giving early outline material to Bill W. in what would become the *Big Book*. Hank included the topic of "sexual relapse," which is not only important for the historical first of linking sexual life with failing at sobriety but also noted for being one of the first uses of "relapse" among recovery circles (White). Sex and recovery, and sex and failing at recovery, have been on the radar since the first days men (it was pretty much exclusively men in those days) have been stepping back and looking at the process of recovery. The sexual scientific community has its own superstitions about sexuality linked with drug and alcohol addiction. I too often hear progressive sexual social scientists write off the recovery community as hopelessly lost in outdated approaches to sexuality and closed-minded responses to overtures to collaborative discourse. As usual, all of these stereotypes inhibit change and keep intractable sexual superstitions about sex and recovery unexamined beyond "what do you think?" conversations among counselors and clients.

If we are to provide counseling approaches beyond patterns of anxiety avoidance defenses and fixed world ideological views on sex and recovery, drug and alcohol counselors will need education, research, and a focus on the right to treatment of men and women with high sex/drug-linked drug dependence that integrates *their* most pressing risk for relapse at every stage of treatment and recovery.

Shame and Counselor Avoidance

Each of the six counselor sex avoidant patterns can contribute to a client experiencing shame about wanting to address sex and recovery. The outcome data from Stepping Stone suggests that shame levels among clients in treatment with high sex/drug linkage will be significantly elevated compared to non–high sex/drug-linked addicted clients. Sexual health relapse prevention counseling interactions, are hypothesized, to reduce shame levels associated with sex/drug-linked behavior overtime.

The experience of shame in the counseling session, combined with the preexisting elevated shame states of high sex/drug-linked addiction, results in a double shame client experience. This mechanism restrains clients from revealing painful and unacceptable concerns related to sex and sobriety. The key here is to have the counseling relationship a place for clients to reveal their shame about sex/drug-linked addiction patterns. Shame creates a wall of isolation from others. To experience shame is to feel not just alone but a relational absence and void from key people, family, or community. Sexual concerns avoided by drug and alcohol treatment providers will magnify the unseen (and almost universally unassessed) high sex/drug-linked shame clients bring to treatment.

ANXIETY MANAGEMENT SKILLS

A key trait of experts in sexual health in recovery is their ability to address sexuality with a common perspective. They can step back from their own feelings, values, ideas, stereotypes, and sex phobic reactions and engage in a process of sexual health communication motivated by reducing and preventing sex/drug-linked relapse.

The three sexual health anxiety management counselor skills to monitor and focus in sex/drug-linked relapse sessions are:

- verbal inquiries,
- affective reactions, and
- clinical judgments

Verbal Inquiries

The Sexual Health in Recovery Assessment and review (covered in Chapters 6 and 7) are opportunities to practice verbal inquiries in a structured format. Once the relationship moves from assessment and treatment planning, therapists may experience a different level of discomfort in addressing sex/drug-linked recovery. Now, the focus shifts from a more guided system to an integration of sexual health in recovery within the overall drug and alcohol counseling. It is now time for counselors to interrupt what may be long-standing patterns of sex avoidance. The good news is that the verbal inquiry skills are applicable in all counseling settings and are not exclusively relevant to sex/drug-linked relapse prevention.

Counselor Self-Assessment
The first skill is to have a mental rating system for your anxiety or tension about addressing sex with clients. Much like an anxiety-scaling technique for clients, counselors will benefit from taking time to anticipate their level of tension in meeting with a specific client and their level of confidence or anxiety.

Have a copy of The Drug and Alcohol Counselor Comfort and Willingness to Discuss Client Sexuality questionnaire from Chapter 4 handy. Take a minute to review the items on the inventory. You may do this once a week, once a month, or daily depending on your level of confidence. Look for items you do well. Ask yourself why it is that you tend to initiate a specific sexual discussion with a particular client.

Cindy, the drug counselor we met in Chapter 1 who lied to her client about her sexual satisfaction in recovery, has begun to use this scale on a weekly basis. Her supervisor, Janice, gave the scale to everyone in the counseling department to anonymously complete. She summarized the cumulative results and presented a sexual health counseling profile for the counseling team. The counseling staff had a high frequency of assessing and initiating therapeutic conversations on sexually transmitted infections, reproduction, HIV, and sexual orientation issues. Less frequent were counselor-initiated discussions on the more pleasure-focused areas of sex in recovery (sexual functioning, sexual satisfaction, relationship enhancement). Cindy liked the structure of the rating instrument and how it organized her priorities for improving her counseling initiation skills. She decided a weekly check-in would be frequent enough for a few months. She might decrease check-in frequency once she increased her confidence in predicting with good accuracy how her answers would look before filling out the form.

Supervision Preparation
Supervisor discussions of specific counselor patterns regarding client sexual disclosures can help minimize anxiety. First, you are not doing this alone. Having a trusted mentor, supervisor, or colleague to support this form of self-assessment is essential to the preparation for change process. Cindy's client, Sabrina, is successfully treating her generalized anxiety disorder and has been clean and sober for more than 10 months. As she was leaving her last session, Sabrina alluded to a "cute" man in her apartment complex. Cindy was determined to be prepared to follow-up this out the door comment with discussion about attractions, dating, and sexuality. In reviewing her responses to the comfort and willingness scale, Cindy noticed she still does not experience herself as very confident in encouraging clients to explore their own sexual issues. She was reminded in supervision that it was her client who brought up the attraction. Cindy was determined to interrupt her pattern of avoiding taking the lead on sex/drug-linked recovery themes. She was tired of having the "caught-off-guard" moment of tension and surprise that she felt each time a client brought up sexuality in the session.

She decided to begin the session by responding to Sabrina's expression of attraction for the man in her apartment complex. Cindy did not want to begin with the focus on the risk part of this feeling. She had learned in her sexual health training to listen to the client's positive, enjoyable feelings of attraction or desire before focusing on the more complex recovery aspects of attraction.

Personal Sexual Health Recovery Success
Cindy remembered how it felt to have her first sober sexual stirrings in her marriage. She recalled how much it meant for her to have a therapist who advocated for her development of a sober sexual relationship with herself as part of becoming sexual with her husband. One session in particular, the therapist spent time discussing what it was like for Cindy to be talking about her unfamiliarity with her sexual arousal and desires with her husband in the therapy. It was so meaningful to have both her therapist and husband just listen. Cindy's therapist was very skilled at asking for Cindy to "be more specific" when she was vague. This was one of those days when Cindy appreciated her commitment to her couple's therapy and to being honest with her supervisor about discussing sex with clients.

Cindy benefits from another anxiety management tool. She is remembering moments in her own recovery when her sex/drug-linked recovery concerns were listened to. She was allowed to articulate her fears about whether her sexual desires would trigger urges to use, that she might not feel sexy or desirable when she was sober. Talking about these issues had been an important part of the beginning of healing for her. Perhaps, the same would be true for Sabrina.

Clarify Vague Sexual Language
Cindy added one more sexual health counseling skill to her plan. She would encourage Sabrina to use specific words and details to describe her feelings or thoughts. Cindy did not want to avoid any of her anxiety by letting Sabrina use vague language.

An important sexual health counseling practice is to clarify clients' reliance on pronouns that stand in the place of specific sexual names, sexual anatomy, sexual thoughts, sexual feelings, and sexual aids or objects. In daily life, we may more commonly say for example:

- "We did it last night." (What does "it" mean?)
- "It was great, I liked it a lot."
- "I would never do that." (What does "that" refer to?)
- "That's sick."

Rarely does someone say:

- "I had oral sex with my girlfriend last night."
- "I enjoyed sex with my partner, particularly because he was really listening to me guide his actions for stimulating my clitoris."

Social customs, privacy, and various boundary concerns create a need for vague language when discussing sexual satisfaction and pleasure.

In counseling, however, this custom can be a barrier to addressing sex/drug-linked relapse. In therapy, the sexual details may be essential for correctly identifying a relapse issue. Counselors will increase confidence and comfort in discussing clients' sex/drug-linked relapse by encouraging clients to use specific sexual terms.

A conversation between Cindy and her client Sabrina elucidates how a counselor intervenes to address this particularly common sexual language anxiety avoidance tactic.

Cindy: I was about thinking about what you said when you ended the last session.

Sabrina: What was that?

Cindy: Well, when you were walking out the door, you said someone was cute.

Sabrina: Oh, that, yeah, well it was just something I said. (Note the use of "it.")

Cindy: What do you mean by "it was just something I said"?

Sabrina: Well, you know, I just wanted you to know I'm not dead.

Cindy: What does "not dead" mean? (Again, note how Sabrina is using a vague metaphor to attempt to discuss her sexual feelings.)

Sabrina: Well, that I saw this guy and for the first time I thought about what it would be like to go on a date.

Cindy: And "what it would be like" means you were thinking about it or having a feeling? (Cindy is asking Sabrina to take responsibility for describing her experience with enough specifics and details to not require Cindy to guess or imagine what Sabrina experienced.)

Sabrina: Oh, come on, are you going to be just like my sponsor and get all in my face about dating in the first year of recovery?

Cindy: No, that is not what I am asking about. I am interested in what you are wanting to say now with me. When you had this idea of a date, did you have a thought or a feeling that you wanted to share with me? (Cindy did not fall for this deflection defense to get Cindy to doubt herself. This territory of Sabrina had already been addressed in therapy. Cindy corrects Sabrina's projection and returns to the question that Sabrina attempted to deflect from.)

Sabrina: Actually, I just wanted you to know that I liked feeling hot for a guy. I was afraid if I felt attraction for a guy, I would just have this instant feeling of wanting to use and I would not be able to control it. I just felt so proud of myself that I could feel an attraction and not go all crazy. I didn't think anyone would think this is okay to feel so soon in my recovery. (Even though Sabrina used another vague pronoun when she said "I would not be able to control *it*," Cindy did not go further. It was time for her to reinforce Sabrina for taking responsibility for her sexual self-expression and for being specific about her personal sex/drug-linked relapse concern. When a client like Sabrina is finally able to articulate a clear sexual health in recovery statement, the counselor needs to let the client rest and experience the feelings of sharing a sexual health detail in the counseling session. There will be plenty of time to address the sex/drug-linked relapse skill set during the session. For now, take just a moment to let the client feel proud and confident of articulating her concern without prematurely moving to action.)

Sabrina: Okay, I am so glad you could make it clear to me what you wanted to share. I want to make sure when we discuss your sexual feelings or experiences in recovery that I know what you are saying and that I understand what you want me to know. That is why I kept asking you to be clear. I just wanted to give you a chance to be specific and clear about what you were saying. Now, we can talk about your sex/drug-linked relapse concern of feeling really attracted to someone.

When requesting more specific language from a client, it is important that the counselor does not give a list of possible answers. If a client says, "It felt good," the counselor's response should not be, "Do you mean the sex felt good or you felt good that he liked how you looked?" It can be a knee-jerk response for counselors to provide a multiple-choice selection to clients who are initially unclear.

A therapist may sense the client's tension and choose to give some examples without allowing for both client and counselor to sit with the awkwardness of not knowing what to say. It is a valuable and esteem-building sexual health moment in counseling to wait, take a breath, and let the client consider what to say. Allowing clients a quiet moment to sit with their own sexual thoughts (and therapists with their personal thoughts) is a good way to model anxiety management for the client. Sitting calmly, letting the client "find the words" and express the thought is an essential sexual health in recovery tool. Clients who increase their confidence is using the language of sexual health in sufficient detail to describe a specific sex/drug-linked relapse risk will increase their confidence in exploring their sexual lives in counseling, 12-step programs, current or future relationships, and most importantly, the quiet moments of their own thoughts.

Affect Regulation

Interdisciplinary research among medical, biological, and social sciences, including clinical psychiatry, psychotherapy and social work, has caused a shift in our understanding of how humans self-regulate their emotions (Schore, 2003). The shift from an emphasis on conscious self-regulation of emotion (we can change the way we feel by changing how we think) to understanding that most moment-to-moment psychological processing that appraises and adapts meaningful situations, events, and changes in the environment involves similar brain mechanisms for implicit learning (Schore, 2003). Listening to hundreds of clients' sexual histories and stories has taught me the importance of barely perceptible nonverbal facial expressions, voice tone, body language, or choice of words as significant sexual health developmental moments. What is learned and the mechanism for this learning are understood by neurobiology to be implicit learning (Schore, 2003). This learning is a confluence of a heightened emotional moment that is rapidly communicated and processed by the brain in a manner not unlike how we learn and remember how to ride a bike. It is a learning that is not specific to language. It operates on brain functions that include emotion and feelings. Incidental learning when we are not always aware of what has been learned is understood to have significant influence in regulation of emotions.

I want to focus on a beginning sexual health–based sex/drug-linked relapse prevention counseling skill for invoking this understanding of emotion regulation in the counseling session. The language of sex is learned both verbally and nonverbally (explicit and implicit learning). We know when we feel attracted to someone is both an explicit learning (oh, when I feel this in my body that is attraction) and an implicit learning (why am I attracted to that person, in this situation at this time?). Sexologists study how sexual development in children and adolescents leads to robust sexual emotions and yearnings postpuberty. Successful self-regulation of sexual feelings is central to both sexual health and dysfunction. Sexual health in recovery counseling provides a space for clients to practice welcoming and regulating emotions connected with sexual behavior, thoughts, history, and desires.

Chapter 9 Improving Counselor Confidence in Talking About Sex

Personalizing sexual words and events based on the client's and counselor's use of "I" statements is the sexual health counseling skill to bring more emotion to sex talk and provide emotion regulation practice in drug and alcohol sex/drug-linked relapse prevention.

Sexual health drug and alcohol counselors will move clients toward a more affective experience by asking them to rephrase or avoid *depersonalizing language* when discussing sexual issues. Depersonalizing language distances the client from feelings or thoughts. Depersonalizing language occurs when the client shifts from first person to second or third person when speaking about emotions or specific sexual details, actions, or interests. The client will organize sentences around words like "it," "you," "someone," "they," and other pronouns that move the focus of the sentence from the client to less specific generalizations or vague references. This depersonalizing defense is an effective emotion regulator. It may also be an implicitly learned language pattern (like riding a bike) that can be brought to self-awareness through counseling interventions that are attuned to this defense and anticipate intervening on this unconscious sexual affect regulation pattern.

Marcus, the 6-year sober HIV-positive addiction counselor is meeting with Frank, the 31-year-old crystal-methamphetamine addict looking for affirmation of his sex/drug-linked relapse prevention plan of limiting his sexual life to masturbation. Frank knows that Marcus is HIV positive. They have seen each other at a Crystal Meth Anonymous (CMA) meeting for HIV-positive men and women. Frank chose to see Marcus for counseling specifically because he knew Marcus is in recovery from crystal meth and is HIV positive.

Marcus began the session by inquiring about Frank's recent sexual health in recovery class.

Frank: Man, you just never know what is on people's minds about sex.

Marcus: Are you talking about yourself? Can you say that again and use "I," see if you notice any difference.

Frank: What? What did I say? (It is common for clients to not be present or pay attention to what they say when they use second-person generalizations. Addressing this serves the dual function of helping the client speak more specifically and be more present in the conversation.)

Marcus: You said, "you never know what is on people's minds about sex." Can you begin the sentence with "I" and see what you notice.

Frank: I had no idea about all the issues some people have about sex.

Marcus: Thanks, now did you notice anything different.

Frank: Well, not really, but I did feel a bit more like I did the night of the class just remembering what it was like to listen to everyone talk.

Marcus: Good, if I notice you not using "I" statements I will point this out to you. Speaking in the first person about issues related to sex is important. In our sessions, I want you to use language that will move you closer to describing your reactions or feelings about sex, especially sex linked with your drug addiction.

Frank: I know what you mean; you hear it all the time at meetings. They tell their stories sometimes like it was someone else it was happening to.

Marcus: Did you hear yourself? "***You*** (with emphasis) hear *it* all the time at meetings." Try this again and use "I," for example say, "I hear it all the time at meetings."

Frank: I do hear it all the time at meetings.

Marcus: Just so we both know what we are talking about, what is the "it" you hear all the time at meetings?

Frank: You know, well, I mean, well . . . let me try this. (He pauses, looks to be concentrating, Marcus waits.). I hear the guys at the meeting say "you" when they are really talking about their own story. I hadn't thought much about this until now, but it does make me wonder if they are really paying attention to what they are saying or are they just telling a story.

Marcus: That's an important observation. I encourage you to notice if this is something you do without thinking when you discuss sex with me.

Frank: Well, okay, I guess. I just wanted you to know how surprised I was by how much people opened up about sex and how many of the group members had the same reactions by their sponsors as my sponsor does when I talk with him about jacking off to online porn.

Marcus: What surprised you? (Frank said an "I" statement to describe his initial comment. When the client follows this up with a feeling word, it is a good time for the counselor to inquire about the emotion.)

Frank: Well, no one called each other a sex addict. Two guys are in recovery for sex addiction, but everyone stayed with the plan. You were right. We talked about the symptoms of out-of-control sexual behavior. They were so open. You could tell how everyone thought it was kind of cool to hear everyone just talk about sex and recovery, especially the guys in recovery for sex addiction. Guys in recovery just don't talk about that stuff. (Marcus notices Frank is not aware of how he shifted from discussing himself to more group generalizations. Because Frank did not exhibit this moment of awareness, Marcus decided to reinforce the sexual health skill one more time. This is also a check for Marcus to confirm that his own anxious feelings listening to Frank's sexual concerns is not being avoided.)

Marcus: Did you notice how you moved away from the first person again? Can you say more about how open you were, how you felt about the openness? What did you feel or think during the symptoms of out-of-control sex discussion?

Frank began to describe to Marcus how he began to tear up a bit in class. Frank felt sad that his masturbation was seen by so many as a problem, something that is wrong. When he read the sentences with the words "problematic sexual behavior" he thought about all the people who just automatically judged his online masturbation as "an addiction." He took out the word "problematic" from the form and filled it out again. He noticed he was less defensive. He began to think about how much time he spends online. He wanted to be honest with himself about this. Maybe even talk it over with Marcus. Frank felt relief when he noticed he could be less defensive and afraid of being judged by others about his online masturbation solo sex life.

"I" statements can be practiced and reinforced with clients whenever sex/drug-linked themes are the focus of counseling.

For example: "What do you do if you have a dream about having sex with your dealer? You know, like, when someone wakes up and has one of those dreams that is so real, you wake up and are amazed because you thought it had really happened."

Take a moment and count the number of second- or third-person pronouns the client used in two sentences! The counselor might respond with a general reinforcement about bringing the sexual health issue to counseling and then address the pronouns. Counselor: "I'm glad you asked about having using dreams that involve sex. I want to talk more about this, but I want you to tell me about this again and use 'I' instead of 'you' or 'someone'." The important task is to generate a more personal, emotional, relational here-and-now interaction between client and counselor. This tool can be a focal point for anxious or low-confidence counselors to practice a sexual health counseling skill with the benefit of increasing confidence and decreasing anxiety over time.

Clinical Judgments

As discussed in Chapter 2, one of the key sex-positive counseling skills is suspending judgmental thoughts and statements. This client-centered counseling skill is not only associated with successful outcomes, it is also an important drug and alcohol confidence builder for addressing client's sex/drug-linked patterns of addiction. When counselors place attention on regulating their judgments, opinions, and reactions about clients' sex/drug-linked concerns in the moment with clients, the counselor is practicing a crucial confidence building skill for addressing sex in recovery counseling.

Counselor Modeling of Suspending Judgment
A significant positive outcome of a counselors suspending judgment during emotionally stimulating sexual health conversation is modeling how suspension of judgment looks and feels. I have come to believe that the counselor's nonjudgmental action is essential for men and women in recovery to learn about their own judgments. When counselors practice not inserting their own sexual opinions and reactions as an emotional regulator for their own anxiety or tension, it liberates the sexual health relapse prevention moment to put the spotlight on the client's beliefs, attitudes, and feelings.

Stephen, who describes his early experiences of childhood nonconsensual sex with a 43-year-old man, is in drug and alcohol counseling with Cindy, a married mother of three in long-term recovery. Stephen's sex/drug-linked history reads like a David Lettermen top 10 list of reasons why it is okay to criticize someone for their sexual behavior: He is gay, attracted to younger men, HIV positive, hepatitis C infected, has never had consensual sex without being under the influence, and now experiencing his first symptoms of a progression in his HIV infection. And most importantly, Stephen wants to maintain a sexual life in recovery. His desire for an active sexual life in recovery is a source of enormous criticism, warning, and fear. Stephen is afraid to talk about this. He is well aware of the most common warnings of sex in early recovery.

Stephen knows very well the basic recovery principle of no new sexual relationships during the first year of recovery. He has discussed this issue at length with many recovering people. He has been reminded of how easy it is to be wrapped up in the newness of a sex partner and lose his focus on his early recovery. In rehab, Stephen learned that the brain response to sex and to crystal meth change neurotransmitters like dopamine and norepinephrine in a very similar manner. This similarity can create a relapse risk when a person in recovery stimulates the brain changes that amphetamine uses once provided through a new sexual relationship. The treatment program emphasized the many risks of altering dopamine levels with sex and new relationships. The relationship becomes the new brain chemistry fix to avoid learning sober-coping mechanisms for emotion regulation and processing. The altered states induced by new relationships (or even falling in love) will prohibit relying on important lifesaving sobriety skills.

Cindy has listened to Stephen discuss these various warnings among his support community. Sex/drug-linked relapse prevention asks Cindy to suspend her own criticisms, judgments, or opinions in response to Stephen's questioning this consistent message about sex and relationships in early recovery.

Suspending Criticism
Suspending judgment interferes with the most common reaction to matters of sexual health: vehement criticism. When counselors stop and regulate their immediate reactions to sexual conversations, they reduce the clients' fear of attack, derision, or moralizing.

Cindy worked closely with her supervisor to expand her capacity for suspending judgment during her conversations with Stephen. Cindy's sex/drug-linked relapse prevention plan was to have Stephen attend a complete cycle of sexual health in recovery psychoeducational group and focus on sex/drug-linked prevention skills identified in his assessment. Stephen was a high risk for sex/drug-linked relapse. Stephen's score in the Sexual Health in Recovery Assessment revealed his equally strong sex-positive attitudes, interest in maintaining good boundaries, and confidence in talking about sex. His many conversations among his support community were an indication of his interest in staying sober and maintaining sexual health.

Cindy wanted to provide sexual health relapse prevention counseling in a manner that will increase Stephen's likelihood of remaining sober. Stephen was managing plenty of opinions about relationships in early recovery. Cindy's goal was to keep the focus on Stephen's critical judgments while listening to Stephen come to terms with a plan for remaining sober and continuing to enjoy his sexuality.

Cindy decided to introduce the Suspending My Judgmental Thoughts and Behavior Worksheet (Figure 9.1) to Stephen before his learning this tool through the curriculum. She did not want to have Stephen wait that long before having this relapse prevention tool.

Cindy: I have a tool from the sex/drug-linked program you are considering to attend. I thought this one relapse prevention tool might be good to learn without having to wait for the class. It is about learning how to deal with judgments about sex in recovery, both your judgments and the judgments of others. Perhaps even the judgments you may think I have your aspirations for sex and recovery.

FIGURE 9.1 Suspending My Judgmental Thoughts and Behavior Worksheet

Suspending judgment is a vital skill for sexual health in recovery. It means learning to delay forming an opinion or judgment about a controversial sexual behavior, attitude, or thought.

Skills

- Observe the sex/drug-linked relapse risk that is on your mind.
- Describe what you notice about your thoughts and feelings when you think about this sex/drug-linked relapse risk. Notice the judgmental thoughts or reactions you have to this sex/drug-linked relapse risk.
- Suspend the judgment and notice how you feel and think when this judgment is suspended.
- Be present by staying in the moment, participating in the moment, and noticing what is happening. How is *what is happening right now* a fact or a situation that is related to sexual health in recovery and avoiding increased risk for sex/drug-linked relapse?
- Take your judgment back when you are done suspending it.

Instructions: Write the sex/drug-linked relapse risk behavior, attitude, or thought that you are preparing to discuss.

_____
_____

Make a check mark next to any of the judgmental behaviors you anticipate you may have about this sexual concern.
____ Interrupt to give opinion or advice.
____ Disgusted sounds or disgusted look on my face because I think it is immoral.
____ Make confrontational, aggressive, and harsh comments.
____ Look for evidence of delusions, impaired judgment, or denial and try to catch self-deception.
____ Feel that I cannot be trustworthy or responsible in my sexual behavior.
____ Laugh, snicker, or express shock.
____ Say sexually titillating or flirtatious comments.
____ Point out what is healthy and what is unhealthy sex.
____ Expect everyone to agree with me about what is healthy or unhealthy sex.
____ Assume I am a sex addict in denial.

(Write a thought or belief not written here.)
_____
_____
_____

Pick the judgment you are most concerned about experiencing with yourself or from others.

Write this judgment on a card or a piece of paper.

Place this judgment in a suspended place (in a book, on a hanger in your closet, on the dashboard of your car, in your medicine cabinet).

Go about your day noticing when you think about this judgment. Remind yourself you have suspended this judgment for the day. Just be present with yourself and notice what it is like to remind yourself that you have suspended this judgment for today.

When you wake up the next day, take your suspended judgment back. Remember this is a skill about suspending judgment, not discarding or changing your judgment.

Chapter 9 Improving Counselor Confidence in Talking About Sex 233

Stephen: You're right. I get judgments all the time. My own judgments are that I must be a fool to not listen to all these people. I just get so upset when I am told to just put sex on the back burner for now. So what is this tool you are talking about?

Cindy: Well, the whole point of the exercise is to learn that it is impossible for people to not have judgments about sex. We all make judgments. The recovery skill is to learn how to put those judgments on hold for a bit, so you can have a more honest and open discussion about sexuality. Let's start by having you write down a sex relapse issue that is on your mind today or recently.

Stephen: So, wait, you want me to talk about something I want to do sexually that may get all those people I talk to about sex all in my face and stuff? Is that what you mean?

Cindy: Well, I guess that is another way to say it, yes, what is on your mind about sex that you think if you talk about it, people in your support circle will react with strong opinions or criticism?

Stephen: Mmm, well, I . . . well I want to say, but it is really embarrassing. I don't talk about this with women. It is usually stuff I talk about with my friends.

Cindy: Ok, let's just practice the worksheet exercise, and you do not need to tell me right away what the subject is that you feel a bit embarrassed to talk about. On the worksheet is a list of judgmental behaviors. (Cindy goes through the list. As she did, Cindy could see a kind of softening, relaxed look in Stephen's body language and facial expression. Acknowledging the range of judgments that Stephen feared he might have about himself had a paradoxical effect of reducing his fear and embarrassment.)

Cindy had Stephen write down his predicted judgments and behavior as if he had spoke about his sexual concern. She asked him to take what he had written and put it in a safe place after the appointment. Cindy explained that this was the suspending his judgment exercise. She directed him to notice his thinking about his possible judgmental thoughts or behaviors throughout the week. When he became concerned with his possible self-criticism and defenses, he would remind himself that he put that judgment away for now. He was going to let go of that concern, wait a week, and then bring the situation back to his next appointment. In his next counseling session Stephen would decide what judgments he wanted to suspend so he could more honestly discuss his sex/drug-linked relapse risk with Cindy.

When Stephen returned the next week, he immediately asked Cindy, "What is your policy on masturbation?"

Stephen wanted to break his silence about masturbation to further his discussion of sex, relationships, and recovery. Both Cindy and Stephen increased their confidence to address important sex/drug-linked relapse concerns by acknowledging judgments and criticism as a part of sexual discussion. To expect no criticism as the only possible situation for discussing a sex/drug-linked relapse concern is unrealistic. What is a more realistic sexual health skill is the ability to suspend judgments. When men and women regulate sexual judgments and criticisms, they will develop increasing levels of self-confidence in exploring sex in recovery.

10

Sexual Health in Recovery Counseling

This final chapter integrates the four core elements of sexual health in drug and alcohol treatment that form the structure and organization for both the Sexual Health in Drug and Alcohol Treatment curriculum (Braun-Harvey, 2009) and sexual health in recovery counseling. The Core Four sexual health themes organize alcohol and drug counseling within a clinical model to address individual client sex/drug-linked relapse risk factors that is consistent with sex-positive counseling modalities.

The Core Four sexual health themes are:

1. sex/drug-linked sexual health,
2. sexual attitudes and values,
3. sexual past, and
4. sexual health

Each core theme encompasses three separate knowledge and skill areas specific to sexual health relapse prevention. Note how the Core Four themes are similar in importance and each of the specific skills within each core is related but not more important than the other.

For each core, I have provided multiple worksheets and exercises from Sexual Health in Drug and Alcohol Treatment (Braun-Harvey, 2009) that you can use with your clients as they contemplate the issues of sexual health in recovery. Most of the recovery worksheets and skill sets are based on cognitive–behavioral learning principles. These worksheets are designed for repetitive learning and multiple application. They can be completed in a counseling session with a client. Some clients may want to do much of this work in private; this is fine.

Sexual health in recovery counseling includes basic counseling knowledge and education within each of the Core Four themes. Increasing counselor confidence in discussing sexual health concerns is essential but not sufficient to effectively address sex/drug-linked relapse. Counselors must have a foundation of sexual education and information available at every stage of experience. Combining sexual knowledge specific to sex/drug-linked relapse with counselor and client comfort and willingness to assess, understand, and prevent sex/drug-linked relapse risk throughout recovery completes the picture for sexual health addiction treatment.

A large part of this book has discussed the emotional, motivational, and attitudinal issues relevant for sexual health–based drug and alcohol counseling. I deliberately left the counseling integrations of sexual health knowledge for the end. Integrating sexual health information and applying it within current drug and alcohol treatment approaches is not an easy action.

SEX/DRUG-LINKED SEXUAL HEALTH

Core 1, *sex/drug-linked sexual health,* focuses on three essential client relapse prevention skills. The first teaches clients to connect sexual situations with their level of relapse risk by developing a skill to think about sex/drug-linked motivations in anticipation of a specific sexual situation.

Sex/Drug-Linked Relapse Risk

To help clients understand their own sex/drug-linked behaviors, I recommend using the Stopping and Thinking About Sex/Drug Situations in Recovery Worksheet (see Figure 10.1). This recovery tool does not generate a correct, ideal, and predetermined client action. Sexual health in recovery is a process of teaching men and women to respect the value of thinking through, contemplating, and considering sex/drug-linked motivations within a specific sexual situation. Sexual health in recovery skill sets do not focus on preordained correct actions or advice in which a person in recovery complies.

Sexual Decisions in Recovery

The second sexual health skill addresses the stage when a client's readiness to become sober is more advanced than his readiness to address sexuality. Men and women in early recovery may be prepared to stop using drugs and drinking but lack interest in changing anything about their sexual behavior. This skill uses consciousness-raising exercises from research on the process of change. The first step in fostering intentional change (Prochaska, Norcross, & DiClemente, 1994)

FIGURE 10.1 Stopping and Thinking About Sex/Drug Situations in Recovery Worksheet

---

What sexual situation or behavior do I need to stop and think about?

_____
_____
_____

Put a check mark next to each sex/drug-linked motivation in this specific sexual situation.

_____ Increase ability to sexually function. Using drugs or alcohol to sexually function.
_____ Change level of sexual interest, desire, or arousal. Using drugs or alcohol to feel interested in sex.
_____ Experience a specific sexual turn-on. Using drugs or alcohol to perform a specific sex act or an unusual or kinky sex act.
_____ Escape from negative or overwhelming feelings. Using sex to get out of a negative or overwhelming feeling and to experience sexual pleasure or excitement instead.
_____ Express feelings of love, affection, and commitment. Using drugs and alcohol to express love to a partner or to receive expressions of love from a partner.

Stop and think for a moment and then rate how often this sexual situation or behavior was linked with using drugs or drinking before recovery:

```
  0    1    2    3    4    5    6    7    8    9    10
Never                                              Always
```

Stop and think for a moment and then rate how likely this sexual situation or behavior will increase your risk for relapse:

```
       0    1    2    3    4    5    6    7    8    9    10
  Not at all likely                                   Very likely
```

Stop and think for a moment and then rate how likely this sexual situation or behavior will increase your likelihood of staying sober:

```
       0    1    2    3    4    5    6    7    8    9    10
  Not at all likely                                   Very likely
```

Read the specific sex/drug-linked situation again. Review the motivations you checked. Review the three ratings. Pause and think for a moment. Now write an answer to the question: Why am I still motivated to pursue this sexual activity?

_____
_____
_____

is to "become conscious of the self-defeating defenses that get in our way" (p. 89). Sexual decisions in recovery will improve when men and women understand how their defenses interfere with honest self-reflection and talking about sex/drug-linked relapse risk as integral to the recovery process.

The "Common Defenses That Interfere With Knowing How Sexual Life Impacts Recovery" (see Figure 10.2) educates and normalizes common defenses of precontemplator clients not ready for entering into the ambiguity of contemplating sexual health. Sexual health counseling understands these defenses (to prevent knowing something about oneself) as barriers to effectively address sex/drug-linked relapse. When client and counselor can articulate, describe, and explore these defenses in counseling it strengthens client consciousness level for sex/drug-linked relapse risk.

The recovery tool Sexual Behavior Consciousness Raising Self-Assessment (see Figure 10.3) inculcates a pattern of pausing to honestly self-reflect on the connection between sexual health consciousness raising and sex/drug-linked relapse risk. The repetition of this tool supports learning sexual health relapse prevention skills through a process of change rather than promoting a universally "correct," "acceptable," or "approved" sexual behavior.

Dating and Sexual Relationships in Recovery

The final area for Sex/Drug-Linked Sexual Health is arguably one of the most contentious and pervasive concerns surrounding sex and recovery. It seems that everyone involved in counseling men and women in recovery worries about the client's current or future sexual relationships with partners or spouses. Sexual relationships are seen as a significant threat to establishing and maintaining sobriety and abstinence in early recovery.

However, men and women must eventually face rebuilding a current relationship, developing a new one, or coming to accept their personal limitations and capacity for love and connection. Sexual health relapse prevention counseling teaches professionals to educate clients about common myths about relationships and dating in recovery and to use self-evaluation skills to counteract these myths. Clients learn that myths, distortions, and misguided information about sobriety and relationships are significant relapse risk factors.

Counselors teach clients to use the Ready for Dating and Recovery Worksheet (see Figure 10.4) to evaluate and rate their relationship skills to reduce the risk of relapse at any time in recovery. This helps clients

FIGURE 10.2 Common Defenses That Interfere With Knowing How Sexual Life Impacts Recovery

---

Minimizing: Acknowledge some level of concern about sexual life but discount this concern as not very significant or very serious.

Rationalizing: Present plausible explanations to justify, excuse, or explain sexual behavior.

Intellectualizing: Avoid painful feelings and emotional reactions, and make the sexual situation less personal by using unemotional intellectual analysis.

Blaming: Focus on events outside of one's self and focus on other people, events, or circumstances as a cause or responsibility for sexual behavior or decisions. Personal responsibility for sexual actions and choices is rejected.

Your Basic Everyday Run-of-the-Mill Denial: Insist that one's sexual decision making is not a significant concern for recovery despite a significant amount of evidence that disputes this conclusion. An ongoing effort to filter out information that might make a person consider changing his or her sexual behavior.

Hostility: Become irritated, mean, critical, angry, sullen, temperamental, or shaming toward anyone who invites you to look at your sexual behavior. The purpose for these reactions is to discourage the person from ever bringing up the subject again.

Diversion: Create a flurry of concern about other issues (like whether or not someone loves you or is attracted to you) to make sure there isn't time or ability to focus on one's sexual behavior and the effect it has on recovery. (Adapted from Anderson, 1981, pp. 11–12)

FIGURE 10.3 Sexual Behavior Consciousness Raising Self-Assessment

This is a brief self-assessment checklist. Each item is a description of a behavior. Rate yourself on the frequency that you have engaged in the behavior in the last 7 days. Choose the number that most closely reflects how frequently you have used this method of sexual behavior consciousness raising. The level of frequency of using these consciousness raising behaviors is a reflection of how ready you are to honestly evaluate your sexual choices and their effects on your sobriety.

1 = Never; 2 = Seldom; 3 = Occasionally; 4 = Often; 5 = Repeatedly

_____ I look for information related to sexual behavior in recovery and understand the sexual behavior guidelines for my treatment program.

_____ I think about the information from sexual health in recovery and used one of the recovery tools.

_____ I talk to people who have successfully changed their sexual behavior and reduced their risk for relapse.

_____ I recall information from the sexual health in recovery class and what other people in the class have said about the benefits of changing their sexual behavior.

The highest score is 20.

The higher your score is, the more ready you may be to look at your sex/drug-linked relapse risk. Generally people who are not interested in how their sexual behavior may place them at risk for relapse have defenses that interfere with honest self-reflection.

If your score is less than 13, it is recommended that you spend more time increasing your awareness and consciousness about your sexual behavior as a factor in maintaining your recovery.

If you scored more than 13, write down an activity you can focus on over the next week to increase the frequency of your consciousness raising behavior.

_____

_____

_____

_____

_____

Adapted from Prochaska et al., 1994, p. 93

FIGURE 10.4 Ready for Dating and Recovery Worksheet

	Not Ready	Getting Ready	Done
Talk about my dating history with a minimum of three people in my recovery support system.			
Talk about my interest in learning more about dating with a minimum of three people in my recovery support.			
Look for information about dating in recovery from books, magazines, Internet recovery chat rooms, therapist, and counselor.			
Talk about dating information I am learning with my recovery support system.			
Use the "Stop, Think, Inform, Listen, and Listen (STILL)" tool when feeling attractions.			
Can identify at least two defensive reactions I tend to have when I talk to my support system about dating or relationships.			
Can identify at least two behaviors or attitudes of a dating partner that would be a serious sign of not supporting my recovery.			
Can identify at least two personal information disclosures I will keep to myself until having three dates.			
Can identify at least two things I do well on dates.			
Before dating, have at least two people in my support system with whom I can talk honestly and openly with about my dating experiences.			
Can identify the two biggest mistakes I could make on the first three dates that could risk my sobriety.			
Can identify the two most important recovery tools for me to use on a date.			

concurrently integrate sex/drug-linked relapse prevention with their relationship recovery work (whether pursuing, sustaining, or choosing to leave a relationship). This sexual health relationship skill-building process can be used immediately or many years into recovery. This multidimensional application provides an alternative to common drug and alcohol treatment and recovery community focus on a one-size-fits-all boundary of 1 year of recovery as the primary relapse prevention focal point.

There is also a separate worksheet for clients who are married or in a committed relationship (see Figure 10.5).

The Stop, Think, Inform, Listen, and Listen (STILL) Sexual Health in Recovery Worksheet addresses the impulsive behavior, decisions, and actions common for men and women in early recovery (see Figure 10.6).

STILL is designed to delay impulsive actions in a relationship or sexual situation by providing a contemplation space for looking at sexual motivations that may be highly linked with drug/alcohol use. Sexual health is about considering and discussing our sexual decisions that are linked with drug and alcohol prior to taking action. This worksheet may be a valuable tool to use during a counseling session to affirm the need for stopping prior to action as a central tool for sex/drug-linked relapse prevention. Sexual health counseling will connect a client's ability to slow down sexual feelings or attractions as essential to acknowledging their specific sex/drug link.

SEXUAL ATTITUDES AND VALUES

Core 2, *sexual attitudes and values*, focuses on three essential interpersonal and intrapersonal relapse prevention skills. First, Core 2 will help counselors better understand each of their client's sexual attitudes and values. This core sexual health in recovery theme examines how counselor and client sexual attitudes and values interact to influence the efficacy of treatment. In other words, every drug treatment professional's sexual health attitudes and values will influence their sex/drug-linked relapse prevention interventions. When it comes to sex, the sexual health messenger can often (intentionally or unintentionally) kill the sexual health message.

Second, Core 2 begins by asking clients to reflect upon their motivations for sex. It then helps clients learn to talk about sexual health issues. The third component helps clients better understand the spiritual and ethical values they may hold with regard to sexuality and sexual activity.

FIGURE 10.5 Recovery in Marriage or Relationship Worksheet

	Not Ready	Getting Ready	Done
Talk about my relationship and marital history with a minimum of three people in my recovery support system.			
Talk about my interest in learning more about relationships and marriage in recovery with a minimum of three people in my support system.			
Look for information about relationships and marriage in recovery from books, magazines, Internet recovery chat rooms, therapist, and counselor.			
Talk about relationship or marriage information I am learning with my recovery support system.			
Use the "Stop, Think, Listen, and Listen (STILL)" tool when feeling attractions.			
Can identify at least two defensive reactions I tend to have when I talk to my support system about my relationship or marriage.			
Can identify at least two behaviors or attitudes of my partner or spouse that would be a serious sign of not supporting my recovery.			
Can identify at least two personal information disclosures I will keep to myself until I have a relapse prevention plan in place.			
Can identify at least two skills I do well in my relationship or marriage.			
Before addressing a significant relationship or marital issue, have at least two support people with whom I can talk honestly and openly with.			
Can identify the two biggest mistakes I could make when addressing a relationship or marital concern that could risk my sobriety.			
Can identify the two most important recovery tools for me to use in my relationship or marriage.			

FIGURE 10.6 Stop, Think, Inform, Listen, and Listen Sexual Health in Recovery Worksheet

Acting impulsively without thinking is a common pattern of behavior for men and women in early recovery. STILL is designed to delay impulsive actions in a relationship. Sexual health in recovery is the ability to slow down sexual feelings or attractions to consider the sex/drug link. Taking the time to consider the sex/drug link of a particular sexual situation is central to sexual health in recovery. STILL can be practiced over and over again. STILL is a relationship skill that can be used at any time in recovery.

There are five steps in STILL.

1. Stop
2. Think
3. Inform
4. Listen
5. Listen

Without the first step, nothing else can happen. Stop!

Knowing when to stop, take a break, or slow down is a very important tool. Only you can decide to take this step. You have to be the one to decide to stop and notice that a sexual feeling, fantasy, impulse, or plan may need to be evaluated in regard to the link with drugs/alcohol. Sexual health in recovery is taking the time to do this evaluation before taking action.

This worksheet is a guide for what to do after you stop an impulse or urge before taking action.

Think: The thinking step involves answering four questions.

1. What sexual behavior/situation am I thinking about?
2. What aspect of this sexual behavior/situation is high risk for drug/alcohol relapse?
3. What aspect of this sexual behavior/situation is low risk for drug/alcohol relapse?
4. Who in my key support circle do I want to ask to listen to me about this sexual behavior/situation?

When you can answer these four questions go to the next step:

Inform: Take your answers and inform a key trusted member of your support system. This cannot be the person with whom you are having the sexual feelings or interest about. Inform your key support person of your situation and answers to the four questions.

Listen: Have him or her listen to your answers to all four questions. The job of your support person is to first listen to your responses. He or she should listen without interruption and should concentrate on hearing your thoughts and assessment of the situation. This is the part where you are listened to.

Listen: The last step is to listen to what your key support person says after listening to you. This is your time to listen without interruption. The key to this skill is to listen. Listening does not mean agreement. Listening does not mean complying. Listening is a form of concentration with the focus on paying attention to what another person is saying. Listening is an effort to hear and take into account what your key support system is saying.

The ability to stop, think, inform, and listen will be a significant skill in improving sexual health in recovery.

Motivations for Sex in Recovery

Research suggests "motivations for engaging in sexual intercourse may be larger in number and psychologically complex in nature" (Meston & Buss, 2007, p. 477). Sexual health in recovery is a process for reevaluating and reestablishing motivations for sex, many of which may be unfamiliar or unexplored. Sexual health counseling contrasts motivations for sex within the culture of addiction and motivations for sex that support recovery and sex/drug-linked relapse prevention.

Okay, now we will do our own exercise. Stop reading this book for a minute. Think about what motivated you to want to have sex with your most recent intercourse partner. It may have been your spouse, your dating partner, or perhaps someone you do not know. Perhaps you have not had sexual intercourse for a long time. More unsettling to consider is that perhaps it may not have been consensual.

Your thoughts and feelings right now are an example of the difficult emotional and psychological terrain we all encounter when we reflect up motivations for sexual intercourse. The same research challenged previous assumptions among many sexologists and therapists when they found over 200 different motivations for sexual intercourse.

For a more comprehensive list, I recommend reading *Why Humans Have Sex?* (Meston & Buss, 2007). Among the top 25 most frequently endorsed motivations for sex between men and women in their study, 20 were the same for the men as for the women. Gender differences were reflected more when subjects reported how frequently and how important specific motivations were for pursuing sexual intercourse. The study confirms as well as challenges many common drug and alcohol counselor gender-based assumptions about why men and why women have sex. Addiction treatment professionals will benefit from learning sexual science to more effectively intervene with sex/drug-linked patterns of addiction. With over 200 different motivations for sex recovering men and women with a high level of sex/drug-linked shame will benefit from counselors normalizing client contradictory or more common and shameful sexual motivations during their untreated drug abuse.

Clients can use the I STILL Want to Have Sex in Recovery Worksheet (see Figure 10.7) to reflect upon their current motivations for sex. Counselors can refer to Lesson 4 in Sexual Health in Drug and Alcohol Treatment that outlines the top 50 motivations for sex as well as sex/drug-linked motivations for sex that are required for clients to complete this exercise (Braun-Harvey, 2009, pp. 116–122).

FIGURE 10.7 I STILL Want to Have Sex in Recovery Worksheet

There are five steps in STILL.

1. Stop
2. Think
3. Inform
4. Listen
5. Listen

This worksheet is a guide on what to do after you stop an impulse or urge, before taking action. If you are reading this worksheet instead of acting impulsively, congratulations; you chose to stop and think.

Think: The thinking step involves identifying sex/drug-linked motivations for sex- and non-sex/drug-linked motivations for sex by rating their risk for relapse.

Take out the list of the Top 50 Motivations for Sex for Either Men or Women. Take out the list of the Top 50 Sex/Drug-Linked Motivations for Sex.

Write down up to five sex/drug-linked motivations for this current potential sexual situation. Items can be from the lists or your own thoughts.

1. _____
2. _____
3. _____
4. _____
5. _____

Write down up to five nonsex/drug-linked motivations. Items can be from the lists or your own thoughts.

1. _____
2. _____
3. _____
4. _____
5. _____

(continued)

FIGURE 10.7 I STILL Want to Have Sex in Recovery Worksheet *Continued*

> Stop and think for a moment and then rate which motivation is the highest risk for relapse. Write it here.
>
> _____
>
> Stop and think for a moment and then rate which motivation is the most consistent with recovery and sobriety. Write it here.
>
> _____
>
> When you have completed this section go to the next step: Inform.
>
> **Inform:** Take your answers and inform a key trusted member of your support system. Do not talk with the person with whom you are having the sexual feelings or interest to complete this step. Inform your key support person of your sexual situation and motivations.
>
> **Listen:** Have him/her listen to your written responses that you filled out about motivations for sex. The job of your support person is to first listen to your responses. He or she should listen without interruption and concentrate on hearing your thoughts and assessment of the situation. This is the part where you are listened to.
>
> **Listen:** The last step is to listen to what your key support person says after listening to you. This is your time to listen without interruption. The key to this skill is to listen. Listening does not mean agreement. Listening does not mean complying. Listening is a form of concentration with the focus on paying attention to what another person is saying. Listening is an effort to hear and take into account what your key support person is saying.
>
> The ability to stop, think, inform, and listen will be a significant skill in improving sexual health in recovery.

Talking About Sexual Health

Drug- and alcohol-dependent clients all too often withhold discussing their sexual worries and problems because they fear their own judgment as well as judgmental responses from professional helpers, sponsors, or fellow clients. Recovering men and women increase their likelihood of staying sober when they learn simple skills for suspending their judgmental sexual attitudes and behavior. When both client and counselor are able to suspend their judgments, many of the essential sexual health in recovery relapse prevention skills will be more useful and successful.

Stephen, whom we met in Chapter 1, is a Nova Scotian gay HIV-positive man in recovery. He is having difficulty grasping this idea of suspending judgments. His counselor asks him to spend the next week obtaining as much information as he can find on what the recovery community thinks about sexually active recovering HIV-positive men. The goal is to collect various viewpoints that may contain judgments about his situation. Stephen returns the following week to discuss two prevalent judgments. He was told that some of his medical providers were perplexed by his priorities. One nurse commented, "I just don't get it how someone who has HIV and is in recovery from drug addiction would be so concerned about sex?" Stephen realized that he felt shame about discussing sexual health concerns during his medical appointments when this specific nurse was on duty. He imagined her reading his chart or talking with other nurses after the appointment. He felt shame just imagining this.

Stephen also noticed a fairly frequent judgment he has about himself: "I am damaged goods. Who will want me?" Stephen was crying as he admitted this, and he glanced up to view his counselor's face. This is the moment for Stephen's counselor to demonstrate suspension of judgment. As I discussed earlier, the suspension of judgment is more often than not an implicit nonverbal experience. The client peaks at the counselor's facial expression. At this moment, they may be less focused on words. If clients see or hear a nonverbal sound that conveys judgment, the counselor's words will be ineffective because of their perceived incongruence with the more significant nonverbal communication.

Here are a few specific counseling skills that increase suspension of judgments about client sex/drug-linked recovery:

- Voice tone: "How do I modulate my voice tone, pitch, volume, and rate of speech?"
- Facial expressions: "Am I aware of how my face looks when listening to sexual stories that may trigger (against my better wishes) judgmental thoughts?"

- Body language: "Do I track how I am sitting? Do I remain still or move about? What does my posture communicate?"
- Language: "Do I concentrate on my word choice as being a summary of the client's language, not my own? Do I ask the client about their judgments by using the words they used to describe their judgment?" For example, a client uses the word "pervert" as their judgment about enjoying anal stimulation. The counselor may say, "I would like to discuss how your interests in anal pleasure may be connected with sex/drug-relapse risk, but I first want to have you say more about, now I am going to use your word, it is not mine, 'pervert.' When you say that word what does it mean?"

Sexual health in recovery suspending judgment counseling skills and confidence in discussing sexuality in recovery is based on research and treatment approaches from Dialectical Behavioral Therapy (DBT). This is a cognitive–behavioral psychotherapy for men and women with substantial and inflexible personality patterns that lead to a wide range of emotional, relational, and behavioral problems. A key DBT psychotherapist skill is the ability to suspend judgment. Sexual health relapse prevention counseling teaches clients to use a three-step process for nonjudgmental behavior borrowed from DBT.

The Suspending My Judgmental Thoughts and Behavior Worksheet (see Figure 10.8) guides men and women to use the three-step process of observing, noticing, and staying present in the moment to identify judgmental thinking, suspend the judgment, experience some time in this suspended judgment mental frame of mind, and then reclaiming the judgment.

Spirituality and Sexuality in Recovery

Sexual health attitudes and values often reflect an uncomfortable tension between moral principles and sexual desires. Many men and women learn sexual moral principles from their religious, spiritual, or cultural traditions early in life and carry those principles into adulthood. Sexual health in recovery is about being aware of the relapse risk consequences of engaging in sexual behavior that conflicts with one's ethics and values. The Religious Institute on Sexual Morality, Justice, and Healing is a multifaith organization dedicated to advocating for *sexual* health, education, and *justice* in faith communities and

FIGURE 10.8 Suspending My Judgmental Thoughts and Behavior Worksheet

Suspending judgment is a vital skill for sexual health in recovery. It means learning to delay forming an opinion or judgment about a controversial sexual behavior, attitude, or thought.

Skills

- Observe the sex/drug-linked relapse risk that is on your mind.
- Describe what you notice about your thoughts and feelings when you think about this sex/drug-linked relapse risk. Notice the judgmental thoughts or reactions you have to this sex/drug-linked relapse risk.
- Suspend the judgment and notice how you feel and think when this judgment is suspended.
- Be present by staying in the moment, participating in the moment, and noticing what is happening. How is *what is happening right now* a fact or a situation that is related to sexual health in recovery and avoiding increased risk for sex/drug-linked relapse?
- Take your judgment back when you are done suspending it.

Instructions: Write the sex/drug-linked relapse risk behavior, attitude, or thought that you are preparing to discuss.

_____
_____

Make a check mark next to any of the judgmental behaviors you anticipate you may have about this sexual concern.

____ Interrupt to give opinion or advice.
____ Disgusted sounds or disgusted look on my face because I think it is immoral.
____ Make confrontational, aggressive, and harsh comments.
____ Look for evidence of delusions, impaired judgment, or denial and try to catch self-deception.
____ Feel that I cannot be trustworthy or responsible in my sexual behavior.
____ Laugh, snicker, or express shock.
____ Say sexually titillating or flirtatious comments.
____ Point out what is healthy and what is unhealthy sex.
____ Expect everyone to agree with me about what is healthy or unhealthy sex.
____ Assume I am a sex addict in denial.

(Write a thought or belief not written here.)
_____
_____

Pick the judgment you are most concerned about experiencing with yourself or from others.

Write this judgment on a card or a piece of paper.

Place this judgment in a suspended place (in a book, on a hanger in your closet, on the dashboard of your car, in your medicine cabinet).

Go about your day noticing when you think about this judgment. Remind yourself you have suspended this judgment for the day. Just be present with yourself and notice what it is like to remind yourself that you have suspended this judgment for today.

When you wake up the next day, take your suspended judgment back. Remember this is a skill about suspending judgment, not discarding or changing your judgment.

society. Thousands of religious leaders from over 50 religious traditions have endorsed their stirring affirmation of the spiritual nature of sexuality. It begins with:

> Sexuality is God's life-giving and life-fulfilling gift. We come from diverse religious communities to recognize sexuality as central to our humanity and as integral to our spirituality. We are speaking out against the pain, brokenness, oppression, and loss of meaning that many experience about their sexuality.
>
> Our faith traditions celebrate the goodness of creation, including our bodies and our sexuality. We sin when this sacred gift is abused or exploited. However, the great promise of our traditions is love, healing, and restored relationships.
>
> Our culture needs a sexual ethic focused on personal relationships and social justice rather than particular sexual acts. All persons have the right and responsibility to lead sexual lives that express love, justice, mutuality, commitment, consent, and pleasure. Grounded in respect for the body and for the vulnerability that intimacy brings, this ethic fosters physical, emotional, and spiritual health. (Haffner, 2010)

Six fundamental principles of sexual health in recovery (adapted from international respected global agreements from the World Health Organization [WHO, 2006] and from the Religious Institute on Sexual Morality, Justice, and Healing [Haffner & Ott, 2005]) provide drug and alcohol counselors and their clients with an ethical and moral compass for creating individual maps for spiritual sexual health in recovery. They are:

1. Consent: is a "voluntary cooperation" (Wertheimer, 2003, p. 124) and the go-ahead to try and reach sexual satisfaction and intimacy with willing partners (see Wertheimer, 2003, p. 125 for more discussion). Nonconsent forces an adult or child to have a sexual experience that he or she does not want or desire.
2. Nonexploitive: Criteria for nonexploitive sex take into consideration the level of unfair advantage of one sex partner over the other, the level of consent between partners, level of harm, and level of mutual advantageousness of the sexual situation for each person (Wertheimer, 2008). Nonexploitation is a sexual health in recovery boundary to prevent harm and reaffirm that sex is always consensual.
3. Protected from sexually transmitted infections (STIs) and unintended pregnancy: All partners are capable of protecting themselves and others from an STI and unintended pregnancy.

4. Honest: All partners present information and express themselves truthfully, directly, and openly. The facts of what you say and do correspond with reality.
5. Mutually pleasurable: Each partner is interested in his or her partner's pleasure.
6. Support process of recovery: Sexual relations and activity supports treatment goals and recovery goals.

These six fundamentals of sexual health form the basis of sex/drug-linked relapse prevention and spirituality in recovery. When any one of these principles is crossed, counselors must address the level of relapse risk associated with this spiritual/sexual health–boundary crossing. These principles are basic to recovery, not only because of the sex/drug-linked relapse risk they represent, but also because they are fundamental to safe and sane sexual relations for everyone on the planet.

Sex that is consensual, nonexploitive, protected from STI and unwanted pregnancy, honest, and mutually pleasurable and that supports the process of recovery is the basis for sex/drug-linked relapse prevention. Sexual health in recovery counseling encourages clients to contemplate the linkages between their sexuality, spirituality, and recovery.

Consent is a principle of sexual health that is present in some form or definition among most cultures on the planet. (It is so essential to sexual health in recovery that it will be covered again, later, as a separate lesson within Core 3.) The exact definition of consent may be up for debate. For example, different governments have different standards for the "age of consent," the age at which a person is legally allowed to engage in sexual activity. Alan Wertheimer (2003) writes extensively on the complexities of consent and sex. He proposes a theory of consent in sexual relations that prioritizes obtaining valid consent both legally and morally. (Some drug and alcohol counselors work with individuals involved in illegal nonconsensual sexual boundary violations such as sex offenders, perpetrators of abuse or incest, voyeurs, exhibitionists, and so forth. For this discussion, I will keep the focus on men and women in recovery without specific legal allegations or convictions as part of their sexual history.) This moral permission involves two competing tensions. Every person has a right to choose with whom he or she consents to have sex. However, each person has his or her own individual responsibility to understand his or her own specific moral dimensions for agreeing to have sex with someone. This is the individual's responsibility. The tension is when the legal and moral consent is not so clear. This is a common situation in the world of drug addiction.

Sexual health counseling and education on consent will help clients make moral decisions about when to consent to sex in recovery. Counselors will need to use very clear language when discussing consent and nonconsent. Avoid common words or phrases like "she wanted it," "I had to," "he made me," "I didn't want to," "I gave in," "I got tired of saying no," and "I just got it over with."

> There is often a fine line between agreeing to have sex in order to keep a persistent partner quiet and being verbally pressured into having sex against one's will. When a women is forced to choose between having sex or ending the relationship, or is made to feel fearful, guilty, or bad about herself for saying no, or is given alcohol or drugs to lower her inhibitions and "give in," then sex moves into the realm of coercion . . . Sexual coercion and rape can and do occur between strangers. But more often than not, they take place with the context of either a potential or existing relationship. (Meston & Buss, 2009, pp. 219–220)

The key sexual health counseling skill is for clients to be clear that consent is basic to all sexual relations and a fundamental principle of sexual health in recovery. Men and women in recovery must learn not only about this fundamental principle but also link consensual sex with maintaining abstinence and recovery.

Exploitation can refer to forcing or offering sex in trade for drugs, food, and shelter to be protected from being a victim of a crime or adults having sex with drug-addicted minors. The key to exploitation is a person with a significant degree of bargaining power using his or her power to obtain sex from the person in a position of inequality. Addiction creates multiple situations of inequality that can be manipulated by either a nonaddicted person or a fellow addict. Addicts may be able to rationally justify exploitive sex. Sexual health in recovery counseling educates clients about the nature of exploitive sex. A significant sex/drug-linked relapse risk is clients being unaware or unprepared for exploitive sex within the recovery community. A goal of sex/drug-linked relapse prevention skill building is to increase client awareness and ability to see attempts to unfairly make use of somebody for sex.

Protection from HIV, STIs, and unintended pregnancy is the third fundamental for sexual health. Beyond the public and personal health issues, the spiritual–sexual health dimension involves protecting self and others from harm. A general list of this sexual health protective measure may emerge in drug and alcohol counseling at various times in recovery. This list includes the following:

- "Do I know my current health status regarding STIs, HIV, and/or pregnancy?"
- "Do I know how to access proper medical attention or treatment?"
- "Do I know how to manage lifelong sexually transmitted infections like herpes, hepatitis, or HIV?"
- "Do I know how and if I want to prevent a pregnancy?"
- "Do I use the chosen method of contraception?"
- "Do I take responsibility to prevent pregnancy and not give full responsibility for contraception to my partner?"
- "Do I seek knowledge and information about these basic sexual health issues when needed?"

Drug and alcohol counselors are not expected to be experts on medical sexual health information. Clients should have access to public health clinics, online education, and other resources for education. However, it is important that the counselor address relapse risks in recovery when these basic boundaries of health are not maintained.

Men and women in recovery with STIs have an additional relapse risk. They may experience elevated shame or embarrassment because of the infection or its symptoms. Recovery may be the first time they have proactively considered treating the symptoms. They may be dealing with a wide range of emotions associated with self-blame for obtaining an STD.

Honesty in sexual relationships is a fundamental principle. Spiritual–sexual health requires that all partners present information and express themselves truthfully. As central as honesty is to recovery, there may be specific complications inherent for men and women with high sex/drug linkage. Movement away from sexual honesty to increasing levels of deception is common when it comes to humans seeking sex (Meston & Buss, 2009). Women and men with high levels of sex/drug-linked addiction may have combined drug use with common forms of dishonesty as routine means for being sexual or being duped into sex. Thus, decreasing dishonesty is essential for sexual health, spiritual health, and the basis for sustained recovery.

Even in the best of sexual situations, some small fibs seem to be part of the picture. Embellishments are not the sexual health problem for men and women in recovery. Honesty as a sexual health fundamental is determining what kind of mischaracterization is essentially human and which a relapse risk is. Sexual health in recovery counseling provides the forum for clients to discuss this. Counselors need to listen to clients struggle with finding their balance between rigorous honesty and honest courtship or marriage.

Another honesty skill is to review previous deception strategies the client practiced to find or have sex with partners. Sex/drug-linked motivations for sex involve a high frequency of deception and dishonesty ("I want to give someone a sexually transmitted disease," "I want to break up my relationship," "I want to hurt an enemy," "I want to get back at my partner for having cheated on me," "I want to manipulate him/her into doing something for me."; Meston & Buss, 2007).

The next principle affirms that sex is pleasurable. Sex as a mutually pleasurable relationship is fundamental for sexual health. Giving pleasure and receiving pleasure has different meaning for different people. For people with sex/drug-linked addiction, sexual pleasure may be fused with drinking and/or using drugs. However, "Drugs and Alcohol are a nightmare for brain function" (Amen, 2007, p. 218). Sexual pleasure and mutual pleasure between partners is often collateral damage in sex/drug-linked relationship destruction. Men and women with high sex/drug linkage may have little experience with sexual pleasure, either giving or receiving without being under the influence of a host of substances.

What may be of particular importance for sexual health in recovery counselors to listen for is the motivation for combining sex and drugs to achieve mutual pleasure. This may be an already established sexual health goal for many recovering people. The sex/drug link is a misguided attempt to shortcut a solution to the now essential sober work of mutually pleasurable sex. Counselors may look for client cues describing drugs and alcohol functioning in the service of mutually pleasurable sex.

When clients have an opportunity to reveal and own this mutual pleasure as a motivation for combining drugs with sex, they have an important sexual health relapse prevention skill at their disposal. They can feel good about having some of the most important and common motivations for sex (the need to be "normal") delinked from their ill-conceived solution (drugs and alcohol). The good news is that they already have this sexual health, sobriety, and spirituality principles established within their vision of sexual health. The relapse prevention work for the counseling is to find alternative means for seeking mutual pleasure in sober sex. This is not the task of a drug and alcohol counselor (unless they have advanced training in sexuality or sex therapy). For the vast majority of drug and alcohol counselors, the intervention is the shame reduction process of clarifying sex/drug-linked addiction as an indication of the recovering person's high value on pleasure and pleasuring one's partner in sex.

The final principle is that a person's sexual life must support his or her recovery program. It assumes that the client will have a future sexual life in recovery. Sexual health in recovery supports each person's individual recovery as well. The process of sexual health in recovery considers and values the consequences of sexuality and sexual relations. Combining recovery with sexual health is a foundation for men and women to forge a foundation of listening to their better judgment as an integral source for sexual satisfaction and pleasure.

The Sexuality and Spirituality in Recovery Inventory (see Figure 10.9) reinforces the universality of basic sexual health boundaries as a lifelong recovery tool. Clients learn to first reflect on the six fundamental ethical and spiritual principles as the basis for relapse prevention. The inventory invites the client to reflect upon 20 deeper and larger sexual ethics and spiritual concepts shared among humanity, not limited to the life process of recovery.

SEXUAL PAST

Recovery is a process that involves looking back at life as part of going forward in sobriety. The following three sexual history elements, which are sex/drug-linked relapse prevention skill areas, may be necessary to address among many of the drug- and alcohol-dependent clients you treat. Core 3 hones the focus to looking back specifically on sexual history elements that are essential for relapse prevention within sex/drug-linked addiction.

Sexual Development

Sexual development is part of everyone's sexual story. As the first sexual health skill for this core, counselors educate clients to understand their sexual development as a combination of physical, behavioral, and physiological milestones that occur from birth to adulthood within an environment of many sexual attitudes, inhibitions, and influences. Stephanie Covington (1991), in her book *Awakening Your Sexuality*, describes current sexual feelings and actions molded and influenced by everything from our past such as family sexual training, childhood and adolescent sexual experiences, choice of partners, and sexual behavior while drinking or using drugs.

FIGURE 10.9 The Sexuality and Spirituality in Recovery Inventory

Rate yourself on each item. Each item is an opportunity to reflect and measure your current sexual behavior as it relates to the six foundations of sexual health in recovery.

First, measure how you are doing on the six fundamentals (rate yourself based on your sexual life since you last filled out this questionnaire). If this is your first time filling this out, rate yourself based on your sexual life since you became sober.

Read each item, think about each item, and take your time. Reflect on how much you agree with each statement.

FIRST REFLECT ON THE SIX FUNDAMENTAL ETHICAL AND SPIRITUAL PRINCIPLES

	Strongly Disagree	Disagree	Agree	Strongly Agree	
1. The physical act of sex has always been consensual.	1	2	3	4	Not sure
2. I have not engaged in sex with someone as a result of exploiting them (or being exploited).	1	2	3	4	Not sure
3. I have protected myself and my partners from sexually transmitted infections (and pregnancy, if desired).	1	2	3	4	Not sure
4. I have been honest with my sexual partners.	1	2	3	4	Not sure
5. I have been focused on my partner's and my own sexual pleasure.	1	2	3	4	Not sure
6. I am supporting my goals for recovery in my sexuality.	1	2	3	4	Not sure

(continued)

FIGURE 10.9 The Sexuality and Spirituality in Recovery Inventory *Continued*

WHEN I REFLECT ON MY SEXUAL ETHICS AND SPIRITUALITY TODAY					
	Strongly Disagree	Disagree	Agree	Strongly Agree	
1. The physical act of sex is not always my ultimate goal.	1	2	3	4	Not sure
2. Sex is an important component of how I express my whole being.	1	2	3	4	Not sure
3. I ask for what I need in my sexual relationships.	1	2	3	4	Not sure
4. I want to build a committed sexual relationship with someone I love.	1	2	3	4	Not sure
5. A sexual experience with my intimate partner can be a way to touch each other's souls.	1	2	3	4	Not sure
6. I like to lose myself and meld with my partner during sex as if the boundary of skin-to-skin contact is lost and a sense of timelessness exists.	1	2	3	4	Not sure
7. Sexual pleasure is a haven for me where I feel free to express myself.	1	2	3	4	Not sure
8. I find a powerful pleasure in hidden, mysterious, and suggestive erotic activity.	1	2	3	4	Not sure
9. My body's erotic nature is a virtue.	1	2	3	4	Not sure
10. I like to abandon myself to my senses during sex and give up my need to understand everything that is happening.	1	2	3	4	Not sure

(continued)

FIGURE 10.9 The Sexuality and Spirituality in Recovery Inventory *Continued*

	Strongly Disagree	Disagree	Agree	Strongly Agree	
11. Sex and sexuality can be a mystical experience.	1	2	3	4	Not sure
12. My body and the sensations my body brings me can serve as my spiritual goals.	1	2	3	4	Not sure
13. Everything I do, everything I contact, every event in my life, has spiritual significance.	1	2	3	4	Not sure
14. Sex is an opportunity to leave ordinary reality behind by entering deeply into sensation, imagination, and passion.	1	2	3	4	Not sure
15. Part of my spiritual practice is to cultivate affection and sensuality.	1	2	3	4	Not sure
16. My spirituality is partly defined by whom I love.	1	2	3	4	Not sure
17. My sexuality is something I make through my everyday experimentation with sensation, sex, and pleasure.	1	2	3	4	Not sure
18. I can use prayer and conscious contact with my Higher Power to develop my spiritual sexual life.	1	2	3	4	Not sure
19. I use my spiritual life to support me in being honest, vulnerable, and open with my sexuality.	1	2	3	4	Not sure
20. My spirituality depends on me fully embracing my sexuality.	1	2	3	4	Not sure

From *A Time to Speak: Faith Communities and Sexuality Education* (2nd ed.), by D. Haffner & K. Ott, 2005. Norwalk, CT: Religious Institute on Sexual Morality, Justice, and Healing. Retrieved May 24, 2009, from www.religiousinstute.org/pubs/TimeToSpeak_07.pdf

Men and women in recovery will increase their likelihood of staying sober when they increase their awareness about the role of drugs and alcohol in their sexual development. Sexual health drug and alcohol counseling supports clients in talking about their sexual development in relation to drug and alcohol use to reveal current patterns that increase risk for sex/drug-linked relapse. Clients, regardless of their level of sex/drug-linked relapse risk, will improve on the process of recovery with this self-knowledge.

Sex/drug-linked men and women's addiction develops parallel with key sexual developmental stages and sexual behavior milestones. This requires substance abuse counselors to integrate client drug and alcohol history with their sexual development among high to very high level of sex/drug-linked patterns of addiction. A person in recovery with a very high sex/drug-linked addiction pattern must have a language and working knowledge not only of the developmental process of addiction but also of sexual development.

Beginning in the 1970s, contemporary sex research began to look at sexual development as a combination of scripts that are written (or more often unwritten) rules for how boys and girls, men and women are to sexually behave. Sexual behavior and, therefore, sexual development is a sequential script in which everyone wants to get their lines correct. Drug and alcohol counselors will set clients at ease by normalizing this early script-learning process. Sexual health–based drug and alcohol treatment for high sex/drug-linked addiction must provide a useful sexual script as an essential narrative for relapse prevention. Without a useful script and good direction, actors must endure the shame of being onstage without a guide. Addicts in recovery may just leave the stage and go use. This is especially true for high sex/drug-linked addiction. A language and structure for linking sexual past with current relapse prevention is the essential script. Drug and alcohol counseling has many traditions incorporating a timeline approach for clients to write scripts for various aspects of their addiction. One sexual health counseling exercise is to have a client just list what they think are important sexual events, changes, or developments that are typical for any boy or girl to experience. A counselor might organize this brainstorming by asking about physical body changes, sexual acts or behaviors, falling in love, developing a meaningful love relationship, discovering our individual range of sexual attractions, and so forth.

As clients discuss their sexual development sequence, it is important to distinguish between milestones in which they had control and those in which they did not. For example, the onset and outcomes of puberty are, for the most part, not within our control. Perhaps, experiences of sexual arousal or erections may be regulated through use of drugs and alcohol. When in life did the person attempt to change, improve, decrease, increase, sustain longer, intensify, prolong, or eradicate involuntary or natural sexual experiences through taking drugs and alcohol?

What sexual developmental milestones are under our control? What sexual choices along the course of sexual development did we follow the expected script? What sexual choices went off script? For many men and women, drug use, drinking, and prescription medications became essential solutions for compromise between societal, family, cultural, religious, gender, biological, entertainment, peer group, legal, parental, and individual sexual scripts. Reviewing sexual history and visually linking these moments of drugging and drinking to balance competing or conflicting sexual scripts will be an important task for high sex/drug-linked recovering men and women.

We often come to understand the most significant sexual scripts in which we are expected to follow only when we are confronted with the reality that we will not comply with the unspoken script.

Gloria, a 56-year-old recovering alcoholic, recalls the many times during her 27 years of marriage when she intentionally drank to "get in the mood for sex" because she felt neither very attracted to her husband nor very much enjoyed him as a sexual partner. Gloria avoided a significant amount of sexual incompatibility through drinking. Now sober, she is unsure what to do about this situation. The sexual development life cycle timeline exercise created an opportunity for Gloria and her counselor to acknowledge and recognize her sex/drug-linked pattern. Rather than focus prematurely on "solving my marriage sex problem," Gloria's counselor focused on relapse prevention. Gloria will use this worksheet to explore her ambivalence about sex with her husband. She begins by distinguishing between drinking and nondrinking sexual interactions with him. Not every marital sexual experience has been while drinking. It became more sex/drug-linked over time. She considers how she will separate out this long-standing marital problem from her sobriety. This may entail the couple talking primarily about the lack of sexual history without one or both partners drinking.

It is important for Gloria to include her script that her husband never protested about her being drunk when they had sex. The shared sex/drug link in a couple's sexual life can often be overlooked when only one member of the couple is in treatment. The relapse risk prevention step is to address the *shared* responsibility for the sex/drug link. A premature focus by the counselor on specific sexual satisfaction concerns may move the couple away from understanding the family system adaptation to Gloria's alcoholism.

How might Gloria's drinking solution to address low sexual satisfaction and desire with her husband be similar to other alcohol-linked relationship conflict patterns? The couple may endure the difficulty of getting this sexual satisfaction difference out in the open if it is in the context of the several other conflicts that have been set aside by Gloria's drinking. This process of bringing to conciousness the couple's conflict avoidance sex/drug-linked script or narrative is an important sexual health in recovery skill. Couples therapy and sexuality trained drug and alcohol counselors place sex/drug-linked themes in the context of each person in the couple's history as well as relationship with drugs and alcohol in their early life sexual development.

Counselors can also use the Looking Back/Looking Forward Exercise with clients (see Figure 10.10). This tool provides a structure for clients to explore ambivalent feelings about a current sexual choice in recovery. Often the uncertainty of a sexual choice, behavior, or desire is connected with our sexual past. Clients who remember their sexual past and look at their future sexual health goals will find clarity in resolving here-and-now ambivalence surrounding a sex/drug-linked relapse risk.

Nonconsensual Sex

The two remaining sexual health counseling skills sets guide drug and alcohol treatment professionals to provide sex/drug-linked relapse prevention tools for clients to address nonconsensual sex and the high frequency of sexual abuse among people in recovery as well as direction for addressing symptoms of out-of-control sexual behavior (OCSB).

Men and women in treatment are likely to have experienced sexual abuse. Experts now recognize childhood sexual abuse as a risk factor in all forms of drug dependence (Rosellini, 2002). "At least two-thirds of patients in drug abuse treatment centers say they were physically or sexually abused as children" (Swan, 1998). Women who experience any type of sexual abuse or nonconsensual sex in childhood may be 3 times more likely than unabused girls to report drug dependence as adults (Kendler et al., 2000). Researchers from the Harvard Medical School and McLean Hospital found that repeated sexual abuse during childhood causes physical changes in the brain that can explain why abused children often develop substance abuse problems (Anderson, Teicher, Polcari, & Renshaw, 2002).

A smaller percentage of recovering men and women may have committed rape, forced nonconsensual, or exploitive sex. Nonconsensual

FIGURE 10.10 Looking Back / Looking Forward Exercise

This exercise can be used when you are thinking twice about a particular sexual behavior. Feeling undecided and uncertain about sexual choices and options is going to happen for all of us from time to time. It will happen more frequently in early recovery. This exercise is a tool to assist you in exploring your ambivalent feelings. By looking back and looking forward, sometimes we do a better job of resolving a present conflict within ourselves.

I feel uncertain and undecided about the following sexual choice, behavior, or desire.

_____
_____
_____

Looking Back

Describe a time in your sexual development before you ever used drugs or alcohol when you engaged in the sexual behavior that you are currently feeling ambivalent about.

_____
_____
_____

If you have never engaged in this behavior without using drugs or alcohol, describe what you remember about the first time you engaged in this behavior.

_____
_____
_____
_____

How did the presence of drugs help or hurt your first time with this particular sexual experience?

_____
_____
_____

(continued)

FIGURE 10.10 Looking Back / Looking Forward Exercise *Continued*

Looking Forward

Describe the choices you would like to make in recovery regarding this particular sexual behavior.

_____
_____
_____

If you have never engaged in this behavior without using drugs or alcohol, describe what you think will be the benefits of being sober during the sexual experience.

_____
_____
_____
_____

If you have never engaged in this behavior without using drugs or alcohol, describe what you think will be the fears and drawbacks of being sober during the sexual experience.

_____
_____
_____
_____

The choice I can consider making today about this sexual behavior that will increase the likelihood of staying sober is:

_____
_____
_____
_____

You can use this worksheet any time you are confronted with a difficult sexual choice. By remembering your past and looking at your hope for the future, you may get clearer about resolving your uncertainty.

sexual relations are a violation of bodily integrity and sexual self-rule and control. This leads to harmful distress and psychological injury. Some sexual abuse survivors may themselves have committed forced sexual violence or rape or use drugs to manipulate another adult or child into sex. Sobriety may lead to an increase in thinking about or remembering sexual abuse or committing nonconsensual sexual violence.

I recently presented a day-long training on sex/drug-linked relapse prevention. Several of the participants worked in a prison sex offender drug and alcohol treatment program. The counselors reported many difficulties in raising sexual health issues among their clients. One counselor discussed the difficulty for men who may have agreed to enter into a consensual same-sex relationship in prison and yet report no pre-incarceration or post-incarceration interest in same-sex attractions or orientation. Other men may be forced into sex or become a sex slave as trade for safety, drugs, or other desired privileges. The counselor was concerned that once these men leave prison, the drug and alcohol recovery community offers no confidential and relapse prevention focused places to discuss their nonconsensual or exploitive sexual activity. Several counselors at the workshop mentioned the high levels of shame experienced by these men because of their experiences while in prison. What are they to do with these experiences? How many men and women in drug and alcohol treatment have initiated or forced nonconsensual sex while high or drunk? This subject may not even be considered in treatment. How often does the omission of nonconsensual sex/drug-linked behavior contribute to treatment failure, treatment termination, or sexual behavior safety concerns in the treatment center?

Experiences of nonconsensual sex among alcoholics and addicts is so common that it is not unreasonable for substance abuse counselors to expect a history of sexual abuse among many of their clients. I hypothesize that even a greater percentage of men and women with high sex/drug-linked addiction patterns have a history of nonconsensual sex, although this has yet to be studied.

Sexual abuse is a violation of bodily integrity (with implications for body image issues that will be addressed in Core 4) and sexual self-rule and control. This leads to harmful distress and psychological injury. If clients with high sex/drug linkage are overly represented among the already disproportionate ratio of nonconsensual and sexual abuse rates among addicts compared to nonaddicts, then clinical counseling skills for nonconsensual sexual history is fundamental to sexual health–based drug and alcohol counseling.

Sex/drug-linked relapse prevention sexual health counseling skills focus clients to develop emotion regulation and self-soothing skills so they can effectively manage feelings and emotions that may arise when discussing or remembering sexual abuse. Sex/drug-linked relapse prevention is *not* sexual abuse counseling, for which a client should be referred to a licensed psychotherapist with the appropriate skills and training. It is essential for drug and alcohol counselors to understand their scope of practice, training, ethics, and professional guidelines when counseling client sex/drug-linked relapse prevention and a history of nonconsensual sex.

Sexual health in recovery counseling focuses the client on relapse prevention skills while addressing one's history of nonconsensual sex. Counseling clients to manage the emotions and feelings linked with historical (or perhaps very recent) nonconsensual sex is the essential tool for clients to develop confidence in slowly addressing sexual abuse, perpetration, or both within the recovery-oriented system of care. Sexual health counseling includes education about common effects of nonconsensual sex in childhood, adolescence, and adulthood (Braun-Harvery, 2009). Nonconsensual sex is a severe boundary violation of personal and physical safety. Sexual health in recovery counseling requires both therapist and client to focus on building emotional and physical safety for effective treatment (and relapse prevention) of individual symptoms and feelings associated with rape, child sexual abuse, or incest.

The sex/drug-linked safety skill is teaching clients easy, brief, and self-soothing exercises that are done in a safe environment (see Figure 10.11). Clients learn to identify a range of thoughts and feelings associated with upset or frightening feelings common to discussing or remembering nonconsensual sex. Clients then implement one or more self-soothing exercises that can be completed in a few minutes and then rerate the intensity of feelings and body sensations. The key relapse prevention tool is to gradually increase client self-efficacy in regulating intense affect states as a precursor to entering into treatment of sexual abuse.

Out-of-Control Sexual Behavior

When I began doing research on sex/drug-linked addiction, the universal assumption among addiction treatment, mental health, and sexology professionals was that I was talking about "sex addicts." The conversation would universally move to clinical content focused on treating co-occurring sexual addiction among men and women who seek drug and alcohol treatment. Granted, men and women in any stage of recovery may be disappointed to discover that abstinence from drugs and alcohol is not the end of their troubling or problematic sexual behavior. Described as sexual addiction, compulsive sexual

FIGURE 10.11 Self-Soothing Checklist

Purpose

This tool can be used anytime you need to take a minute or two to relax and gather your thoughts. It can be useful if you are having feelings that upset, concern, or frighten you. Knowing you have the ability to change how you feel in your body may help you be more effective in approaching whatever early recovery situation you may find yourself in.

Directions

Check in with your thoughts and feelings. Do not judge or criticize yourself for these sensations. Put a check mark next to each current thought or body sensation.

_____ Heart beating faster
_____ Rapid thoughts in mind
_____ Imagining a catastrophe or frightening thing will happen
_____ Feeling ashamed or embarrassed
_____ Feeling hopeless
_____ Feeling discouraged
_____ Feeling afraid
_____ Thoughts flooded, cannot think clearly
_____ Thoughts of using
_____ Thoughts of fleeing to just get away
_____ Thoughts of hitting or hurting someone
_____ Memory of sexual abuse or trauma that I can't stop thinking about
_____ Memory of being hurt or injured that I can't stop thinking about
_____ Memory of being high that I can't stop thinking about

Rate the intensity level of your body sensations (1 = lowest to 10 = highest)

Circle one number   1   2   3   4   5   6   7   8   9   10

Do one or several self-soothing exercises.

Belly Breathing

- Place the palm of one hand on your belly and the palm of the other hand on your chest.
- Breathe through your nose and out your mouth.
- Take deep slow breaths by using your diaphragm.

(continued)

FIGURE 10.11 Self-Soothing Checklist *Continued*

- Deep breaths will move your lower palm out, with little movement from the palm on chest.
- Do this for several minutes.
- Imagine the breath coming in relaxing you and the breath going out releasing your distress.

Clasp Your Hands

- Stand straight.
- Cross left ankle over your right ankle.
- Stretch arms over your head.
- Cross right wrist over left wrist.
- Turn hands so palms are touching.
- Clasp your fingers.
- Twist hands down and toward your ribs.
- Rest hands on chest.
- Hold position for 2 minutes while breathing through your nose.

Tense-Relax-Breath-Tense-Relax-Breath

- Sit in a chair with your feet on the floor or lay on your back on the floor.
- Briefly tense each of the body parts in order: feet, lower legs, thighs, buttock, pelvis, abdomen, lower back.
- After each brief moment of hard tension, release the tension completely and feel the muscle soften and relax.
- Briefly tense each body part in order: hands, forearms, upper arms and shoulders, belly, back, neck, face.
- Now take some deep breaths and imagine tension leaving your body when you breathe out.
- Repeat.

Elephant Hang

- Stand straight, shoulders back, arms at your sides.
- Keep your knees straight; slowly and gently bend at the waist with your arms moving toward your toes.
- Stop at a 90-degree angle.
- Gently sway your arms back and forth.
- Take deep breaths.
- Slowly raise back to starting position.
- Repeat.

Re-rate the intensity level of your body sensations (1 = lowest to 10 = highest)

Circle one number   1   2   3   4   5   6   7   8   9   10

behavior, and hypersexuality, OCSB among men and women in recovery is a combination of sexual urges, thoughts, and conflicted sexual ambivalence. It is often marked by repeating harmful sexual behaviors despite multiple and ongoing negative consequences. If left untreated, OCSB will be a significant risk for relapse. Sexual health counseling takes measured steps in addressing symptoms of OCSB. First, clients should obtain an accurate diagnosis to be sure that they are not jumping to conclusions by labeling themselves as "sex addicts" or "sexually compulsive." The Sexual Symptom in Recovery Worksheet (see Figure 10.12) is a self-evaluation instrument that clients use to assess patterns of sexual behavior that continue despite placing recovery at high risk. This sex/drug-linked recovery tool is used at 7-day intervals to gain perspective over time about patterns of problematic sexual behavior. Counselors can review each item on this scale in one or more sessions with a client to teach them how to accurately use the tool, and then they can have the clients report the weekly score over several weeks or months to establish patterns rather than quick judgments.

SEXUAL HEALTH

The fourth core sexual health in recovery counseling skill area is *sexual health*. This core represents three common sexual health concerns among the general population, which are also essential sexual relapse risks if left unattended in the recovery counseling process. These three areas do *not* represent the entire range of possible sexual health concerns within the recovery community. However, I do believe they do represent a common source of difficulty, shame, and consternation among counselors and clients alike.

Sexual Functioning in Recovery

Sexual functioning in drug and alcohol recovery is an important (and often overlooked) component of relapse prevention. The vast majority of Americans lack basic knowledge about why and how our sexual responses function (or not). However, people in recovery may have a history of abusing drugs or alcohol as a homemade remedy for sexual performance. Drugs and/or alcohol that reduce sexual inhibitions, increase sexual excitation, or both are common sex/drug-linked chemical aphrodisiacs. Shame stemming from sex/drug-linked abuse patterns as a treatment plan for sexual functioning may decrease when this behavior is seen as a misguided attempt to improve sexual health.

FIGURE 10.12 Sexual Symptoms in Recovery Worksheet

The following questionnaire is aimed at evaluating problematic sexual behaviors *during the past 7 days*. Please read the questions carefully before you answer. Write a short description of the problematic sexual behavior you are evaluating:

_____

_____

Sexual health in recovery is taking the time to assess patterns of sexual behavior that continue despite placing your recovery at high risk.

1. If you had urges to engage in problematic sexual behaviors, on average, how strong were your urges to drink and use? Please circle the most appropriate number.

None	Mild	Moderate	Severe	Extreme
0	1	2	3	4

2. How many times did you experience urges to engage in problematic sexual behaviors? Please circle the most appropriate number.

None	Once	Two to three times	Several to many	Constant to near constant
0	1	2	3	4

3. How many hours (add up hours) were you preoccupied with your urges to engage in problematic sexual behaviors? Please circle the most appropriate number.

None	1 or less	1 to 7	7 to 21	More than 21
0	1	2	3	4

4. How much were you able to control your urges? Please circle the most appropriate number.

Completely	Much	Moderate	Minimal	No control
0	1	2	3	4

5. How often did thoughts about engaging in problematic sexual behaviors come up? Please circle the most appropriate number.

None	Once	Two to three times	Several to many	Constant to near constant
0	1	2	3	4

(continued)

FIGURE 10.12 Sexual Symptoms in Recovery Worksheet *Continued*

6. Approximately how many hours (add up hours) did you spend thinking about engaging in problematic sexual behaviors? Please circle the most appropriate number.

None	1 or less	1 to 7	7 to 21	More than 21
0	1	2	3	4

7. How much were you able to control your thoughts of problematic sexual behaviors to prevent using or drinking? Please circle the most appropriate number.

Completely	Much	Moderate	Minimal	No control
0	1	2	3	4

8. Approximately how much total time did you spend engaging in problematic sexual behaviors? Please circle the most appropriate number.

None	1 or less	1 to 7	7 to 21	More than 21
0	1	2	3	4

9. On average, how much anticipatory tension and/or excitement did you have *shortly before* you engaged in problematic sexual behaviors? If you did not actually engage in such behaviors, please estimate how much tension and/or excitement you believe you would have experienced if you had engaged in problematic sexual behaviors. Please circle the most appropriate number.

None	Mild	Moderate	Severe	Extreme
0	1	2	3	4

10. On average, how much excitement and pleasure did you feel when you engaged in problematic sexual behaviors? If you did not actually engage in such behaviors, please estimate how much excitement and pleasure you would have experienced, if you had. Please circle the most appropriate number.

None	Mild	Moderate	Severe	Extreme
0	1	2	3	4

11. How much emotional distress (stress, anguish, shame, guilt, embarrassment) has your problematic sexual behavior caused you? Please circle the most appropriate number.

None	Mild	Moderate	Severe	Extreme
0	1	2	3	4

12. How much risk of relapse (thoughts of using drugs or drinking, secretly planning to get high and have sex, using drugs, drinking) has your problematic sexual behavior caused you? Please circle the most appropriate number.

None	Mild	Moderate	Severe	Extreme
0	1	2	3	4

Adapted from Raymond, Lloyd, Miner, and Kim (2007); SSAS, Program in Human Sexuality, University of Minnesota.

Sexual health counseling evaluates client motivation to use drugs and/or alcohol to influence sexual excitation and sexual inhibition. Some drugs increase arousal, sustain arousal, or allow for prolonged arousal. Other drugs decrease inhibition, lessen inhibitions, or (in the extreme) eliminate inhibitions via unconsciousness or blackout. Sex/drug-linked relapse prevention teaches clients to consider their personal delicate balance between what turns them on sexually as well as what puts the brakes on their arousal. The Sexual Health Recovery Scale for Men (see Figure 10.13) and The Sexual Health Recovery Scale for Women (see Figure 10.14) are checklists that can be used throughout recovery. The higher the sex/drug-linked pattern of addiction, the more important improving sexual functioning is to maintain long-term recovery. These checklists allow clients and counselors to target specific sexual functioning concerns to reduce relapse risk. They reflect gender differences within some subscale items specific to sexuality and substance abuse. Sexual health in recovery counselors will benefit from knowing why and how gender-specific and informed approaches for recovering men and women can improve treatment outcomes and can increase client retention.

Sexual Boundaries in Recovery

Sexual boundaries are central to many of the other concerns addressed in sexual health counseling. Sexual health boundaries are essential for men and women to begin and sustain their recovery. Sex/drug-linked relapse prevention requires counselor and client to develop and practice sexual boundaries that enhance and support recovery. Unprofessional counselors who exploit and/or harm clients by violating sexual boundaries with clients are a disturbing source of relapse for men and women in recovery. Clients with significant impairment in regulating sexual boundaries with members of their personal and professional recovery support system are at extremely high relapse risk.

Sexual health counselors need to define the continuum of boundaries: boundary challenges, boundary crossings, and boundary violations (Gutheil & Brodsky, 2008).

Boundary challenges are the typical daily situations and interpersonal challenges that require a person to be very clear about his or her boundary and communicate the boundary to others. The person to whom the boundary is clearly stated must choose to cooperate, respect, and honor the request or not. It can be as simple as "That's my glass of soda, get your own" or "Those are my new socks, I do not want you to wear them."

FIGURE 10.13 Sexual Health Recovery Scale for Men

This is a 30-item self-assessment checklist. Each item is a description of a sexual behavior, thought, or experience. Rate yourself on the frequency that you have experienced each situation in the last 3 months. The level of frequency of these sexual activities can improve your sexual functioning and increase your chances of maintaining your recovery.

1 = Never; 2 = Seldom; 3 = Occasionally; 4 = Often; 5 = Repeatedly

_____ I find sex pleasurable.
_____ I talk about my sexuality with my doctor as it relates to health care.
_____ I talk about my sexual functioning concerns with informed and knowledgeable persons.
_____ I am able to keep my healthy sexual boundaries.
_____ I fantasize about sex.
_____ I have interest in having sex.
_____ The sex I have had while sober is satisfying.
_____ I feel free to be sexual without drugs or alcohol.
_____ I have orgasms.
_____ Having an orgasm is an important part of having sex.
_____ I am unlikely to stay aroused during sex if there is a risk of unwanted pregnancy.
_____ I can get or keep an erection.
_____ I can control my arousal so I only orgasm when I am ready.
_____ I stay erect when I put on a condom.
_____ I like how I can wait to have an orgasm until I am ready.
_____ I feel intimate and close with my partner during sex.
_____ I feel relaxed and comfortable after having an orgasm.
_____ My desires to have sex are an enjoyable part of my daily life.
_____ I have an interest in specific sexual turn-ons.
_____ My sexual behavior is compatible with my recovery program.
_____ I enjoy sex when I am sober.
_____ I feel more confident that my sexual behavior will not lead to a relapse.
_____ I take responsibility for my sexual satisfaction and pleasure.
_____ I take responsibility to communicate to my sex partner what I need sexually.
_____ I enjoy masturbation.
_____ I usually think ahead about the potential consequences for having sex.
_____ I have not allowed myself to just not care about my sexual behavior.
_____ I like how I feel intensely passionate when I have sex.
_____ I stop my sexual behavior when my partner is hurt or feeling pain.
_____ I am interested in learning more about how my body responds to sexual arousal.
_____ Total score

The highest possible score is 150. Any score above 90 is a fairly good sign that your sexual functioning is a strong support of your recovery. Scores of less than 60 may be an indication of sexual functioning as a risk factor in relapse. Review any item you rated less than 3 and circle the items that you think play a role in increasing your risk for relapse. Focus on at least one of the circled items in your next 3 months of recovery.

FIGURE 10.14 Sexual Health Recovery Scale for Women

This is a 31-item self-assessment checklist. Each item is a description of a sexual behavior, thought, or experience. Rate yourself on the frequency that you have experienced each situation in the last 3 months. The level of frequency of these sexual activities can improve your sexual functioning and increase your chances of maintaining your recovery.

1 = Never; 2 = Seldom; 3 = Occasionally; 4 = Often; 5 = Repeatedly

_____ I find sex pleasurable.
_____ I talk about my sexuality with my doctor as it relates to health care.
_____ I talk about my sexual functioning concerns with informed and knowledgeable people.
_____ I am able to keep my healthy sexual boundaries.
_____ I fantasize about sex.
_____ I have interest in having sex.
_____ The sex I have had while sober is satisfying.
_____ I feel free to be sexual without drugs or alcohol.
_____ I have orgasms.
_____ Having an orgasm is an important part of having sex.
_____ I am interested in sex.
_____ I make sexual choices around the cycle of my period.
_____ I can control my arousal so I only get off when I am ready.
_____ I enjoy my partner paying attention to me when having sex.
_____ I like how I can wait and have an orgasm when I am ready.
_____ My genitals respond when I feel aroused.
_____ I feel comfortable during sexual intercourse with a sex partner.
_____ I enjoy having clitoral stimulation.
_____ My desires to have sex are an enjoyable part of my daily life.
_____ I have an interest in specific sexual turn-ons.
_____ My sexual behavior is compatible with my recovery program.
_____ I enjoy sex when I am sober.
_____ I feel more confident that my sexual behavior will not lead to a relapse.
_____ I take responsibility for my sexual satisfaction and pleasure.
_____ I take responsibility to communicate to my sex partner what I need sexually.
_____ I enjoy being sexually playful.
_____ I enjoy being seductive.
_____ I like how I feel when I have feelings of sexual desire.
_____ I like how I feel intensely passionate when I have sex.
_____ I stop having sex when I am hurt or feeling pain.
_____ I am interested in learning more about how my body responds to sexual arousal.
_____ Total score

The highest possible score is 150. Any score above 90 is a fairly good sign that your sexual functioning is a strong support of your recovery. Scores of less than 60 may be an indication of sexual functioning as a risk factor in relapse. Review any item you rated less than 3 and circle the items that you think play a role in increasing your risk for relapse. Focus on at least one of the circled items in your next 3 months of recovery.

Boundary crossings occur when a person's emotional limits or personal space boundary is crossed by another. The other person may become physically, emotionally, or mentally closer than is desired. Most likely there was a previously established or assumed boundary that in the immediate moment has been altered or crossed without agreement or consent. Emotional reactions to a boundary crossing may include confusion, doubt, and tension.

Boundary violations are the most severe and always result in harm because control of one's own boundaries (self-determination) were nonconsensually relinquished to someone else. People will commit boundary violations when they are interested in exerting a significant amount of power over another person. This is done either by a physical/sexual boundary intrusion or an emotional boundary intrusion.

Counselors can introduce clients to the Unhealthy Boundaries handout (see Figure 10.15) as an educational resource for ongoing sex/drug-linked boundary relapse prevention.

The Sexual Boundaries in Recovery Inventory (see Figure 10.16) is a sex/drug-linked relapse prevention tool that allows clients to discern the common daily sexual boundary challenges that must be managed successfully in recovery. This recovery tool also provides self-reflection on sexual boundary crossings that may intermittently be experienced within the recovery community, residential treatment, friends, family, workplace, church, or community at large. Sexual boundary violations may be infrequent, yet they are so highly correlated with client relapse that counselors need to be prepared for a fast and acute intervention whenever a client reports a current or recent experience of engaging in, or being the target of, a sexual boundary violation.

It is my hope that integrating sexual health in recovery will lead to a decrease in sexual boundary violations by professional helpers.

Relationship With My Body

All too often, drugs and alcohol are used to reduce, eliminate, or alter feelings and thoughts about our bodies in order to experience sexual pleasure or functioning. Men and women with high sex/drug-linked addiction and elevated scores on the body image assessment subscore may be unprepared to address their link between their body image and their drug and alcohol abuse. Sexual health counseling provides skills to face body image conflicts and shame as part of maintaining abstinence. Sexual health in recovery is the ability of women and men to maintain a positive body image.

FIGURE 10.15 Unhealthy Boundaries

A boundary is the personal space that you keep between yourself and others. Boundaries let everyone know your areas of privacy.

Sexual and Physical Boundaries Protect Our Bodies
- Who can touch you?
- How can they touch you?
- Where can another person touch you?

Emotional and Spiritual Boundaries Protect Private Thoughts and Emotions
- What feelings do I want to share with this person?
- What feelings am I not ready to share?
- Who are the people I trust with my deepest feelings?

Characteristics of rigid boundaries: These can lead to isolation and loneliness, keeping people very distant, and not letting anyone get close.
1. Whenever possible, avoid talking about personal feelings.
2. Whenever possible, avoid talking about personal needs.
3. Whenever possible, avoid talking about deep emotions and feelings with recovery support network.
4. Difficulty keeping friends.
5. Difficulty choosing friends.
6. Avoid close relationships.

Characteristics of too loose or weak boundaries: These can lead to hurt and pain.
1. Displaying inappropriate affection.
2. Whenever possible, avoid saying "no."
3. Whenever possible, avoid disagreeing.
4. Whenever possible, go along with what others say or want.
5. Say or do sexually suggestive things in front of others.
6. Share too much personal information about yourself.
7. Share personal information about yourself before you are ready.
8. Being tricked into being used or abused.
9. Whenever possible, avoid conflict.
10. Having many sexual experiences.
11. Continuing with a sexual experience even though you don't want to.
12. Taking responsibility for others' feelings.

The following are behavioral examples of people violating your boundaries:
1. Interrupting your conversations.
2. Taking your possessions.
3. Teasing that hurts you.
4. Asking personal questions that are inappropriate.
5. Gossiping about you.
6. Always hanging around you and invading your private space.
7. Saying offensive or vulgar things.
8. Doing offensive or vulgar things.
9. Always trying to sit or stand too close to you.
10. Forcing you to do something sexual.
11. Physically abusing you.
12. Sexually abusing you.
13. Inappropriate language and touch.

Some content adapted from Peter and Dowd (2000).

FIGURE 10.16 The Sexual Boundaries in Recovery Inventory

Take a few minutes to reflect on your day. Did you experience any sexual boundary issues today? The checklist offers a few examples of sexual boundary challenges, sexual boundary crossings, and sexual boundary violations. If you experienced a boundary challenge, crossing, or violation, check your level of concern in response to this boundary issue.

Remember the sequence for resolving any sexual boundary issue is:

1. The sexual boundary issue is identified and described clearly.
2. Talk about the boundary issue with the person who was involved in the boundary challenge or crossing. Talk with a trusted helper after a boundary violation.
3. The boundary challenger, or crosser, listens and negotiates a resolution. The helper asks if your are safe, if you are hurt, and how you are feeling.

Sexual Boundary Challenges	Very Concerned	Somewhat Concerned	No Concern
Sharing the bathroom			
Interrupts when you are talking			
Talks about himself or herself without asking how your are doing			
Makes sexual jokes in response to sex/drug-linked relapse concerns			
_____			
_____			

Sexual Boundary Crossings	Very Concerned	Somewhat Concerned	No Concern
Offensive sexual comments			
Being constantly sexualized			
Sexual stories or exploits			
Intrusive sexual questions			
Gossiping about client's sex life			
_____			
_____			

(continued)

FIGURE 10.16 The Sexual Boundaries in Recovery Inventory *Continued*

Sexual Boundary Violations	Very Concerned	Somewhat Concerned	No Concern
Sex with another client			
Sex with a newcomer to AA/NA			
Sponsor wanting to have sex			
Counselor asked me for a date			
Masturbated with someone in the treatment program			
Sex that could lead to contracting HIV or another STI			
_____			
_____			

Definitions

Sexual boundary challenges: One person is very clear about his or her boundary and clearly communicates the boundary or request. The other person is given the challenge. The person listening to the request has the challenge of choosing to cooperate, respect, and honor the request. This is sexual boundary challenge.

Sexual boundary crossings: Your own sexual limits, boundaries, or personal sexual space are crossed by another person. He or she is physically closer, emotionally closer, or mentally closer than you want him or her to be. The previously established sexual boundary has been altered. When a sexual boundary has been altered without our consent, we usually have feelings and reactions.

Sexual boundary violations: These are the most severe sexual violations, and they always result in harm. Harm and pain results from the loss of control of one's boundaries. Violations of sexual intrusion can happen by breaching a physical or emotional boundary. A physical boundary is defined by our skin, body, and self. I decide how I am touched, who touches me, and where I am touched. An emotional boundary is defined by our age, role, relationship with those around us, our personal requirements for safety, and how we want to be treated.

Remember: "Boundaries bring order to our lives. As we learn to strengthen our boundaries, we gain a clearer sense of ourselves and our relationship to others. Boundaries empower us to determine how we'll be treated by others. With good boundaries, we can have the wonderful assurance that comes from knowing we can and will protect ourselves from the ignorance, meanness, and thoughtlessness of others." (Katherine, 1993, p. 17)

FIGURE 10.17 Body Self-Talk in Recovery

This tool is designed to assist in retraining your self-commentary on your body image. For a relationship with your body to be satisfying and fulfilling, the ratio of positive to negative body statements must be about five positive statements for every negative statement. Relentless body contempt and body criticism will maintain a negative mindset that will contribute to relapse. Positive, complimentary body self-talk and honest acknowledgement of what is disappointing about your body is first-aid directly applied to the wound of body hatred. An honest complaint without harsh judgment may reduce shame-based body self-talk. Changing your body attitudes to a much more frequent positive self-talk is a practical way to prevent relapse and improve sexual health in recovery.

Directions
1. Read the list of items related to your body and your body functioning. Find an item you are noticing having negative, harsh, or punitive self-talk about today. Circle that item.

Hair	Attractiveness	Waist
How others like my body	Body build (muscles)	Height
Thighs	Breast/chest (pecs)	Eyes
Legs	Lips	Skin
Hips	Arms	Teeth
Face	Weight	Sex (male or female)
Skin color	Stomach	Penis/labia/vulva
Buttocks		

List your own (be specific):
_____

2. Is the body talk contempt or criticism? Contempt: Is the body talk demeaning? Insulting? Name calling? Mean?
3. Criticism: Always? Never? Blaming? Piling on every negative body criticism? Complaint: What am I dissatisfied with right now?

Write your complaint here:
_____

I feel dissatisfied about (list body part or feature here) today because (list the immediate situation that is happening right now):
_____

4. Is this a disappointment that I associate with using drugs/alcohol?   Yes   No
5. I can train myself to have a more balanced and satisfying relationship with my body. When I have body contempt or criticism, I will balance this harsh judgment with five positive statements about my body:

Write your positive statements here:
1. _____
2. _____
3. _____
4. _____
5. _____

I recommend that body image conflicts be treated as a high priority in early recovery. A negative body image, highly linked with drug or alcohol abuse, will be an ongoing threat to recovery, especially when the client begins to explore sexual relationships. Sexual health in recovery counseling increases client awareness of negative body self-talk and a recovery tool to assist in retraining self-commentary on body image to more balanced ratio between negative and positive messages. Counselors can teach clients to use the Body Self-Talk in Recovery Worksheet (see Figure 10.17) to identify destructive body self-talk and use proven relationship skills to minimize the harm from negative body self-talk.

These twelve sexual health in recovery relapse prevention skill sets are the basis for sexual health in recovery counseling among the wide range of clients at every stage of the ongoing process of recovery.

References

CHAPTER 1

Braun-Harvey, D. (2009). *Sexual health in drug and alcohol treatment: Group facilitator's manual*. New York: Springer Publishing Company.

Center for Substance Abuse Treatment. (2007). *National Summit on Recovery: Conference report* (DHHS Publication No. SMA 07-4276). Rockville, MD: Substance Abuse and Mental Health Services Administration.

Haynes, L., Calsyn, D., & Tross, S. (2008). Addressing sexual issues in addictions treatment. *Counselor, The Magazine for Addiction Professionals, 9*(4), 28–36.

Office of the Surgeon General. (2001). *The Surgeon General's call to action to promote sexual health and responsible sexual behavior*. Retrieved January 25, 2009, from http://surgeongeneral.gov/library/sexualhealth

Pan American Health Organization, Regional Office of the World Health Organization. (2000). *Promotion of sexual health: Recommendations for action*. Retrieved September 27, 2008, from http://www.paho.org/English/HCP/HCA/PromotionSexualHealth.pdf

Rawson, R., Washton, A., Domier, C., & Reiber, C. (2002). Drugs and sexual effects: Role of drug type and gender. *Journal of Substance Abuse Treatment, 22*(2), 103–108.

World Association for Sexual Health. (1999). *Declaration of sexual rights*. Retrieved September 27, 2008, from http://www.worldsexology.org/about_sexualrights.asp

World Health Organization. (1975). *Education and treatment in human sexuality: The training of health professionals* (Technical Report Series No. 572). Retrieved September 27, 2008, from http://www2.huberlin.de/sexology/GESUND/ARCHIV/WHOR.HTM

World Health Organization. (2002). *Sexual health working definitions*. Retrieved August 23, 2008, from http://www.who.int/reproductive-health/gender/sexualhealth.html

World Health Organization. (2006). *Defining sexual health: Report of a technical consultation on sexual health, 28–31 January 2002*. Geneva, Switzerland: Author.

CHAPTER 2

Center for Substance Abuse Prevention, Substance Abuse and Mental Health Services Administration. (2009). *Identifying and selecting evidence-based interventions. Revised guidance document for the strategic prevention framework state incentive grant program* (HHS Publication No. SMA 09-4205). Rockville, MD: Author.

Center for Substance Abuse Treatment. (2007). *National Summit on Recovery: Conference report* (DHHS Publication No. SMA 07-4276). Rockville, MD: Substance Abuse and Mental Health Services Administration.

Germain, M. (2006, February). *Stages of psychometric measure development: The example of the Generalized Expertise Measure (GEM)*. Paper presented at the Academy of Human Resource Development International Conference, Columbus, OH. Retrieved July 24, 2010, from http://www.eric.ed.gov:80/ERICWebPortal/search/detailmini.jsp?_nfpb=true&_&ERICExtSearch_SearchValue_0=ED492775&ERICExtSearch_SearchType_0=no&accno=ED492775

Miller, W. R., & Rollnick, S. (2002). *Motivational interviewing: Preparing people for change* (2nd ed.). New York: Guilford Press.

Rollnick S., & Miller, W. R. (1995). What is motivational interviewing? *Behavioural and Cognitive Psychotherapy, 23*, 325–334.

CHAPTER 3

Braun-Harvey, D. (2009). *Sexual health in drug and alcohol treatment: Group facilitator's manual*. New York: Springer Publishing Company.

California Certification Board of Alcohol and Drug Counselors. (2008, November). *Certification handbook*. Retrieved July 25, 2010, from http://www.caadac.org/media/cert_handbook_rev_11-2008.pdf

DiClemente, C. (2003). *Addiction and change: How addictions develop and addicted people recover*. New York: Guilford Press.

Marlatt, G., & Donovan, D. (2008). *Relapse prevention: Maintenance strategies in the treatment of addictive behavior*. New York: Guilford Press.

Miller, W. R., & Rollnick, S. (2002). *Motivational interviewing: Preparing people for change* (2nd ed.). New York: Guilford Press.

Rollnick, S., Mason, P., & Butler, C. (1999). *Health behavior change: A guide for practitioners*. Edinburgh, Scotland: Churchill Livingstone.

CHAPTER 4

Amodeo, M., Chassler, D., Oettinger, C., Labiosa, W., & Lundgren, L. (2008). Client retention in residential drug treatment for Latinos. *Evaluation and Program Planning, 31*(1), 102–112.

DiClemente, C. (2003). *Addiction and change: How addictions develop and addicted people recover*. New York: Guilford Press.

Harris, S., & Hays, K. (2008). Family therapist comfort with and willingness to discuss client sexuality. *Journal of Marital and Family Therapy, 34*(2), 239–250.

Levine, S., Risen, C., & Althof, S. (2003). *Handbook of clinical sexuality for mental health professionals*. New York: Brunner-Routledge.

Rollnick, S., Mason, P., & Butler, C. (1999). *Health behavior change: A guide for practitioners*. Edinburgh, Scotland: Churchill Livingstone.

CHAPTER 5

Braun-Harvey, D. (2009). *Sexual health in drug and alcohol treatment: Group facilitator's manual.* New York: Springer Publishing Company.

Covington, S., Burke, C., Keaton, S., & Norcott, C. (2008). Evaluation of trauma-informed and gender-responsive intervention for women in drug treatment. *Journal of Psychoactive Drugs*, (SARC Suppl. 5), 387–398.

Harder, D., & Zalma, A. (1990). Two promising shame and guilt scales: A construct validity comparison. *Journal of Personality Assessment*, 55(3–4), 729–745.

La Pera, G., Carderi, A., Marianantoni, Z., Peris, F., Lentini, M., & Tagg, F. (2008). Sexual dysfunction prior to first drug use among former drug addicts and its possible causal meaning on drug addiction: Preliminary results. *Journal of Sexual Medicine*, 5(1), 164–172.

National Institute on Drug Abuse. (2009). *Principles of drug addiction treatment: How does drug addiction treatment help reduce the spread of HIV/AIDS, hepatitis C (HCV), and other infectious diseases?* Retrieved January 30, 2010, from http://www.drugabuse.gov/podat/faqs3.html

Rawson, R., Washton, A., Domier, C., & Reiber, C. (2002). Drugs and sexual effects: Role of drug type and gender. *Journal of Substance Abuse Treatment*, 22(2), 103–108.

Tangeny, J., Youman, K., & Boyle, S. (2009). Proneness to shame and proneness to guilt. In M. Leary & R. Hoyle (Eds.), *Handbook of individual differences in social behavior* (pp. 192–209). New York: Guilford Press.

Wyatt, G. (2007, May). *How does trauma contribute to substance abuse and HIV infection among ethnic women?* Paper presented at the National Institute on Drug Abuse Science Meeting, Bethesda, MD.

CHAPTER 6

Braun-Harvey, D. (2009). *Sexual health in drug and alcohol treatment: Group facilitator's manual.* New York: Springer Publishing Company.

Prochaska, J., Norcross, J., & DiClemente, C. (1994). *Changing for good: A revolutionary six-stage program for overcoming bad habits and moving your life positively forward.* New York: Avon Books.

CHAPTER 7

Anderson, C., Teicher, H. L., Polcari, A., & Renshaw, P. (2002). Abnormal T2 relaxation time in the cerebellar vermis of adults sexually abused in childhood: Potential role of the vermis in stress-enhanced risk for drug abuse. *Psychoneuroendocrinology*, 27(1–2), 231–244.

Bang-Ping, J. (2008). Erectile dysfunction associated with psychoactive substances. *Chonnam Medical Journal*, 44(3), 117–124.

Best, K. (2005). Nonconsensual sex undermines sexual health: Young and old, females and males are at risk. *Network, 23*(4). Retrieved April 2, 2010, from http://www.fhi.org/en/RH/Pubs/Network/v23_4/nt2341.htm#Traditions

Braun-Harvey, D. (2009). *Sexual health in drug and alcohol treatment: Group facilitator's manual*. New York: Springer Publishing Company.

Carpenter, D., Janssen, E., Graham, C., Vorst, H., & Wicherts, J. (2008). Women's scores on the Sexual Inhibition/Sexual Excitation Scales (SIS/SES): Gender similarities and differences. *Journal of Sex Research, 45*(1), 36–48.

Centers for Disease Control and Prevention. (2010). Sexually transmitted diseases. In *Healthy people 2010: Volume II: Objectives for improving health (Part B, focus area 25)* (2nd ed.). Retrieved August 8, 2010, from http://www.healthypeople.gov/document/html/volume2/25stds.htm

Consumer Reports. (2004). *Drugs vs. talk therapy*. Originally published October 2004. Retrieved August 8, 2010, from http://www.consumerreports.org/health/free-highlights/manage-your-health/depression/talktherapy.htm

Kendler, K. S., Bulik, C. M., Silberg, J., Hettema, J. M., Myers, J., & Prescott, C. A. (2000). Childhood sexual abuse and adult psychiatric and substance use disorders in women: An epidemiological and cotwin control analysis. *Archives of General Psychiatry, 57*(10), 953–959.

Loebstein, R., & Koren, G. (1997). Pregnancy outcome and neurodevelopment of children exposed in utero to psychoactive drugs: The Motherisk experience. *Journal of Psychiatry and Neuroscience, 22*(3), 192–196.

National Alliance on Mental Illness. (2003). *Dual diagnosis and integrated treatment of mental illness and substance abuse disorder*. Retrieved March 27, 2010, from http://www.nami.org/Template.cfm?Section=By_Illness&Template=/TaggedPage/TaggedPageDisplay.cfm&TPLID=54&ContentID=23049

National Institute on Drug Abuse. (2010). *HIV, hepatitis and other infectious diseases*. Retrieved August 8, 2010, from http://www.drugabuse.gov/consequences/hiv/

Rosellini, G. (2002). *A women's guide to sex and recovery*. Retrieved March 6, 2009, from http://www.doitnow.org/pdfs/807.pdf

Saisan, J., Smith, M., & Segal, J. (2009). *Child abuse and neglect: Recognizing and preventing child abuse*. Helpguide.org. Retrieved August 8, 2010, from http://helpguide.org/mental/child_abuse_physical_emotional_sexual_neglect.htm

Sanjuan, R., Langenbucher, J., & Labouvie, E. (2009). The role of sexual assault and sexual dysfunction in alcohol/other drug use disorders. *Alcoholism Treatment Quarterly, 27*(2), 150–163.

Swan, N. (1998). Exploring the role of child abuse in later drug abuse. *NIDA Notes, 13*(2). Retrieved May 22, 2009, from http://www.drugabuse.gov/NIDA_Notes/NNVol13N2.exploring.html

Wilson, J., & Thorp, J., Jr. (2008). *Global Library of Women's Medicine* (ISSN: 1756-2228) DOI 10.3843/GLOWM.10115. Retrieved August 8, 2010, from http://www.glowm.com/?p=glowm.cml/section_view&articleid=115#850

CHAPTER 8

Braun-Harvey, D. (2009). *Sexual health in drug and alcohol treatment: Group facilitator's manual*. New York: Springer Publishing Company.

Calsyn, D., Berns, S., Hatch-Maillette, M., & Tross, S. (2009). *Real Men Are Safe (REMAS): A gender-focused HIV and sexual risk reduction intervention for men in substance abuse treatment.* Seattle, WA: CTN Pacific Northwest Node, Alcohol & Drug Abuse Institute, University of Washington. Available at the CTN Dissemination Library http://ctndisseminationlibrary.org/display/397.htm

Calsyn, D., Crits-Christoph, P., Hatch-Maillette, M., Doyle, S., Song, Y., Coyer, S., et al. (2010). Reducing sex under the influence of drugs or alcohol for patients in substance abuse treatment. *Addiction 2010, 105*(1), 100–108.

Centers for Disease Control and Prevention. (2009). *Promising evidence interventions: Safer Sex Skills Building [SSSB]. Divisions of HIV/AIDS Prevention, National Center for HIV/AIDS, Viral Hepatitis, STD, and TB Prevention.* Retrieved June 20, 2010, from http://www.cdc.gov/hiv/topics/research/prs/resources/factsheets/sssb.htm

Covington, S., Burke, C., Keaton, S., & Norcott, C. (2008). Evaluation of a trauma-informed and gender-responsive intervention for women in drug treatment. *Journal of Psychoactive Drugs,* (SARC Suppl. 5), 387–398.

Harris, S., & Hays, K. (2008). Family therapist comfort with and willingness to discuss client sexuality. *Journal of Marital and Family Therapy, 34*(2), 239–250.

Katherine, A. (1993). *Boundaries: Where you end and I begin.* New York: Simon and Schuster.

McGovern, M. P., Matzkin, A. L., & Giard, J. (2007). Assessing the dual diagnosis capability of addiction treatment services: The Dual Diagnosis Capability in Addiction Treatment (DDCAT) index. *Journal of Dual Diagnosis, 3*(2), 111–123.

Song, Y., Calsyn, D. A., Doyle, S. R., Dierst-Davies, R., Chen, T., & Sorensen, J. L. (2009). Predictors of condom use among men enrolled in drug treatment programs. *AIDS Education and Prevention, 21*(5), 460–473.

Tross, S., Calsyn, D., Miele, G., Cohen, L., Campbell, A., El-Bassel, N. (2009). *Safer Sex Skills Building.* New York: CTN Long Island Node, New York State Psychiatric Institute. Available at the CTN Dissemination Library http://ctndisseminationlibrary.org/display/398.htm

CHAPTER 9

Barthalow, P., & Weis, D. (1998). *Sexuality in America: Understanding our sexual values and behavior.* New York: Continuum International Publishing Group Ltd.

Burroughs, A. (2004). *Dry: A memoir.* New York: Picador.

Grob, J. (2009). If you don't show your disgust, your emotions may stay negative. *ScienceDaily.* Retrieved June 12, 2010, from http://www.sciencedaily.com/releases/2009/03/090312093916.htm

Haynes, L., Calsyn, D., & Tross, S. (2008). Addressing sexual issues in addictions treatment. *Counselor, The Magazine for Addiction Professionals, 9*(4), 28–36.

Harris, S., & Hays, K. (2008). Family therapist comfort with and willingness to discuss client sexuality. *Journal of Marital and Family Therapy, 34*(2), 239–250.

Levine, S., Risen, C., & Althof, S. (2003). *Handbook of clinical sexuality for mental health professionals.* New York: Brunner-Routledge.

Prochaska, J., Norcross, J., & DiClemente, C. (1994). *Changing for good: A revolutionary six-stage program for overcoming bad habits and moving your life positively forward.* New York: Avon Books.

Schore, A. (2003). *Affect regulation and repair of the self.* New York: W. W. Norton & Company, Inc.

White, W. (n.d.). *Confessions of an A.A. history buff.* Retrieved June 12, 2010, from http://www.facesandvoicesofrecovery.org/pdf/White/Confession_of_an_AA_History_Buff.pdf

CHAPTER 10

Amen, D. (2007). *Sex on the brain: 12 lessons to enhance your love life.* New York: Harmony Books.

Anderson, D. J. (1981). *The psychopathology of denial.* Minneapolis, MN: Hazeldon Educational Service, USA.

Anderson, C., Teicher, H. L., Polcari, A., & Renshaw, P. (2002). Abnormal T2 relaxation time in the cerebellar vermis of adults sexually abused in childhood: Potential role of the vermis in stress-enhanced risk for drug abuse. *Psychoneuroendocrinology, 27*(1–2), 231–244.

Braun-Harvey, D. (2009). *Sexual health in drug and alcohol treatment: Group facilitator's manual.* New York: Springer Publishing Company.

Covington, S. (1991). *Awakening your sexuality: A guide for recovering women.* Center City, MN: Hazelden.

Gutheil, T., & Brodsky, A. (2008). *Preventing boundary violations in clinical practice.* New York: Guilford Press.

Haffner, D. (2010). *Religious declaration on sexual morality, justice, and healing.* Religious Institute on Sexual Morality, Justice and Healing. Westport, CT. Retrieved August 14, 2010, from http://www.religiousinstitute.org/religious-declaration-on-sexual-morality-justice-and-healing

Haffner, D., & Ott, K. (2005). *A time to speak: Faith communities and sexuality education, second edition.* Religious Institute on Sexual Morality, Justice, and Healing, Norwalk, CT. Retrieved May 24, 2009, from www.religiousinstitute.org/pubs/TimeToSpeak_07.pdf

Katherine, A. (1993). *Boundaries: Where you end and I begin.* New York: Simon and Schuster.

Kendler, K. S., Bulik, C. M., Silberg, J., Hettema, J. M., Myers, J., & Prescott, C. A. (2000). Childhood sexual abuse and adult psychiatric and substance use disorders in women: An epidemiological and cotwin control analysis. *Archives of General Psychiatry, 57*(10), 953–959.

Meston, C. M., & Buss, D. M. (2007). Why humans have sex. *Archives of Sexual Behavior, 36,* 477–507.

Meston, C. M., & Buss, D. M. (2009). *Why women have sex: Understanding sexual motivations—from adventure to revenge (and everything in between)* (pp. 219-220). New York: Times Books.

Peter, V., & Dowd, T. (2000). *Boundaries: A guide for teens.* Boys Town, NE: The Boys Town Press.

Prochaska, J., Norcross, J., & DiClemente, C. (1994). *Changing for good: A revolutionary six-stage program for overcoming bad habits and moving your life positively forward.* New York: Avon Books.

Rosellini, G. (2002). *A women's guide to sex and recovery.* Retrieved March 6, 2009, from http://www.doitnow.org/pdfs/807.pdf

Swan, N. (1998). Exploring the role of child abuse in later drug abuse. *NIDA Notes, 13*(2). Retrieved May 22, 2009, from http://www.drugabuse.gov/NIDA_Notes/NNVol13N2.exploring.html

Wertheimer, A. (2003). *Consent to sexual relations.* Cambridge, United Kingdom: Cambridge University Press.

Wertheimer, A. (2008). *Exploitation. Stanford encyclopedia of philosophy.* Retrieved August 15, 2010, from http://plato.stanford.edu/entries/exploitation/

World Health Organization. (2006). *Defining sexual health: Report of a technical consultation on sexual health, 28–31 January 2002.* Geneva, Switzerland: Author.

Index

AASECT. *See* American Association of Sexuality Educators, Counselors and Therapists.
Abstinence, as sexual recovery concept, 40
Addiction and Change: How Addictions Develop and Addicted People Recover, 54
Affirming sexual pleasure, 31–32
  masturbation, 95
  official policy and, 97–98
Alcohol use, 106–107
Ambivalence, 48–52
  continuum of, 50–52
  motivation, 49
  resolution of, 50
  self-assessment, 52
  self-efficacy, 49–50
American Association of Sexuality Educators, Counselors and Therapists (AASECT), 29
American Psychological Association, 42
Anxiety management, 221–234
  clinical judgment, 229–234
  personal sexual health recovery, 223
  sexual language clarification, 223–226
  supervision preparation, 222–223
  verbal, 221–226
Arguing, 73
Assessment-Based Treatment for Traumatized Children: A Trauma Assessment Pathway, 157

Avoidant pattern disruption, 213–221
  counselor avoidance, 220–221
  shame, 215–216, 220–221
  shyness, 216–217
  silence, 214–215
  silliness, 215
  superstition, 219–220
  suppression, 217–219
Awakening Your Sexuality, 256

Behavior, sex/drug-linked relapse and, 115
Body image relationships, 275, 280
Boundaries, sexual behavior, 19–20
Boundary challenges, 272
Boundary crossings and violations, 275
Burroughs, Augusten, 214, 218

California Association of Alcoholism and Drug Abuse Counselors, 64
CBT. *See* cognitive behavioral therapy.
Center for Substance Abuse Prevention, *Discovering Sexual Health Program*, 40
Center for Substance Abuse Treatment (CSAT), 5, 95
  guiding principles of recovery, 5–7
Centers for Disease Control and Prevention, 207
Chadwick Center for Children and Families, 157

289

Client behavior, counselor's
  concerns re, 33–34
Client disclosures, 191
Client motivation, 34–37
  motivational interviewing, 34
Clinical judgment, 229–234
  suspending criticism, 231–234
  suspending judgment, 229–234
Cognitive behavioral therapy (CBT),
  109–110
Confidential identification system,
  Sexual Health in Recovery
  Assessment and, 138
Consent, 251, 252–253
Core Four sexual health, 235, 236–242
  dating while in recovery, 238, 241,
    242
  sex/drug-linked relapse risk, 236,
    237
  sexual attitudes and values,
    242–256
  sexual decisions in recovery, 236,
    238, 239–240
  sexual relationships in recovery,
    238, 241, 242
Counsel avoidance, 220–221
Counseling, 28–31
  affirming sexual pleasure, 94–95
  American Association of Sexuality
    Educators, Counselors and
    Therapists, 29
  environment, 89–92
  *Family Therapist Comfort With and
    Willingness to Discuss Client
    Sexuality* questionnaire, 85
  retention rates, 90
  screening information, 91
  self-reflection, 82–89
  Sexual Attitude Reassessment, 29
  treatment center environment
    readiness, 93
Counseling skills, sex-positive and,
  190–197
Counselor advocacy responses, 71–76
  arguing, 73
  expert, 73

  hurried, 76
  labeling, 74
  preeminence, 76
  shaming, 74
Counselor confidence, 64–76
  advocacy responses, 71–76
  recovery vs. sexuality, 68–71
  subject avoidance, 65–66
  treatment denial, 66–68
Counselor readiness, 212–213
Counselor self-assessment, 221–222
Counselor sexual knowledge, 210
  anxiety levels, 211
  comfort level, 210–211
Covington, Stephanie, 8, 64, 256
CSAT. *See* Center for Substance
  Abuse Treatment.
Cultural competency
  gender responsiveness, 207
  sex-positive drug and alcohol
    counseling, 206–208

Dating, while in recovery, 238, 241,
  242
DBT. *See* Dialectical Behavioral
  Therapy.
Depersonalizing language, 227
Desire, 24–25
Deviant behavior, 27
Dialectical Behavioral Therapy
  (DBT), 109, 249
DiClemente, Carlo, 54
Discovering Sexual Health Program, 40
Drug and alcohol use, 106–107
Drug and Alcohol Use Assessment,
  121, 122–124
Drug-linked addiction, sex and,
  relapse levels, 82
Drugs, sexual behavior, link to, 4
Dry: A Memoir, 214, 218

*Education and Treatment of Human
  Sexuality: The Training of
  Health Professionals*, 8

Emotional expression, 26–27
Emotional regulation, 25–26
Environment, counseling and, 89–92
Evaluation of a Trauma-Informed and Gender Responsive Intervention for Women in Drug Treatment, 207
Evidence-based sexual behavior concepts, 40–43
    American Psychological Association, 42
    Stepping Stone drug treatment facility, 41
    Substance Abuse and Mental Health Services Administration's Center for Substance Abuse Prevention, 40
Expert opinion, 73

Family Therapist Comfort With and Willingness to Discuss Client Sexuality questionnaire, 85

Gender responsiveness, 207
Guiding principles of recovery, 5–7

Handbook of Clinical Sexuality for Mental Health Professionals, 212
Handbook of Sexuality for the Mental Health Professionals, 84
Harm reduction principles, 37–40
    out-of-control sexual behavior, 38
Health Behavior Change: A Guide for Practitioners, 50
High level sex/drug-linked addiction relapse, 181–184
    readiness to change, 182
High-risk sexual concerns, 192
HIV/AIDS, 163–164
HIV prevention, 207
    National Drug Abuse Treatment Clinical Trials Network, 207

HIV recovery and, 18
Honesty, 252, 254–255
Human sexuality, importance of, 32–33

Implicit learning, 226–229
    depersonalizing language, 227
Inferior behavior, 27
Integrated Substance Abuse Programs, UCLA, 118
Intervention, 53

Journal of Psychoactive Drugs, Evaluation of a Trauma-Informed and Gender Responsive Intervention for Women in Drug Treatment, 207

Killen-Harvey, Al, 157

Labeling, 74
Levine, Stephen, 84, 212
    Handbook of Sexuality for the Mental Health Professionals, 84
Looking Back/Looking Forward Exercise, sexual development and, 262, 263–264
Low-risk sex/drug-linked addiction relapse, 177, 179

Masturbation, 95, 108, 175, 198, 233, 234
Medication side effects, 165–166
MI. *See* Motivational interviewing.
Mid range sex/drug-linked addiction relapse, 179–181
Motivation, ambivalence and, 49
Motivational interviewing (MI), 34, 47
Mutual pleasure, 252, 255–256

National Child Traumatic Stress Network (NCTSN), 157
National Drug Abuse Treatment Clinical Trials Network, 207
National Institute on Drug Abuse (NIDA), 116–117
  Principles of Drug Addiction Treatment: A Research Based Guide, 116
NCTSN. *See* National Child Traumatic Stress Network
NIDA. *See* National Institute on Drug Abuse
Nonconsensual sex, 166–168, 262, 265–266, 267–268
  out-of-control sexual behavior, 262
  self-soothing checklist, 267–268
  sexual abuse, 265
Nonexploitation, 251, 253

OCSB. *See* Out-of-control sexual behavior
Office of the Surgeon General, 9
Out-of-control sexual behavior (OCSB), 38, 168–169, 262, 266, 269, 270–271

Pan American Health Organization, 9
Personal Feelings Questionnaire (PTF) Revised Form, 111
Personal sexual health recovery, 223
Perverted behavior, 27
Policies, treatment centers and, 100
Preeminence, counselor advocacy responses and, 76
Pregnancy, 162–163
Principles of Drug Addiction Treatment: A Research Based Guide, 116
Principles of recovery, 5–7
  relapse and other setbacks, 7
Privacy issues, Sexual Health in Recovery Assessment and, 137–138
PTF. *See* Personal Feelings Questionnaire.

Rationalization, 60–61
Rawson, Richard, 118
Readiness to change, 182
Rebellion, 57–58
Recovery
  ally in, 44–45
  HIV and, 18
  principles of, 5–7
  sex-negative, 12
  sexual health and, anecdotes, 10–17
  sexuality and, 17–18, 61–71
Recovery precontemplation, 54–64
  rationalization, 60–61
  rebellion, 57–58
  reluctance, 54–56
  resignation, 58–60
  reveling, 61–64
Recovery support process, 252, 256
Relapse, 7
  emotional response to, 4
Relapse levels, sex and drug-linked addictions, 82
Relapse prevention intervention, 44
Relapse prevention planning, 199–202
  Sexual Boundaries in Recovery Inventory, 195–196
  Stopping and Thinking About Sex/Drug Situations in Recovery Worksheet, 200–202
Religious Institute on Sexual Morality, Justice and Healing, 249, 251
Reluctance re sexual health counseling, 54–56
REMAS intervention, 207
Resignation, 58–60
Retention rates, 90
Reveling, 61–64
Risky sexual behavior, 116–118
  National Institute on Drug Abuse, 116–117
  sexual functioning, 117–118
Rollnick, 50, 51

Index

Safer Sex Skills Building: A Manual for HIV/STD Safer Sex Skills Groups for Women in Outpatient Substance Abuse Treatment, 207
Same-sex activity, 114
SAMHSA. *See* Substance Abuse and Mental Health Services Administration.
SAR. *See* Sexual Attitude Reassessment.
Satcher, David, 9
  The Surgeon General's Call to Action to Promote Sexual Health and Responsible Sexual Behavior, 9
Scoring, Sexual Health in Recovery Pathway (SHRP), 138–148, 170, 173–175
Screening candidates, 91
Self-discrepant sexual behavior, 115–116
Self-soothing checklist, 267–268
Self-efficacy, ambivalence and, 49–50
Sex, in recovery motivations, 245–247
Sex addiction, 168–169
Sex/drug-linked addiction relapse, 82
  behavior vs. values, 115
  beliefs, 113–116
  client's perceived risk, 176–177
  cognitive behavioral therapy, 109–110
  definition of, 4
  Dialectical Behavioral Therapy, 109
  drug and alcohol, 106–107
  health attitudes, 113–116
  masturbation, 108
  Personal Feelings Questionnaire Revised form, 111
  prevention goals, 177–184
    high-level, 181–184
    low risk, 177, 179
    midrange, 179–181
  risk of, 105–119, 236, 237
  risky behavior, 116–118
  sex-positive, 114
  Sexual Health in Drug and Alcohol Treatment: Group Facilitator's Manual, 114
  Sexual Health in Recovery Assessment, 105
  sexual partners, 107–108
  sexual secrets, 110–113
  shame, 110–113
  Stepping Stone client assessment, 105
Sex/drug-linked recovery, 121, 127–132
Sex-negative, 12
  definition of, 27, 28
  deviant, 27
  inferior, 27
  normal behavior, 27
  perverted, 27
Sex-positive, 1, 15, 27–37, 114
  definition of, 27, 28
  drug and alcohol counseling, 189–208
    client disclosure, 191
    high-risk sexual concerns, 192
    sexual health relapse prevention, 191
Sex-positive concepts, 27–38
  affirming sexual pleasure, 31–32
  client behavior, 33–34
  client motivation, 34–37
  human sexuality, 32–33
  recovery ally, 44–45
  relapse prevention intervention, 44
  shame reduction intervention, 43–44
  suspending judgment, 28–31
Sex-positive counseling disruption, implicit learning, 226–229
Sex-positive counseling skills, 190–197, 209–213
  anxiety levels, 211
  anxiety management, 221–234
  avoidant pattern disruption, 213

Sex-positive counseling skills *(cont.)*
  comfort level, 210–211
  counselor readiness, 212–213
  sexual knowledge, 210
Sex-positive drug and alcohol counseling
  client disclosure, 191
  cultural competency, 206–208
  cultural competency, gender responsiveness, 207
  HIV prevention, 207
  relapse prevention planning, 194, 197, 199–202
  sexual pleasure affirmation, 197–202
  supervision, 202–206
Sex-positive supervision, 202–206
  sexual lives, 205–206
Sexual abuse, 113, 166–168, 265
Sexual arousal, 24–25
Sexual Attitude Reassessment (SAR), 29
Sexual attitudes and values, 242–256
  sex in recovery motivations, 245–247
  sexual health discussions, 248–249
  sexuality in recovery, 249, 251–256
  spirituality in recovery, 249, 251–256
Sexual behavior
  boundaries, 19–20
  drugs, link to, 4
  out-of-control, 38, 168–169
  risky, 116–118
  treatment centers, 18–20
Sexual boundaries in recovery, 272, 275
  boundary challenges, 272
  boundary crossings, 275
  boundary violations, 275
  inventory tools, 276–279
Sexual Boundaries in Recovery Inventory, 195–196, 276–279

Sexual decisions in recovery, 236, 238, 239–240
Sexual development, 256, 260–262
  Looking Back/Looking Forward Exercise, 262, 263–264
  milestones in, 261
Sexual dysfunction, 164–165
Sexual functioning in recovery, 24, 117–118, 269, 272
  body image relationships, 275, 280
  Sexual Health Recovery Scale for Men, 272, 273
  Sexual Health Recovery Scale for Women, 272, 274
Sexual health, 269, 272–280
  definition of, 8–9
  functioning in recovery, 269, 272
  history of, 8–9
  Office of the Surgeon General, 9
  Pan American Health Organization, 9
  recovery, anecdotes, 10–17
  sex-negative, 12
  sex-positive, 12, 15
  sexual boundaries in recovery, 272
  World Association for Sexual Health, 9
Sexual Health Assessment, 121, 125–126
Sexual health attitudes, 113–116
  inconsistency in, 115–116
  responsibility in, 115
  same-sex activity, 114
  self-discrepant, 115–116
  sexual abuse, 113
Sexual health beliefs, 113–116
Sexual health discussions, 248–249
  Dialectical Behavioral Therapy, 249
Sexual Health in Drug and Alcohol Treatment, 189
Sexual Health in Drug and Alcohol Treatment, 235
  Group Facilitator's Manual, 64, 114, 121

Sexual Health in Recovery
  Assessment, 105, 108–110,
    121–155
  administration of, 135–137
    discussion of, 137
    employee completion of, 136
    initial completion, 136
    reverse scoring of, 147–148
    scoring of, 138–145
    shame reduction procedures,
      135
  Drug and Alcohol Use
    Assessment, 121, 122–124
  feedback, 157–185
  Group Facilitator's Manual, 121
  interpretation of results,
    148–150
  key measurements, 134–135
  limitations re, 154–155
  principles of progress, 134–135
  privacy issues, 137–138
    confidential identification
      system, 138
  scoring guidelines, 133
  Sex/Drug-Linked Recovery
    Section, 121, 127–132
  shame, 113
  staff input, 152–154
  treatment team discussions re,
    151–152
Sexual Health in Recovery
  counseling
  Core Four sexual health, 235
  nonconsensual sex, 262, 265–266,
    267–268
  out-of-control sexual behavior,
    266, 269, 270–271
  sexual health, 269, 272–280
  sexual past, 256, 260–269
Sexual Health in Recovery Pathway
  (SHRP), 158, 159
  feedback, 169–176
    scoring, 170, 173–175
  form, 171–172
  importance of, 53–54
  relapse, 176

sex/drug-linked addiction,
  175–176
sexual health services, 158, 160–169
sexuality discussions, 175–176
Sexual health recovery, 223
  addressing issues, 96–98
  effectiveness of, 100–102
  program policies, 100
  statement of affirming sexuality, 97
  treatment center effectiveness,
    100–102
  treatment center motivation, 98–100
Sexual Health Recovery Scale for
  Men, 272, 273
Sexual Health Recovery Scale for
  Women, 272, 274
Sexual health relapse prevention, 191
Sexual health services, 158, 160–169,
  177
  HIV/AIDS, 163–164
  nonconsensual sex, 166–168
  out-of-control sexual behavior,
    168–169
  pregnancy, 162–163
  psychiatric medication sexual side
    effects, 165–166
  sexual dysfunction, 164–165
  sexually transmitted diseases, 164
Sexual knowledge, counselors and, 210
Sexual language clarification,
  223–226
Sexual lives of counselors, 205–206
Sexual partners, 107–108
Sexual past, 256, 260–269
  sexual development, 256, 260–262
Sexual pleasure
  affirmation, 94–95, 197–202
  importance of, 95–96
  masturbation, 198
  Stepping Stone, 94
Sexual recovery concepts, 22–46
  abstinence, 40
  desire, 24–25
  emotional expression, 26–27
  emotional regulation, 25–26
  evidence based, 40–43

Sexual recovery concepts (cont.)
  harm reduction principles, 37–40
  sex-positive, 27–37
  sexual arousal, 24–25
  sexual functioning, 24
  turn-ons, 25
Sexual relationships while in recovery, 238, 241, 242
  Stop, Think, Inform, Listen and Listen, 242, 243, 244
Sexual secrets, 110–113
Sexual turn-ons, 24–25
Sexuality, recovery vs., 68–71
Sexuality and Spirituality in Recovery Inventory, 256, 257–259
Sexuality in recovery, 249, 251–256
Sexually transmitted disease, 8, 164
  protection, 251, 253–254
Shame, 110–113, 215–216, 220–221
  assessment of, 112
  Sexual Health in Recovery Assessment and, 113
Shame reduction intervention, 43–44, 112, 139
  Stepping Stone facility, 43
Shaming, 74
SHRP. *See* Sexual Health in Recovery Pathway.
Shyness, 216–217
Silence, 214–215
Silliness, 215
Spirituality in recovery, 249, 251–256
  consent, 251
  disease protection, 251, 253–254
  honesty, 252, 254–255
  mutual pleasure, 252, 255–256
  nonexploitation, 251, 253
  principles, 251–256
  Religious Institute on Sexual Morality, Justice and Healing, The, 249, 251
  support process, 252, 256
  World Health Organization, 251

Statement of affirming sexuality, 97
Stepping Stone drug treatment facility, 41, 89, 91, 94–95, 110
  client assessment, 105
  statement of affirming sexuality, 97
  Zians, Jim, 41
STILL. *See* Stop, Think, Inform, Listen and Listen.
Stop, Think, Inform, Listen and Listen (STILL), 242, 243, 244
Substance Abuse and Mental Health Services Administration (SAMHSA), 157
  Center for Substance Abuse Prevention, *Identifying and Selecting Evidence-based Interventions*, 40
Substance abuse, number of, 4
Superstition, 219–220
Suppression, 217–219
Surgeon General's Call to Action to Promote Sexual Health and Responsible Sexual Behavior, The, 9
Suspending criticism, clinical judgment and, 231–234
Suspending judgment, 28–31
  counseling, 28–31
  counseling modeling, 229–234

TAP model. *See* Trauma Assessment Pathway.
Trauma Assessment Pathway (TAP) model, 157
  Sexual Health in Recovery Pathway, 158, 159
Treatment, denial of, 66–68
Treatment center
  boundaries, 19–20
  counselor motivation, 98–100
  effectiveness, 100–102
  environment readiness, 93
  sexual behavior and, 18–20

UCLA, Integrated Substance Abuse Programs, 118

Values, sex/drug-linked relapse and, 115
Verbal inquiries, anxiety management and, 221–226

WHO. *See* World Health Organization.

Why Humans Have Sex?, 245
World Association for Sexual Health, 9
World Health Organization (WHO), 8, 251
Education and Treatment of Human Sexuality: The Training of Health Professionals, 8

Zians, Jim, 41